401(k) Fiduciary Solutions

Expert Guidance for 401(k) Plan Sponsors on

How to Effectively and Safely Manage

Plan Compliance and Investments by Sharing

the Fiduciary Burden with Experienced Professionals

★ ★ ★ ★ ★

by

Christopher Carosa

THANK FOR ALL !

Pandamensional Solutions, Inc.

Mendon, New York

This book contains both original and previously published work. Some material contained herein represents the opinions of the individuals quoted and not necessarily the opinion of the author. In some cases, for metaphorical purposes, this work contains fiction. In such circumstances, names, characters, places and incidents are either the product of the author's imagination or are used fictitiously. Any resemblance to actual events or locales or persons, living or dead, is entirely coincidental.

Limit of Liability/Disclaimer of Warranty: While the publisher and the author have used their best efforts in preparing this book, they make no representations or warranties with respect to the accuracy or completeness of the contents of this book and specifically disclaim any implied warranties or merchantability or fitness for any particular purpose. No warranty may be created or extended by sales representatives or written sales materials. The advice and strategies contained herein may not be suitable for your situation. This book is sold with the understanding that the publisher and author are not engaged in rendering legal, accounting, investment or any other advice. If expert assistance is required, you should consult with the proper professional where appropriate. Neither the publisher nor author shall be liable for any loss of profit or any other commercial damages, including but not limited to special, incidental, consequential or other damages. If you actually read this, go to "X" in the Index right now.

ISBN-10: 1938465008
ISBN-13: 978-1-938465-00-0

What Others Are Saying About Christopher Carosa's
401(k) Fiduciary Solutions:

"The collection of material Mr. Carosa has compiled in *401(k) Fiduciary Solutions* is nothing short of extraordinary. Chris digs deeply into an expansive set of topics to extract the practical insights diligent fiduciaries can use on a daily basis as they work with their retirement plans."

> – Mike Alfred, Co-Founder & CEO
> BrightScope, Inc.
> San Diego, California

"In four acts, nine sections, 76 chapters and 320 pages, Chris provides a treasure trove of practical and invaluable information and insights for plan sponsors and financial advisors to 401(k) plans. If you wear either of these hats you MUST read this book."

> – Harold Evensky, CFP, AIF, President
> Evensky & Katz
> Miami, Florida

"*401(k) Fiduciary Solutions* provides clear, concise, must-know information to help 401(k) plan sponsors successfully navigate their fiduciary responsibilities and truly serve the best interests of plan participants. Consistent with his stellar reputation as Chief Contributing Editor of *FiduciaryNews.com*, author Chris Carosa demonstrates a knack for cutting through the clutter of investment, administrative and regulatory issues plan sponsors face to uncover the essence of what the reader needs to know and points to great resources for more information."

> – Blaine F. Aikin, CEO,
> fi360

"What sets this book apart from others I've seen in this space is the thoroughness of Chris's research, the variety of experts interviewed, and the breadth and depth of the topics covered. Additionally, the book flows seamlessly from expert to expert and topic to topic. If you are a plan sponsor or in any way provide service and advice to plan sponsors this is a must-have book for your library."

> – Roger Wohlner, Co-founder
> Retirement Fiduciary Advisors
> Arlington Heights, IL.

"Provocative yet conversational, Chris Carosa's book will terrify plan fiduciaries before guiding them on a simple path out of the darkness."

> – Jan Sackley, Fraud Examiner, PI,
> Fiduciary Consultant
> Fiduciary Foresight, LLC
> Kalamazoo, Michigan

"Candid and forthright, Mr. Carosa proves he writes what he knows. The pithy and concise narrative translates the technicalities of the 401(k) fiduciary area into a relatable expertise."

> – Jenny Ivy, Managing Editor
> BenefitsPro.com
> Denver, Colorado

"Having now spent about half my professional life writing and editing the writing of others in the retirement plan industry, I can tell you that EVERYONE has one good column in them, but frequently only one. To craft, as Chris Carosa has on a regular basis, information on a complex subject that is readable, timely, and instructive — as well as occasionally controversial — is a rare gift."

> – Nevin E. Adams, JD
> Director, Education and
>   External Relations
> Employee Benefit Research Institute
> Washington, D.C.

Dedication

For my grandmother, who insisted any talent, knowledge or insights God may have blessed upon me would be worthless unless I made a concerted effort to share them with others.

ACKNOWLEDGEMENTS

First and foremost, I would like to thank the readers of *FiduciaryNews.com*, without whose encouragement and enthusiasm this tome would not have been possible. I also want to thank Mark Frisk for all his help during the initial launch of *FiduciaryNews.com*, for insisting I write this book and for reviewing its pages with the literary eye of a booksmith.

I was delightfully surprised with my goddaughter's offer to design the cover of the book. Teresa is a gifted artist and her simple yet powerful graphics far surpassed my own imagined drafts and received rave reviews from the experts I showed it to. I'm sure you'll see why when you study its elements more carefully.

Any book covering such a wide subject as this relies on stalwart research, and I have Joe LoMando to thank for that. Joe dug deep and the fruits of his research are reflected in the quality of the analysis shown in the chapters covering some of the more important papers published in the field of behavioral economics. Joe even helped out in proofing.

Of course, it goes without saying I owe a great deal to my wife Betsy, who started and owns Pandamensional Solutions, Inc, the publisher of this book and of *FiduciaryNews.com*. She is not only my muse, but also the distributor of the fruits of that creative inspiration.

Christopher Carosa
Mendon, New York
April 27, 2012

TABLE OF CONTENTS

FOREWORD

I've been active on social media for about three years. One of the first people to whom I gravitated was Chris Carosa. As a fee-only financial advisor who strongly believes in the Fiduciary Standard, I find Chris' writings to be a natural for me to read, follow, and share. Chris is the ultimate Renaissance man. Besides his acclaimed blog *FiduciaryNews.com*, Chris manages money and writes in the non-financial realm as well.

401(k) Fiduciary Solutions is a must-read for both organizations sponsoring a 401(k) plan and professionals who provide services to those plan sponsors.

In writing this book, Chris has interviewed a wide and exhaustive range of sources in the 401(k) world. Chris spoke with attorneys, providers of 401(k) plan rankings, 401(k) advisors, and many other sources. These interviews provide a broad perspective on the array of issues facing plan sponsors in today's increasingly complex 401(k) landscape.

Moreover, rather than a dry tome on what could be a very dry subject, Chris uses his literary skills to make this book an easy read. Besides being a recognized authority on Fiduciary matters, Chris has written a novel and two stage plays as well.

As one who serves as an advisor to a number of 401(k) plan sponsors, I'll be turning to Chris' book as a vital reference tool for years to come. The variety of topics covered as well as the depth of research make this a "must have" manual. Add to this the relevance and preciseness of the solutions offered and you have a book that serves the needs of all major parties involved in the management of 401(k) plans.

This book showcases Chris' knowledge of the fiduciary issues facing plan sponsors. What sets this book apart from others that I've seen in this space is the thoroughness of Chris's research, the variety of experts interviewed, and the breadth and depth of the topics covered. Additionally the book flows seamlessly from expert to expert and topic to topic. If you are a plan sponsor or in any way provide service and advice to plan sponsors, this is a must-have book for your library.

Roger Wohlner is based in Arlington Heights, IL. He serves as a financial advisor to retirement plan sponsors, endowments and foundation, as well as to high net worth individual clients with Asset Strategy Consultants. Additionally Roger is the co-founder of Retirement Fiduciary Advisors as full-service advisory firm with a focus on providing investment and retirement advisor to the participants of 401(k) and other defined contribution retirement plans. Roger is an avid social media user and blogs at Chicago Financial Planner and for US News on their Smarter Investor blog.

PREFACE

Some time ago I met an electrical engineer at a FIRST robotics competition. After sharing our experiences as mentors for the young innovators who built and ran the robots, we spoke of our enthusiasm for promoting science, technology, engineering and mathematics. My fellow mentor was somewhat surprised to learn that I took my Physics and Astronomy degree and promptly entered the field of investments and portfolio management.

Well, it wasn't too prompt. It also started during the height (make that the nadir) of the 1982 recession. I was desperate to accept any job. The offer from the investment firm just happened to be the first (and only) one that came along. Now, although the company was a successful investment adviser, my job was a rung below that of mail clerk. A glorified data entry typist, each day I would enter the data for the previous day's trades from which I'd print authorization letters my company would then send to the banks holding the clients' assets, instructing them they were authorized to settled said trades.

I thought this was an incredible waste of time and energy, not to mention personally demeaning. It didn't take a rocket scientist (ironic given my degree suggests I could indeed have become a rocket scientist) to determine we could build a rather powerful computer database out of the data I entered. Indeed, within a few short years, I had created such a system, which allowed my employer to move from using paper ledgers to enjoying the wonderful world of computing. Not only did it put me in a higher pay grade, it also got me out of typing those darned authorization letters. This turned out to be a good thing because with the implementation of the Depository Trust Company about the same time, authorization letters became obsolete.

(Not in the mind of the SEC, though, and a year or so later I helped draft a no-action letter to that government agency explaining this new electronic approval system.)

That same analytical thinking placed me in the perfect position for my superiors to tap me to help create their mutual funds, head up the firm's entire operations area (after being named a Managing Director at the ripe old age of 26), set up internal custodian operations, create and build their affiliated trust company (as Executive Vice President and Senior Trust Officer) and, ultimately, build and help oversee several common trust funds (as a member of the Trust and Investment Committee).

After all that hard work, and the desire to spend more time with my family, I decided to create my own firm. This firm would be a scaled down version of my former employer. As such, with a fully integrated information system from the get go, it would be more manageable with fewer people. The Internet certainly helped.

Truth be told, my original intention upon leaving my old firm was to write a book to help everyday investors make better decisions. After 150 pages of outline, I figured it was too long and would never sell. With a young family in need of daily feeding, I had to think of some way to provide for them. I looked to the only business model I knew I could turn profitable in the shortest amount of time.

I told the electrical engineer this whole story and a little bit more. Rather than dying from boredom, he seemed genuinely intrigued. A moment later his eyes fell to the floor and flitted back and forth as he shyly inquired, "Do you mind if I ask you a personal question — about me, I mean, not you?"

"Sure," I said. He had my curiosity.

Still somewhat embarrassed, he asked, "Do I have enough to retire?"

This is what I knew about him: He worked for a large firm but wasn't top management. He had been working since graduate school and was in his mid-fifties. His oldest child was about to start college and he had a couple more. He lived in a modest house in a small rural community that's more Midwest than east or west coast. It's more rustbelt than sunbelt.

Here's what I know about that question: I hated it. I've read so many stories of people not having enough to retire. I've met so many people who never thought of saving for retirement. I really hate being the bearer of bad news.

Perhaps he saw this in my hesitation when he meekly offered, "My 401(k) plan is well north of a million dollars."

I smiled and explained that, although he wasn't alone in his savings level, he was much better off than many of his counterparts.

After the robotics tournament, I thought about his situation and how so many people really do share his good fortune. In fact, Thomas Stanley and William Danko's 1996 bestseller *The Millionaire Next Door* describes the phenomenon I'm talking about. It's about how everyday people, living a life of modest discipline, can accumulate retirement assets into seven figures. And I mean seven figures even *after* the 2007-2009 market debacle.

Unfortunately, while the 401(k) plan offers an excellent means for workers to meet their retirement needs, it remains a far too underutilized tool. Two reasons rise to explain this. First, the average worker does not take advantage of the clear economic opportunity afforded by the 401(k), specifically through the employer match. Academic research shows people regularly — and inexplicably — turn away from these no-strings-attached free money offers.

Academic research also suggests reliable solutions to prevent these poor decisions, which brings us to our second problem. Typical 401(k) plan sponsors find themselves consumed by the rigors of the particular rat race in which they've chosen to compete. They simply can't spend the time needed to fine-tune their retirement plan. Worse, to the extent they do devote that time to their 401(k) plan, they expend far too much of it trying to avoid fiduciary liability.

That got me to thinking. What if I interviewed folks from across the country who could reveal best-of-breed solutions and then share those solutions with 401(k) plan sponsors throughout the land? I got the chance to do precisely this thanks to Pandamensional Solutions, Inc., which publishes *FiduciaryNews.com*, a website providing essential information, blunt commentary and practical examples for ERISA/401(k) fiduciaries, individual trustees and professional fiduciaries. This led to other publishing venues and, with more than 300 articles published in paper, print and on the web, I soon found my readers asking for a book; hence the birth of this volume, *401(k) Fiduciary Solutions — Expert Guidance for 401(k) Plan Sponsors on how to Effectively and Safely Manage Plan Compliance and Investments by Sharing the Fiduciary Burden with Experienced Professionals.*

I hope you find this book as enjoyable to read as it was for me to write and as useful a tool as there can be in today's challenging and ever changing 401(k) environment.

Act I:

THE SET-UP

SECTION ONE:

– INTRODUCTION –

DO YOU KNOW WHAT YOU NEED TO KNOW, OR DO YOU ONLY THINK YOU KNOW WHAT YOU NEED TO KNOW?

Hooray for the 401(k)!

Congressional overlords loom like the Sword of Damocles over the unknowing heads of millions of American workers striving to save for retirement in these troubled economic times. If we believe the reports ("Will Congress Balance Budget on Backs of Future Retirees?" *BenefitsPro*, October 5, 2011), the failed "Supercommittee" of Congressmen and Senators considered reducing tax incentives for retirement plan salary deferrals. No doubt, if accepted, this act would have hampered the proven ability of those deferrals to encourage individuals to save for post-employment years. Investors fought hard a decade ago to get lawmakers to allow deferral rates to increase with inflation. It seems as if Washington wants to bring us back to the future.

Appropriately, I write this as we've just finished the feast of Thanksgiving. Since this particular week signifies the traditional start of the Christmas Season, why not imagine — George Bailey style — what life would have been like had the 401(k) never existed.

Let's call the plan sponsor "Clarence." (The plan sponsor's name is not really Clarence. If you don't remember, Clarence was George Bailey's guardian angel. The real plan sponsor did not grant permission to disclose the plan's name, but he described his plan as Clarence does now.) Clarence might point out, without the 401(k), then, sometime in 1994, a construction company in Buffalo, New York would not have established a self-directed retirement plan exclusively for laborers (management would have had its own plan). That means by 2011, more than 17 years since this 401(k) plan's non-inception, during the worst decade of stock market performance in the modern era, though earning modest salaries, those employees, through regular contributions and consistent investment, would no longer each now have more than half a million dollars in retirement assets.

However, *with* a 401(k) plan, in a time period representing only about half the typical career length, these workers would already have in excess of $500K each to their names, and be well on their way to a comfortable retirement.

If Congress doesn't change the rules, it's possible these employees will have retirement assets in excess of a million dollars when they call it a career. If Congress changes the rules, all bets are off. For these men and women, the 401(k) plan has been a benefit that will help them lead better lives with less dependence on (increasingly cash-strapped and unreliable) government programs. In fact, they may end up being net givers (in terms of paying taxes) instead of net takers. This is what a 401(k) success story looks like.

Timothy R. Yee of Green Retirement Plans, Inc., in Oakland, California has no problem disclosing his name to Clarence. Yee spoke of a 52-year-old woman whose retirement assets are worth $1.1 million — and she continues to contribute (now the maximum) to her 401(k). According to Yee, she "has been saving as much as she can since she started work at 22. She is relying on her retirement plans along with a diversified portfolio and disciplined contributions to get her to where she wants to be."

Where would she be today had the 401(k) never existed? If Congress makes it more difficult to save for retirement, she might not be able to afford to retire in California. As it stands, she has, perhaps, another decade of work left. With the current 401(k) deferral allowance, this woman has a good chance to exceed $2 million dollars when she retires. This is what a 401(k) success story looks like.

From one coast to the other, the well-traveled Clarence, no doubt now with weary red eyes, listened to Elle Kaplan,

CEO & Founding Partner of Lexion Capital Management LLC in New York City. Without the 401(k), Kaplan's client, the widow of an air conditioner repairman, would not now have "a net worth of well over a million dollars." How did this happen? Kaplan says of the deceased husband, "From the age of 18 until his death in his 50's, he contributed to a 401(k)." Needless to say, had the husband not suffered an untimely death, the opportunity offered by the 401(k) savings plan would have yielded an even larger portfolio. Still, this is what a 401(k) success story looks like.

Finally, Clarence, a bit of an old-fogey, decides to take the Twentieth Century Limited to Chicago, where he meets up with famed fee-only financial adviser Roger Wohlner, CFP®. Wohlner reveals to Clarence, "I have several clients who over the years have accumulated seven figure (or close to it) balances in their 401(k) plans. None of these clients were senior executives or even high earners. Rather, they saved and invested on a regular basis over the course of their working lives and were able to accumulate the funds needed for them to enjoy retirement."

With no 401(k), these workers would never have had the chance to amass million dollar retirement portfolios. They would have been more likely to depend solely on Social Security or a potentially meager company pension plan. Thanks to the 401(k), though, these folks can live independently through their own means. This is what a 401(k) success story looks like.

Of course, not all believe the 401(k) has been a positive, but many negative stories stem from either employees failing to take advantage of their 401(k) or plan sponsors failing to follow-through on their fiduciary duty (see the next chapter). For many, however, their 401(k) savings have been a boon to their net worth, despite the ups and downs of the market. Perchance it's best if, on his next trip, Mr. Clarence goes to Washington. It'll be a shame if

Congress tries to "fix" what ain't broke and penalize working Americans in the name of atoning for its own mistakes.

After all, through these last nearly forty years, the 401(k) plan has allowed many to live a wonderful life. It's the gift that keeps on giving.

And that, Charlie Brown, to mix a Christmas metaphor, is what 401(k) is all about.

Time Magazine is Wrong!

As a 401(k) fiduciary concerned about reducing personal fiduciary liability, you should be extremely worried. Shortly after the nadir of the three-year stock market debacle from 2007-2009, *Time Magazine* published a completely irresponsible article ("Why It's Time to Retire the 401(k)," Stephen Gandel, October 7, 2009). The publisher might have sold more copies as a result, but a fiduciary may be justifiably afraid that trial lawyers, sights set on suing 401(k) plan sponsors and fiduciaries, might be the ones buying them.

In brief, the article spins a tear-jerker of a tale about a 68-year old who, rather than playing golf in his retirement, now must eke out a living by repairing broken golf carts ("of the rich and famous" is almost certainly implied, if not outright stated). Why must this elderly gentleman continue to work? *Time* decides the villain must be the evil 401(k) plan!

As if on cue, the story's author evokes a blatant party line mantra when he cites the 401(k) as a Reagan-era "executive perk — one more way to dodge Uncle Sam." No. The 401(k) was created to give regular Joes a chance to take control — and responsibility — for their own future. Rather than relying on corporate pensions (a.k.a., legalized Ponzi schemes, q.v., the Social Security System), which might disappear instantly for reasons unrelated to an employee's own actions (corporate takeover, buy-out or bankruptcy), the 401(k) freed the average worker from his employer's chains.

Ironically, on the same day the newsweekly published its piece, *Plan Sponsor Magazine* defied *Time's* emotional diatribe with an empirical counterpunch ("Long-Term 401(k) Balances are Up Despite Recession," October 7, 2009). This article pointed out that the average 401(k) balance grew 41.6% in the five years ending December 31, 2008. In addition, in the face of the worst recession in at least a generation, the median 401(k) balance grew a whopping 11.4% over the same period!

Still, while the real 401(k) growth numbers look good to the average fiduciary, the only numbers that matter are circulation statistics. *Time Magazine* has a wider — and potentially more influential readership — than *Plan Sponsor Magazine*. And notably, emotional arguments tend to tug at the synapses a bit harder and a bit longer than dry figures.

So, for any trawling litigators seeking to influence friendly juries in a case against an ERISA/401(k) fiduciary, the *Time* article offers a very good starting point.

And ill-prepared fiduciaries should be shaking in their boots, leaving them to ask...

AM I AN ERISA/401(K) FIDUCIARY?

You may be an ERISA/401(k) fiduciary and not know it. You don't have to be a named trustee or even a high-level executive to be deemed a fiduciary. What's more, you might think merely hiring an outside service provider might remove that "fiduciary" label and its inherent liability. Unfortunately, the U.S. Department of Labor (DOL) says this just ain't so, even as it seeks to broaden the definition of "fiduciary" to include more classes of service providers.

According to the DOL in its online fiduciary resource (http://www.dol.gov/elaws/ebsa/fiduciary/introduction.htm), "Fiduciaries are those individuals and/or entities who manage an employee benefit plan and its assets. Employers often hire outside professionals, sometimes called third-party service providers, or use an internal administrative committee or human resources department to manage some or all of a plan's day-to-day operations. Employers who have hired outside professionals or who use internal committees/resources still have fiduciary responsibilities."

Furthermore, ERISA Section 3(21)(A) states:

Except as otherwise provided in subparagraph (B), a person is a fiduciary with respect to a plan to the extent

(i) he exercises any discretionary authority or discretionary control respecting management of such plan or exercises any authority or control respecting management or disposition of its assets,

(ii) he renders investment advice for a fee or other compensation, direct or indirect, with respect to any

*moneys or other property of such plan, or has any
authority or responsibility to do so, or*

*(iii) he has any discretionary authority or
discretionary responsibility in the administration of
such plan. Such term includes any person
designated under section 1105 (c)(1)(B) of this title.*

Subparagraph (B) merely states that a mutual fund (and
its associated parties) does not become a fiduciary just
because a plan invests in it.

So, while a plan may have a named fiduciary or trustee,
other employees, officers and directors may assume the
obligations of a fiduciary. Any individual, irrespective of
title, becomes an ERISA/401(k) fiduciary immediately
upon exercising any type of discretion or control over plan
administration or plan assets. This includes the so-called
"chain of command" (see the March 26, 2009 *MarketWatch*
article "Who's Minding Your Retirement Plan?" or the
February 2, 2012 *Forbes* story "Who's On The Hook for
Decisions Made in Your 401(k)?" for more on this), which
may extend the definition of fiduciary all the way up to the
board of directors.

So, the first step to reducing your personal fiduciary
liability it to fully understand under what conditions you
may be acting as a fiduciary.

And if you have any doubts why this might be
important, just wait to see what's in the next chapter.

401(K) PLAN SPONSORS AND THE RISK OF FIDUCIARY LIABILITY

s a 401(k) plan sponsor...

➢ are you concerned...

- ...you don't know what you need to know about your 401(k) plan?
- ...about fiduciary responsibilities, but aren't exactly sure what it means in terms of your specific plan?
- ...your service vendors might have hidden conflicts of interest?

➢ are you unsure...

- ...your 401(k) funds are the right choices?
- ...what fees are being paid and where they are going?
- ...that you don't know enough to ask the right questions?

➢ Then you've got to ask yourself one question:

- Are you doing enough to reduce your fiduciary liability?
  ...or ...
- Do you only *think* you're doing enough to reduce your fiduciary liability?

Do you realize why these headlines should disturb you?

- "US Department of Labor obtains judgment to distribute $1.35 million to participants of Minneapolis-based Northland Inn's 401(k) plan," (DOL Release Number: 11-1511-CHI, October 19, 2011)
- "US Labor Department sues Wisconsin-based B & K Builders, co-owners to recover more than $114,000 for company's employee benefit plans," (DOL Release Number: 11-383-CHI, October 17, 2011)
- "US Department of Labor sues architectural design company to restore more than $135,000 in assets to company's 401(k) plan," (DOL Release Number: 11-684-ATL (235), May 23, 2011)
- "US Labor Department sues trustee of defunct Mentor, Ohio, company to recover $97,000 in profit sharing plan assets," (DOL Release Number: 11-562-CHI, May 11, 2011)
- "US Labor Department obtains judgment requiring repayment of $1.25 million to defunct Florida home health care company's 401(k) plan," (DOL Release Number: 11-0245-ATL, March 10, 2011)
- "US Labor Department sues Wisconsin-based Coin Builders LLC and president to recover more than $1.3 million for company's profit-sharing plan," (DOL Release Number: 11-0279-CHI, March 9, 2011)

Those were just a few small ones initiated by the DOL; here are some of the bigger settlements, mostly dealing with excessive fees:

- "Bechtel Settles 401(k) Fee Case for $18.5M," (*PLANSPONSOR Magazine*, October 14, 2010)
- "Court OKs $16.5M Caterpillar 401(k) Fee Pact," (*PLANSPONSOR Magazine*, August 12, 2010)
- "Parties Settle $15.1M General Dynamics 401(k) Fee Case," (*PLANSPONSOR Magazine*, August 6, 2010)

Indeed, according to a Fact Sheet released by the DOL in February of 2011, nearly four out of five investigations resulted "in monetary results for plans or other corrective action" totaling in excess of one billion dollars in fines. As if all this weren't bad enough, the DOL now says it will hold 401(k) plan sponsors liable even if it is their service providers who fail to comply ("DOL Tells Employers When They Must Fire Advisors to 401(k) Plans," *RIABiz*, February 10, 2012). Life just got a lot harder for 401(k) plan sponsors.

This historical litany of litigation, however, represents the mere tip of the fiduciary liability iceberg, according to several leading ERISA attorneys. Stephen Miller, Counsel at McDermott Will & Emery LLP in Chicago, explained the evolution of the 401(k) lawsuit to me.

"For years," he says, "many plan sponsors decided the potential for liability on 'stock drop' cases outweighed the possibility of ultimate victory, which resulted in numerous multi-million dollar settlements in breach of fiduciary duty lawsuits. This string of settlements created an environment where suits against 401(k) plans could be very profitable for plaintiffs' lawyers, and in part spawned the next string of lawsuits involving breaches of fiduciary duties, this time related to administrative fee offerings."

Today, it's not any final court settlement that troubles benefit plan lawyers, it's the precedent-setting rulings coming from the courts. "I think the Edison-Tibble case is alarming because a plan sponsor can be liable for not using the right revenue sharing funds," says Ary Rosenbaum of The Rosenbaum Law Firm P.C. in Garden City, New Jersey. The court ruled in the Edison-Tibble case that the plaintiff's suit, which claimed the plan sponsor used higher-cost retail funds instead of lower-cost institutional funds, could move forward.

Matthew J. Borror, ERISA Attorney at the Law Office of Matthew J. Borror in Campbell, California, sees another case as a watershed. "In my view," he says, "LaRue remains the seminal court case because it allows for recovery despite the fact that the breach did not affect the entire plan." Unlike the Edison-Tibble case, which focuses on fees and investment due diligence, the LaRue case centers on administrative negligence. Specifically, the plaintiff was allowed to pursue the case against the plan sponsor, who he alleges failed to transfer his funds in a timely manner.

Why don't we see that many court judgments? As Miller alludes, many plan sponsors feel it's less costly to settle. Indeed, Rosenbaum points out that the $15 million claim against General Dynamics was a settlement. "The money came from their insurers and other sources," he says.

"It's not the courts or the DOL that pose the greatest risk to employers," says Borror. "The greatest risk to employers is that their plan is vulnerable to a reasonable claim that it subjects participants to account-balance losses due to excessive fees, insufficient investment monitoring or failure to transfer employee deferrals into the plan in a timely manner." Borror feels most plan sponsors determine that the costs of defending themselves will exceed the cost of settlement at some level. Therefore, if they can settle at or below that level, it's cheaper than going to court.

Miller thinks companies can win by going to court as "the cases are usually very defendable because the plaintiff's burden to prove a breach is very high." He says, "Recently employers have been on a roll, successfully defending stock drop and administrative fee litigation, especially where the case has been taken to trial or at least through dispositive motions." As a result, we haven't seen many high damage awards coming from court rulings. Miller says, "The greatest 'damages' have typically arisen through settlements."

Despite employers' success at trial, dangers still lurk in the foggy night of the court. Miller says, "One type of case that more consistently presents significant fiduciary liability going forward involves improper or negligent notices of plan activities or amendments under ERISA Section 204(h). This type of claim typically is tagged on to a stock drop or administrative fee claim involving a pension plan, and can take on a life of its own if the procedures for giving the necessary notices were improper or lacking. Put another way, the 204(h) claims can turn an otherwise defendable case into real potential fiduciary liability due to a failure to comply properly with ERISA's procedural notice requirements."

Rosenbaum sees the DOL's new Fee Disclosure Rule as opening the floodgates of litigation. "With fee disclosure regulations coming up," he says, "I think you will actually see an upswing in lawsuits as plan sponsors will now have to be more diligent as it concerns paying reasonable fees because now they know how much they are being charged. They will run out of excuses."

"The ERISA plaintiffs' bar is a creative group, always seeking new avenues to bring participant-related lawsuits seeking liability from employers under 401(k) plans," says Miller. "The administrative fee lawsuits appear to be slowing down recently, given a few positive court judgments for employers and regulatory activity by the DOL. ERISA's notice provisions are always a ripe area for lawsuit activity, as ERISA's complex regulatory system presents many hurdles employers sometimes do not always cross cleanly. Also, the recent CIGNA case may give new wind to 'stock drop' cases, where plaintiffs' attorneys try to argue that legal damages for stock losses are really 'restitution damages' under plans. Time will tell where the plaintiffs' bar focuses next. We try to advise our clients to follow ERISA's notice and regulatory rules as closely as possible to make them undesirable possible defendants."

With trillions of dollars tied up in corporate retirement plans, there's no doubt trial lawyers see a ripe target for both class action suits as well as individual actions. And it's the plan sponsor who typically wears the bulls-eye for any perceived sleight. Borror predicts that "participants will continue to claim their account balances have been materially reduced due to failure of the fiduciary to either ensure the fees charged were reasonable in relation to the services provided, or to select and to monitor the retirement plan service providers with the skill of a prudent professional."

With the potential of claims coming from so many directions, what's a 401(k) plan sponsor to do?

"The costs of responding to any of these claims are astronomical when compared to the costs of making affirmative corrections," says Borror. He offers this conclusion: "In short, any employer who even mildly suspects his or her plan is vulnerable to such a claim should have the plan reviewed by an independent professional."

In our next chapter, we present an outline for action.

WHY YOU MUST READ, UNDERSTAND AND IMPLEMENT THE SUGGESTIONS IN THIS BOOK RIGHT NOW

Have you ever stopped to consider why most 401(k) books, articles and seminars are intended solely for employee investors, not employer sponsors? Think about it. Employees vastly outnumber employers. The mathematics therefore suggest publishers could sell many more books by targeting individual investors as opposed to plan sponsors. And speaking of numbers, TV and other media are much more likely to interview an author who writes for this broader range of viewers, readers and listeners rather than one addressing the specific concerns of a small niche.

But it gets more compelling when you dig down deeper. You see, by addressing the employee audience, it's easier (and sometimes convenient), to paint the employer as a villain. But face it, even 401(k) plan sponsors want to know the secrets of successful investing. That makes them also more likely to buy a general 401(k) investing "How-to" book instead of a book offering them specific *401(k) Fiduciary Solutions*. Ironic, isn't it?

In the maelstrom of regulatory and industry confusion, the most important thing a 401(k) plan sponsor can use is a "How-to" book on Zen and the Art of 401(k) Maintenance. (The Zen part is because of all the aforementioned confusion; the Maintenance part is for actually getting the job done; and the Art part is, well, it's because this whole business is more art than science, no matter what your local friendly neighborhood vendor says.) *401(k) Fiduciary Solutions* is just that book. It's a pleasant combination of heartland philosophy structured in a way that presents real-life solutions with a touch of academic flourish tossed in.

Whether you're just starting a plan or have been running one for years, no matter if your plan contains ten employees or tens of thousands of employees, even if your plan assets range from several thousand dollars to several hundred million dollars, the book you hold in your hand is for you. *401(k) Fiduciary Solutions* contains 21st Century tips for the plan fiduciary.

Why is *401(k) Fiduciary Solutions* a "must read" for every 401(k) plan sponsor? Because, ultimately, they're the ones held accountable for any mistakes in the plan. And, as you've no doubt noticed from various nefarious headlines, naïve plan sponsors can make tempting targets for both regulators and salivating class-action attorneys. (Remember the part mentioned earlier about painting employers as villains?)

The outline of the book unfolds with the utmost of simplicity. I divide the book into three overarching acts for a total of nine common sense sections. (After all, if Charlton Heston only needed ten injunctions to solve his Mideast crisis, I figure I ought to use fewer.) And here's the best part, if you've read the book from the beginning and made it this far, you're just about done with the first section! For those like my brother, who enjoy dissing the author's intent by reading the book in a rather random order, you can read a summary of what you just missed in the first section in a moment.

Three Acts, Nine Sections, 80 Chapters, 320 pages

While most dramatic works contain elements of three acts (sometimes compressed to only one or two acts and sometimes stretched to five acts if you're getting paid by the word), I choose this structure not to overdramatize the subject, but to give readers a chance to more quickly find what they're looking for. Here's a brief overview of the key structural elements of *401(k) Fiduciary Solutions*.

Act I — The Set-Up

Act I contains two sections. It is meant to provide a brief background of the 401(k) arena. After reading this Act, you should be able to explain to your coworkers, your wife and your clergyman some of the more salient issues 401(k) plan sponsors face and why it might be prudent to address them. Quickly. As in now. As in yesterday.

Section One represents the introductions. Here we cover both the successes of the 401(k) and some popular misconceptions pertaining to the perceived failure of the 401(k). We then ever so briefly describe who can be held accountable for being a fiduciary. Next, and with greater depth, including commentary from leading ERISA attorneys, we detail the risks posed by fiduciary liability. In case we haven't piqued your interest, we end with a blunt "why you need to read this book" chapter, which is what you're reading now. If *401(k) Fiduciary Solutions* were a shopping mall, you'd be standing in front of a big "You Are Here" sign right now.

Section Two discusses benchmarking and why establishing a baseline is key to the 401(k) plan sponsor's success. It concisely lists the important elements of the plan that plan sponsors should review with both internal and external experts. It then quickly covers the five areas 401(k) plan sponsors must address to reduce fiduciary liability and suggests a general framework for measuring them. Finally, it offers specific insights on benchmarking from well-known industry experts that even the smallest plans can use.

Act II — The Arena

This represents the bulk of *401(k) Fiduciary Solutions*, with five full sections packed with action, adventure and the kind of hands-on stuff you can use to convince the folks in accounting to reimburse you for the cost of the book. This portion of the book discusses in detail each of the five areas of fiduciary liability. The typical reader will revisit the sections contained within this Act, no doubt leaving their pages more dog-eared than the rest.

Section Three reviews Regulatory Compliance. This is where 401(k) plan sponsors usually start, and not without good reason. The (primary) federal and (sometimes) state regulatory complex lays the groundwork for the basic foundation of the plan. From ERISA to the 2006 Pension Protection Act, the government defines the parameters for creating and maintaining plans. Along the way, tidbits like 404(c) and the Uniform Prudent Investor Act pop up to spice up the specific stylings of your 401(k) plan.

Section Four examines Service Vendor Conflicts of Interest. Here it's critical to focus on both the independence of providers (are they watching each other?) and the existence of any potential conflicts of interest. Sure, fees are important, but sometimes a higher fee can help protect 401(k) plan investors from far greater worries. This is the area where benchmarking first rears its head. After all, in the end, you want to know how your vendors stack up against their peers and competitors.

Section Five fully dissects the Investment Policy Statement (IPS). The IPS is the road map for the plan and the plan's investors. A well-written IPS will help guide the plan sponsor to both select appropriate investment options and to frame the investment menu in a manner that best helps employees make the optimal decision (or, at the very least, discourage them from making sub-optimal decisions). The ideal IPS is tied to the corporate vision and mission, has a meaningful and clear objective, is communicated, is measurable and allows for independent due diligence.

Section Six explains Investment Due Diligence. While the IPS lays out the framework, the Investment Due Diligence process represents the sound execution of that framework. It must document both the selection process as well as the monitoring process. It should contain consistent analysis and comparisons. Finally, its critical components should be reviewed periodically (twice a year is fine, but quarterly might be overkill).

Section Seven addresses Trustee and Employee Education. A well-rounded plan with the perfect array of investment choices will die on the vine if the plan sponsor fails to provide adequate education for employees. It's important this education be consistent and regular and that it be tied to the themes and framework identified in the IPS. It should cover both investment options and plan administration and it makes sense to customize it to the specific demographics of the plan employees. Lastly, don't forget to provide education to the plan sponsor and its trustees. Often, employees will ask those insiders questions before going to the plan recordkeeper or other service provider.

Act III — The *Dénouement*

This is not just a feeble attempt to impress everyone with my knowledge of French. (Disclosure: I have none. The only French phrase I actually know was taught to me by a girl when I was a freshman in college. It is *"Je te trouve agaçant!"* which roughly translates to "I find you annoying.") Rather, *"dénouement"* merely represents what English professors say instead of "this is how the story wraps up." For our purposes, it means a straightforward set of actionable marching orders and some handy-dandy checklists for all those who so thoroughly enjoy checking lists.

Section Eight summarizes what *401(k) Fiduciary Solutions* is all about and, as an added bonus, actually suggests a series of tasks you can undertake right now to make your 401(k) plan better than it was before. (Yes, we have the technology…) I'll offer a few specific suggestions you can ask of your service providers. Well, maybe the DOL had a part in these suggestions.

Section Nine really isn't much at all, except the part of the book you're most likely to visit the copy machine for to make those copies you're really supposed to get permission from me before you make them. This is the appendix section of *401(k) Fiduciary Solutions*. It contains all those lovely checklists you've been hearing so much about. (Just kidding about the copying! Feel free to copy away with those checklists!)

In the end, you should explore these areas with the objective of discovering something you don't know (no matter how smart you are, there's always something you don't know). It also helps to use the checklists for each area to help you keep score in order to measure how well you're doing. The checklists also help kick start any action plan that might be undertaken to improve your 401(k) plan.

Of course, this little book can't cover each area with the depth and reach required to be truly helpful (what do you expect from something that costs so little?). On the other hand, it does point you in the right direction to get started. On the other, other hand, if you're really interested, you might just want to subscribe to *FiduciaryNews.com*, where, as Chief Contributing Editor, I provide "essential information, blunt commentary and practical examples for ERISA/401(k) fiduciaries, individual trustees and professional fiduciaries."

SECTION TWO:

– BENCHMARKING –

YOU CAN'T KEEP SCORE WITHOUT A SCORECARD!

BENCHMARKING: THE KEY TO A 401(K) PLAN SPONSOR'S FIDUCIARY COMPLIANCE REVIEW

Benchmarking is the key component of any 401(k) plan sponsors fiduciary compliance review. The Department of Labor isn't looking for perfection from plan sponsors, but it does want to be assured they're at least on the right path. Knowing how one's 401(k) plan stacks up against one's peers certainly places the plan sponsor on the road to fiduciary diligence. Unfortunately, far too few 401(k) plan sponsors conduct these fiduciary self-assessments. And that's a shame because, once the first review is completed, the others follow more easily each subsequent year.

How does one go about undertaking a fiduciary compliance review? It starts with a thorough vetting of the plan history. Reviewing the plan's history helps the 401(k) plan sponsor document and justify the various aspects of the company's retirement plan. For smaller companies, where the individuals who first established the plans still remain, this represents a simple process that, once done, need only be updated periodically. In this chapter, we'll identify and briefly discuss the areas a 401(k) plan sponsor needs to evaluate pertaining to the plan's history.

Plan Origins — Plan sponsors establish plans for specific reasons. In most cases, the reasons have to do with providing employee benefits in order to attract the best employees. If an employer can provide a better retirement plan, it should find workers more willing to join that company. Think of the "hip" firms in Silicon Valley that provide a literal menu of benefits (meaning, they regularly provide meals to employees). This benefit addresses some very basic employee needs (i.e., eating) while giving the company what it wants (i.e., dedicated employees who spend more time at the office being more productive). Ultimately, the origin of the plan finds itself in the plan's mission statement, and this should be included in the plan's investment policy statement, as we'll find out later in *Section Five*.

Plan Evolution — No doubt the typical 401(k) plan changes over time. These changes can derive from changes in the company, changes in its workforce, or external changes like new or different regulations. For example, the 2006 Pension Protection Act permitted (and encouraged) 401(k) plans to begin doing things they weren't permitted to do before. Likewise, in December 2011 we saw the new Participant Advice guidelines come from the DOL. The year 2012 offers yet more changes as the new Fee Disclosure Rule may radically alter the way service providers provide their services, and the expected new Fiduciary Rule may change how the plan is structured. So, change is good and it's expected. More importantly, it needs to be documented. Documentation will allow those responsible for the plan in the future to better understand the reasons and implications of these changes.

Standard Provisions — Many 401(k) plans use prototype plan documents. Plan sponsors choose these because: a) they are more readily available today than they were in the past; b) today's prototypes offer the maximum in flexibility, so plan sponsors can customize their plans; and, c) a third party usually has the responsibility for keeping the prototype up-to-date. Even better news, prototype plan documents often come in a "fill-in-the-blank" format, making it easier for plan sponsors to document the standard provisions within their plans. Understanding the nature of these provisions is important for the next two areas.

401(k) Plan Sponsor Fiduciary Liability — Often, the standard provisions chosen in the plan document will outline the nature and scope of the fiduciary liability undertaken by the plan sponsor. For example, plan sponsors who offer employer matching will take on more fiduciary liability than those who don't. It's critical, then, for plan sponsors to know how each standard provision impacts their personal fiduciary liability. The reason for this is not so much as to eliminate fiduciary liability, but to manage it and, when possible, reduce it.

Comparing Your Plan with Your Competitors' Plans — If the goal is truly to provide a benefit that makes the plan sponsor's firm a better workplace than the plan sponsor's competitors, then: a) plan sponsors must know what's unique about their plan; and, b) plan sponsors must know what their competitors offer. Of course, it's often difficult for one plan sponsor to gather intelligence on another plan sponsor. This is where reliance on third party benchmarking providers becomes important. This is really the meat of the subject in the next two chapters of this Section.

Creating a written record of the 401(k) plan's history forms the foundation for a good fiduciary compliance review. It can also reveal some cracks — like missing or outdated information — that might need to be filled in before moving on. Ultimately, it sets the table that will allow plan sponsors to independently benchmark their plans.

But before we can talk about how 401(k) plan sponsors can best benchmark their plans, we'll need to identify what we'll be grading.

ARE 401(K) PLAN SPONSORS MAKING THE FIDUCIARY GRADE?

Remember those dreaded days after the end of the school term? When you received your report card? Some looked forward to that time as the opportunity for confirmation of a job well done. Most, though, feared the awful sting of rebuke and criticism. The reality lay somewhere in between. On one hand, you learned what you did right. On the other hand, you learned what you needed to learn.

It makes sense for 401(k) plan sponsors to push aside any childhood neurosis and grade their plan on each of the Five Areas of Fiduciary Liability:

1) Regulatory Compliance — State and Federal;
2) Independence of Providers — Service Vendors Conflicts of Interest;
3) Integrated Investment Policy Statement;
4) Documented Investment Due Diligence; and,
5) Trustee and Participant Education.

We'll have plenty to discuss with each of these areas in the following Sections. In this chapter, we focus on the grading mechanism itself. The "Fiduciary Report Card" approach helps provide a framework for the kind of self-assessment 401(k) plan sponsors need to undertake in order to continually improve their retirement plans.

Patrick C. Burke, Managing Principal of the Burke Group, a retirement, actuarial and compensation consulting firm located in Rochester, New York, feels this Fiduciary Report Card approach helps ensure that plan sponsors focus on "best in breed" service providers, one of the "Characteristics of Ideal Plan Structure" identified in Northern Trust's October 2010 study. It enables plan sponsors to identify and remove bad apples before they spoil the basket. Burke says, "Bundled providers', brokers', and financial intermediaries' operating models cannot be considered best in class due to their inherent and unsolvable conflict. This would include any Registered Investment Adviser who participates in a revenue-sharing or 12(b)-1 compensation package. They are primarily in the investment business, which excludes their ability to be conflict free, a basic requirement of any plan sponsor that desires to achieve best in class status. These firms are the classic example of a fox in sheep's clothing."

Burke explains how he's seen companies use an evaluation device like the Fiduciary Report Card. "The leading plan sponsors create a framework of comparable measurements that they review minimally twice per year," he says. "The report is viewed as being as important as the plan document and its governmental filings. Creating and maintaining a comprehensive fiduciary framework is where a provider can be of great value."

Still, he's concerned too few companies employ independent measurement systems. They instead rely too heavily on the kindness of their providers, who often only go through the motions. "Firms that are a source of comparative data are essential," says Burke. "I have only seen a handful of effective solutions. Most go at this as an extension of the marketing department, which underserves the client and expose the client to more risk."

Burke also brings up an important omission in the discussion of benchmarking 401(k) plans. The media, regulators and even 401(k) plan sponsors may place too much emphasis on fees and investment performance. While these criteria are important measurements, Burke feels it's just as important to benchmark the less sexy data like "participation rates, average deferrals, average account balances, diversification, loans/hardship withdrawals, compliance, operational timing and execution, and participant trading patterns" to name more than a few.

It's often a failure in these less talked about areas that can give plan sponsors gastric distress (a.k.a. "agita") during a DOL audit. How much further below average does a plan have to go before it triggers a red flag with the DOL? "Not much," says Burke. "I have seen the DOL assess fines for clients that were remitting employee contributions in four days and they determined it should have been done in two. We have been approached by attorneys representing large groups of participants regarding operational deficiencies of plan sponsors. When the average retiree has an account balance of $65K, which they do, somebody is going to pay."

Still, Burke shares the majority's concerns about fees. He points out "the DOL seems to be paying particular attention to fees, lately, and buddy deals." Without the protection of the fiduciary standard, plans can find themselves, ironically, both victimized and punished at the same time. "The money being made by the providers has addicted many to dubious representations that are rationalized through slick marketing," offers Burke. "This is best understood when you compare the cost of managing a pension plan is less than half of the average 401(k) plan costs." Burke states, "Since 401(k) plans generate in excess of $66B of investment fees annually, $33B more than they should, do you believe the industry can kick its bad habits? Doubtful."

A Fiduciary Report Card can help identify these success gaps. The question, though, remains "what is the best way 401(k) plan sponsors can benchmark their plans?" Coincidentally, this is the title of the third and final chapter of this Section.

The Best Way 401(k) Plan Sponsors Can Benchmark Their Plans

It's evident all 401(k) plan sponsors ought to periodically benchmark their plans. Benchmarking provides a clear vista from which to survey the 401(k) plan. This helps identify weaknesses that can be corrected and addresses important fiduciary liability issues.

We've established the concept of creating a Fiduciary Report Card to facilitate this process. Now comes the question of exactly what kinds of structures and procedures 401(k) plan sponsors should invoke to benchmark their plans.

For some plans, the best solution means, ideally, hiring dedicated, full-time professionals to monitor the plan and keep it updated. Large companies can afford a staff devoted to this work. But in the age of lean and mean, with constant pressure on the bottom line, is this really the best solution for them? In this sense, smaller companies may have an edge. They have a demonstrated need to find the most effective solution to address all needs, not just those associated with benchmarking their retirement plan. Small companies, who already have a culture of outsourcing to providers, therefore possess a comparative advantage.

In many cases, the best solution for 401(k) plan sponsors will be to hire a professional fiduciary who focuses solely on the ins and outs of 401(k) plans. Rich Lynch, COO at fi360, says, "Practically speaking, nearly all plans should outsource benchmarking, because typically they do not have sufficient expertise to do it themselves." Unlike even dedicated in-house staff, who suffer from knowing only one plan, the professional fiduciary will have up-to-date information on benchmark data across a broad array of plan environments. Since the ERISA field is constantly evolving, issues can pop-up first in one segment of plans before impacting other segments. An experienced outside provider will often see things that can impact a company's 401(k) plan before an inside employee can."

There's another reason why companies find hiring outside consultants attractive. As bidding for services will be competitive, presumably the plan will pay a reasonable cost for demonstrably value-added services. Independent firms might possess economies of scale that companies, by themselves, cannot obtain. Of course, there's another plus to hiring an outsider. If there's ever an issue with the provider, it's a lot easier to remove outside providers than to fire an employee.

The issue, then, becomes one of deciding how to obtain outsourced data. Lynch says it's important to get the most recent data, but who you get the data from is also important. He says, "The downside is the outsourced entity may have biases that limit their ability to be objective."

Mike Alfred, Co-Founder and CEO at BrightScope, located in San Diego, California and a leader in the area of 401(k) benchmarking, offers this blunt warning: "The worst source of benchmarking information is usually a company's current provider. Unfortunately, most plan sponsors rely solely on their providers probably because they don't believe they have an alternative and don't fully understand the conflicts of interest inherent in the retirement plan business. There are a growing number of independent firms that offer ratings, data, and analysis on 401(k) plans. There are a number of different approaches and methodologies and each has its own strengths and weaknesses."

Both Lynch and Alfred agree provider data can be useful, but only if they've obtained it from a verifiable source. Alfred says plan sponsors "should not rely on data from their provider unless that firm has partnered with an independent third party for data and reporting. That is the only way a plan sponsor can be sure the benchmarks created are robust and unbiased." Lynch adds, "The gold standard for ensuring those claims are credible is if the consultant can provide an external, objective assessment of their fiduciary practices."

In lieu of hiring a consultant or rating firm, 401(k) plan sponsors have other alternatives. David Huntley, publisher of the *401(k) Averages Book*, suggests, "For plan level statistics, participation, contribution rates, loan frequency and more, the Profit Sharing Council of America's annual survey is an excellent resource. For investment performance, Morningstar and Lipper have been doing that for a long time and have great tools. For plan expenses we have published our book since 1995 and think it is an excellent resource as well."

As Huntley suggests, it's important for benchmarking to be as precise as possible. This is especially true in the area of fees. Alfred points out, "To the extent possible, you must break out the administrative and recordkeeping fees separately. Bundled providers will scream bloody murder but it's the only way to do an apples-to-apples comparison." Still, Huntley feels, "Even with clearer disclosure about how the fees are broken down, plan sponsors should not lose sight of the total expenses their participants are paying and what the value of the services the participants are receiving is."

Alfred is more sanguine on fees, especially with the DOL's new Fee Disclosure Rule that will soon be implemented. "Most plan sponsors have no idea what their participants are paying," he says. "I think many of them will be surprised to learn just how little they've known all these years."

All of which may provide a major move on the part of plan sponsors toward clear, independent benchmarking. As Huntley advises, "The decision to outsource benchmarking needs to a third party, to use your provider's resources, or to conduct the project on your own is an important one and should be done with the same consideration as other decisions you make about your plan. Even if you decide to fully outsource this function you will want to be an active participant in the findings and continue to monitor the results."

BRIGHTSCOPE'S MIKE ALFRED PROVIDES INSIGHT INTO 401(K) PLAN BENCHMARKING

On December 14, 2010, BrightScope, a popular provider of independent retirement plan ratings and investment research, announced its second annual BrightScope Top 30 Ratings List covering 401(k) plans with more than $1 billion in assets. BrightScope obtains an increasing amount of its data directly from plan sponsors and recordkeepers, and augments these primary sources with data from publicly available sources such as the Department of Labor and the Securities and Exchange Commission. BrightScope has rated more than 55,000 401(k) plans, spanning more than 30 million workers and over $2 trillion in assets. Mike Alfred, CEO and co-founder of BrightScope, was kind enough to sit down and talk with me about the list (which appears following this interview).

Carosa: Mike, once again, thanks for providing us with this interesting ranking. Why did you choose to limit BrightScope's Year-End Top 30 Ratings List to only companies with 401(k) plans in excess of $1 billion?
Alfred: We wanted to make sure the companies on the list were recognizable to the general public.

Carosa: It appears most if not all of these plans are associated with publicly traded companies. Is there a reason for that or is it just a coincidence?
Alfred: There is a strong correlation between the size of a plan, the market capitalization of a company, and the likelihood of being public.

Carosa: Is it easier to get the information you need to rate a plan if the sponsoring company is publicly traded?
Alfred: Not really.

Carosa: Are the 401(k) plan issues faced by private companies different from the issues faced by larger companies?

Alfred: Large public companies are probably more likely to be sued. But otherwise, the issues should be similar.

Carosa: Do smaller 401(k) plans have structural disadvantages compared to these billion dollar-plus plans? If so, can you identify some of them?

Alfred: Yes. It's generally harder to structure a plan with ultra-low fees when you don't have the economies of scale provided by a large asset base. But we've seen many plans under $5M that compete favorably with plans over $1B on fees. Other than fees, the structural disadvantages relate more to the size of the company (profitability, salary levels, etc.) than to the size of the plan.

Carosa: Since economies of scale naturally reduce expenses for all mutual fund shareholders, can you think of any reason the price breaks some mutual funds can offer larger 401(k) plans should not be extended to all 401(k) plans (or all other shareholders, for that matter)?

Alfred: I think this is basically the idea behind multiple employer plans. There probably isn't a great reason why this shouldn't happen.

Carosa: Are smaller 401(k) plans different enough from the large plans in your Top 30 list that BrightScope might consider using a different rating algorithm to measure them?

Alfred: I don't think so. The bottom line is that employees that invest within a small company 401(k) plan are generally going to be at a disadvantage relative to their big company counterparts. If we rated plans differently based on size, we would be obscuring this fundamental truth.

Carosa: Do you think it might be helpful to offer a Top 30 list for both mid-sized and small plans (much the same way the S&P places companies into large, mid-cap and small categories)?

Alfred: Potentially. We listen to the market and no one has ever asked us to do this before.

Carosa: In your Top 30 list, the bottom 20 companies are separated by only two points. What differences will the typical employee see between plans separated by only two points?

Alfred: The actual differences between what the employees experience in two different plans with similar BrightScope ratings could be quite dramatic. For example, two companies might both have an 85 rating, but in one plan all of the investment options could be all active and in the other they could be all passive. The ratings could be very similar simply because in both companies the salary deferrals are very high even though the fee structures could be different by more than 50 basis points. We focus on rating outcomes, not features, and there are many ways to get to retirement.

Carosa: Lastly, how would you suggest 401(k) fiduciaries use the Top 30 list?

Alfred: I think fiduciaries can learn a lot from these top plans. In pretty much all cases, these plans have very high participation, salary deferrals, and company contributions. There are some obvious things like automatic enrollment that can make a huge difference to your BrightScope Rating over time. But to get some insight into some of the less obvious factors driving these great results, you may have to go speak with the companies directly. I've found that many of them are willing to share their strategies and approaches because they are proud of their plans.

Carosa: Thanks, Mike. As always, you've given our readers something to chew on.

Here's BrightScope's list of 2010's Top 30 401(k) plans:

2010 Rank	2009 Rank	Plan Name	BrightScope Rating™
1	1	Savings Plan of Saudi Arabian Oil Co.	93.17
2	N/A	Southern California Permanente Medical Group	89.96
3	4	Southwest Airlines Pilots' Retirement Savings	89.04
4	10	Amgen Retirement and Savings Plan	88.40
5	2	United Airlines Pilots' Directed Account Plan	88.30
6	9	Emp. Savings & Ret. Plan of Credit Suisse	87.35
7	20	Bayer Corporation Savings & Retirement Plan	87.26
8	12	BP Employee Savings Plan	86.99
9	N/A	Nucor Corporation P/S & Ret. Savings Plan	86.97
10	25	Avaya, Inc. Savings Plan for Salaried Employees	86.88
11	21	UBS Savings and Investment Plan	86.73
12	28	IBM 401(k) Plus Plan*	86.66
13	8	ExxonMobil Savings Plan	86.45
14	N/A	sanofi-aventis US Savings Plan	86.42
15	N/A	Anadarko Employee Savings Plan	86.35
16	N/A	Novartis Pharmaceuticals Corporation	86.26
17	N/A	Bechtel Trust & Thrift Plan	86.17
18	7	Chevron Employee Savings Investment Plan	85.95
19	N/A	Genentech, Inc. Tax Reduction Investment Plan	85.59
20	N/A	Altria Deferred Profit-Sharing Plan	85.35
21	6	ConocoPhillips Savings Plan	85.22
22	N/A	American Airlines, Inc. Pilot Ret. Benefit Plan	85.11
23	27	Federal Express Corporation Pilots' Ret. Plan	85.10
24	N/A	Shell Provident Fund	84.80
25	N/A	Sun Microsystems, Inc. Tax Deferred Ret. Plan	84.72
26	23	GlaxoSmithKline Retirement Savings Plan	84.68
27	N/A	Cisco Systems, Inc. 401(k) Plan	84.66
28	N/A	Goldman Sachs 401(k) Plan	84.56
29	N/A	AstraZeneca Savings and Security Plan	84.53
30	13	Pfizer Savings Plan	84.52

* denotes a change in plan name since 2009

And so the curtain closes on Act I. We've now set the stage for Act II and its five sections, each devoted to one of the five areas of fiduciary liability. Be prepared for some heavy lifting as these next chapters contain the meat and potatoes of *401(k) Fiduciary Solutions*.

ACT II:

– THE ACTION –

SECTION THREE:

– REGULATORY COMPLIANCE –

"IT'LL NEVER HAPPEN TO ME..."
UNTIL IT DOES!

2010 WHITE PAPER REVEALS THE THREE GREATEST FIDUCIARY LIABILITY THREATS TO 401(K) PLAN SPONSORS

THe summer of 2010 saw the Chubb Group of Insurance Companies and Morgan, Lewis & Bockius LLP release a special report on the risk of fiduciary liability lawsuits. It may just scare the you-know-what out of the average 401(k) plan sponsor. In a press release dated August 12, 2010, Chubb states "The U.S. Labor Department reported 910 corrected violations resulting from the 1,042 investigations of violations of the Employee Retirement Income Security Act (ERISA) it conducted in 2009." That's roughly 4.5 corrected violations for every business day of the year. And who said regulators have been sitting on their hind ends?

Making matters worse, the current economic setting only heightens fiduciary liability. "Business owners and managers need to understand the fiduciary liability exposures they face, especially in an environment where they are likely to reduce staff or employee benefits," said Christine Dart, vice president and manager for worldwide fiduciary liability at Chubb. "Employees who still have jobs may not be inclined to 'rock the boat,' but those who find themselves overboard are more likely to take legal action against employers, especially if their 401(k) plans sustained losses before they were terminated."

Charles Jackson, a labor and employment partner and co-chair of the ERISA Litigation Practice at Morgan, Lewis & Bockius LLP, warns, "The U.S. Supreme Court's ruling in LaRue v. DeWolff and regulatory changes have helped empower individual plan participants to bring actions for losses to their own accounts, paving the way for other claims against the fiduciaries."

Below we summarize the three most significant litigation threats to 401(k) plan sponsors revealed in the report (portions of this summary are extracted directly from the report):

1. **"Stock drop" cases that allege plan fiduciaries acted imprudently in offering an employer stock fund or misrepresented the risks associated with investments in a plan sponsor's stock** — With more than 200 such cases filed in the past decade, it's easy to understand why these legal actions represent a large percentage of class action filings under ERISA. First, the market itself has been volatile and unpredictable. Second, a number of high profile ERISA class action attorneys actively solicit these kinds of claims from retirement plan participants.

2. **"Fees and expense" cases alleging the plan fiduciaries breached their obligations to the plan and its participants by charging or permitting excessive fees and expenses for plan services provided by third parties, such as investment management, recordkeeping, and custodians** — These fees claims come in three basic forms. The most common form is suits filed by class counsel directly against employers, their officers and directors, and sometimes service providers, contending that 401(k) plan fiduciaries were "asleep at the switch" in allowing plan service providers to be paid excessive amounts for their services and in failing to inform participants of the intricacies of compensation arrangements. A second type of claim (actually a subset of the first) is the "proprietary fund" case. Proprietary fund lawsuits allege plan fiduciaries improperly bought, on behalf of the plan investment, products of affiliated entities of plan

service providers. A third category of claims is "gatekeeper" cases, which have been brought as national class actions by fiduciaries of small to midsize plans against bundled service providers such as insurance carriers, alleging that improper revenue-sharing agreements provided unlawful "kickback" payments to the carriers, based on the percentage of plan assets invested in a particular fund.

3. **Investment imprudence cases alleging that plan fiduciaries breached their duties to invest plan assets prudently, breached their duty of loyalty, had conflicts of interest, and/or engaged in prohibited transactions** — The report suggests including a Section 404(c) provision and hiring an outside fiduciary may relieve the fiduciaries from liability for damages for "any loss or any breach" where participants exercise control over assets allocated to their accounts.

Author Kerry Pechter was kind enough to share his story on this subject with me. For a list of five recommendations from the Chubb report, we encourage you to read his *Retirement Income Journal* story "How to Reduce the Threat of Fiduciary Liability Lawsuits," (August 18, 2010).

Here's the direct link to the full report "Who May Sue You and Why: How to Reduce Your ERISA Risks and the Role of Fiduciary Liability Insurance," as provided by the Chubb press release:

http://www.chubb.com/businesses/csi/chubb12107.pdf

5 CRITERIA 401(K) PLAN SPONSORS MUST CONSIDER WHEN HIRING AN ERISA ATTORNEY

With many changes looming from Washington regulators — from mandatory fee disclosure to redefining fiduciary liability — 401(k) plan sponsors will likely need to turn to independent experts for advice. Among those most likely to be called are ERISA attorneys. Too often a plan fiduciary only considers those service providers he more often contacts (e.g., third-party administrators, recordkeepers, investment advisers, brokers, etc...). The ERISA attorney, however, often provides plan information and regulatory interpretation. If the consequences of choosing the wrong ERISA attorney can prove catastrophic, what criteria should the 401(k) plan sponsor and fiduciary use to select an ERISA attorney?

I asked several experienced ERISA attorneys from across the country how they might approach this issue. As you might expect, picking the wrong attorney can lead to dire repercussions. "Not only do you risk losing the tax-qualified status attributable to 401(k) plans, which can be devastating both to the participants and the plan sponsor," says Edward A. Marshall, Attorney at Law, Arnall Golden Gregory LLP, "but, even short of a total loss of such status, noncompliance with ERISA can result in significant penalties." Individual plan sponsors and fiduciaries have still greater worries, advises Marshall. He says, "Lack of proper guidance from counsel can greatly increase exposure to personal liability for breach of fiduciary duty and for engaging in prohibited transactions (which are defined broadly by ERISA)."

The first step to picking an ERISA attorney involves drawing up a list of possible candidates. Rather than merely going to Google or the Yellow Pages, industry experts suggest asking people you know. Business consultant

William P. O'Malley, Managing Director at RSM McGladrey, Inc., says, "The best way is for the employer to discuss the matter with the law firm that it regularly uses as general corporate counsel. That firm may have those capabilities in house or may have one or more standing referral relationships." Ary Rosenbaum of the Rosenbaum Law Firm, P.C. thinks "the best way is by word of mouth. Ask an adviser or a TPA for the names of independent attorneys they refer work to." Marshall agrees. He says, "The best place to start is by relying on your existing firm relationships and referrals from your peers in the pension plan community to identify skilled counsel with experience in ERISA and ERISA litigation."

As a 401(k) plan sponsor, you already have existing relationships from which to obtain referrals. Many of the experts we spoke to felt generating a list of four to six names is sufficient. With that list in hand, Attorney Jeff Mamorsky of international law firm Greenberg Traurig offered the following five criteria to consider as you compare different ERISA attorneys. Mamorsky says the ideal candidate should be:

1. Experienced in plan design, drafting, regulatory approval and technical requirements (IRS, DOL and Pension Benefit Guaranty Corporation (PBGC)), the compliance issues of ERISA fiduciary duties, the establishment of best-practice plan governance procedures and in negotiations with service providers and vendors.

2. Experienced in operational compliance with plan documents and all applicable law to comply with tax (IRS) and ERISA (DOL) requirements.

3. Experienced in representing plan sponsors in ERISA participant and governmental litigation and adversarial proceedings with the IRS, the DOL and the PBGC.

4. Experienced in assisting plan sponsors establish best-practice operational internal control procedures to comply with new financial statement requirements (SAS 115) and IRS and DOL compliance requirements.

5. Experienced in conducting "mock" IRS and DOL audits to qualify for self-audit voluntary correction without the imposition of monetary sanctions and in the preparation of plan sponsors in the event of governmental examination.

While these five criteria appear generic, it's important to realize different plans and different ERISA scenarios will have different answers to each of these criteria. For example, Rosenbaum points out you might be dissatisfied if, as a single employer 401(k), "You picked an attorney with a limited background in single employer 401(k) plans who may be more experienced with multi-employer pension plans, which is a completely different animal."

And don't be fooled by the title "ERISA attorney," for the term ERISA refers to a large range of concerns. O'Malley says, "An employer needs to determine that the potential attorney does indeed have ERISA expertise and that the lawyer has that expertise with respect to that part of ERISA that applies to the employer's situation. For example, if the U.S. Department of Labor is investigating the employer's 401(k) plan, then a lawyer who specializes in defending employers with respect to ERISA healthcare claims may not have sufficient experience to represent the employer with respect to the 401(k) plan."

Finally, we get to the issue of fees. Surprisingly, the attorney experts I spoke with warned of the infamous "billable hour" albatross that drags on the industry. Rosenbaum advises, "Either hire an attorney who offers flat-fee billing or a guesstimate of what costs will be. Many ERISA attorneys bill by the hour and some use that method with abuse where a client is spending needless amounts of money for something rather simple." In a similar vein, O'Malley warns that the strength of a large firm may also be its greatest weakness and says, "Many of the largest law firms in the country have very strong ERISA departments. However, those great resources come at a price that may be more expensive than what a particular sized employer may need. For example, if the employer is a medical corporation there are many small and medium-sized law firms that do a great deal of tax and ERISA work for professional firms and such firms often have the skill needed at an appropriate price."

In the end, picking an appropriate ERISA attorney is definitely a caveat emptor situation. "You will want to identify counsel with specialized expertise in ERISA, which is a notoriously complex and dynamic statute," says Marshall. Preferably, he says, "The firm you select should have regulatory, transactional, and litigation experience in ERISA matters, because prudent implementation of the statute's requirements is shaped as much by regulatory policy as it is by understanding emerging trends in ERISA litigation. Finally, you should ensure the firm you select has experience with plans comparable to your own in terms of the number of participants and size of the plan's assets."

Perhaps the greatest thing to remember is you aren't limited to one firm or one ERISA attorney. Attorney Tod Yeslow of Mitchell, Williams, Selig, Gates & Woodyard, P.L.L.C. reminds us, "Keep the names of candidates who have a specialized skill or talent that you may need for future reference, for you are never limited to using just one employee benefits/ERISA lawyer."

ARY ROSENBAUM DISCUSSES THE MAJOR AREAS OF REGULATORY COMPLIANCE AND THE 3 BIGGEST COMPLIANCE OBSTACLES FOR 401(K) PLAN SPONSORS

Long time readers of *FiduciaryNews.com* (and quite a few chapters of this book) will quickly recognize the name of Ary Rosenbaum. I often turn to him when in need of a quick quote on legal matters within the fiduciary realm. Rosenbaum, as mentioned earlier, is an ERISA/retirement plan for his firm, The Rosenbaum Law Firm P.C., located in Garden City, New York. He helps plan sponsors reduce their plan cost, facilitate administration, and limit their fiduciary liability. Here's what I like about him: He charges only a flat fee. I find that attractive in an attorney. But that might just be me.

Rosenbaum is an oft-quoted expert in retirement plans, having appeared, besides in *FiduciaryNews.com*, in *Fortune Magazine*, *The Stamford Advocate*, bankrate.com, smartmoney.com, *Long Island Business News*, *PLANSPONSOR Magazine*, *DailyFinance.com*, American Express Open Forum, *Marketwatch.com*, *Pittsburgh Post-Gazette*, *The Wall Street Journal* and *Investment News*. He's a prolific writer whose articles have been made available in numerous publications. Rosenbaum has also written more than 90 articles for his blog. He's also a well-respected speaker, having been invited to make presentations at venues throughout the country.

Rosenbaum is a graduate of Stony Brook University (B.A., Political Science, 1994), American University Washington College of Law (J.D., 1997), and Boston University (L.LM, Taxation, 1998). He is licensed to practice in New York, Massachusetts, and California and is currently an accredited provider of continuing education for

New York accountants and attorneys. He lives in Oceanside with his wife and two kids.

With this impressive resume, we thought Rosenbaum would be the perfect person to interview about state and federal regulatory matters as they pertain to retirement plans. As you read the interview, you'll see his advice is both succinct and practical, a testament to his on-target real-life work experience. I thought you might be impressed to learn more of what's beyond the standard bio.

Carosa: Ary, I'm sure the readers of *401(k) Fiduciary Solutions* would appreciate your insights and forthright comments. Tell us how you gained such a breadth of knowledge about retirement plans.

Rosenbaum: While I do have an L.LM in taxation and took two courses on retirements plans at Boston University School of Law, I learned how retirement plans truly operate while working for nine years as an attorney for third-party retirement plan administration firms.

Carosa: So you actually worked in the practical side of the business. How does this compare to the experience of the typical ERISA attorney and what did you discover there?

Rosenbaum: Many ERISA attorneys have spent their entire career at law firms with very little experience in the day-to-day administration of retirement plans. I had hands-on experience in seeing many of the issues and problems retirement plans go through on a daily basis. It is this experience where I saw the abuses of the retirement plan industry that has made me a leading supporter of 401(k) fee transparency, as well as cutting down a plan's sponsor cost and potential liability because I know the tricks of the trade. While ERISA and retirement plans are a complicated topic for most plan sponsors, I've learned how to break down important and technical concepts into a language plan sponsors can understand.

Carosa: As you know, ERISA was passed in 1974 — almost two generations ago. No doubt some of today's plan sponsors weren't even born yet. What is the nature and purpose of ERISA? What are the most important elements that came out of ERISA?

Rosenbaum: The nature and purpose of ERISA is to protect the rights of retirement plan participants and to make sure employers meet their obligations as retirement plan sponsors. Under ERISA, retirement plans must provide for vesting of employees' pension benefits after a specified minimum number of years. ERISA also requires the employers who sponsor plans to satisfy certain minimum funding requirements. In addition, ERISA created the Pension Benefit Guaranty Corporation (PBGC), which provides coverage in the event that a terminated defined benefit plan does not have sufficient assets to provide the benefits earned by participants.

Carosa: So ERISA appears to have initially focused on pension plans (and traditional profit-sharing plans). Yet it spawned the 401(k) plan. What is the nature and purpose of the 404(c) provision of ERISA?

Rosenbaum: The purpose is to have the employer minimize their fiduciary liability if participants elect the investments under their account, usually under a 401(k) plan.

Carosa: What's the most important thing to know about 404(c)?

Rosenbaum: 404(c) isn't a suicide pact, meaning that plan sponsors have obligations under a participant-directed plan. Giving participants a choice of [at least three] investments options isn't enough. The plan sponsor has to develop an investment policy statement (IPS), review the investment options to make sure it still meets the requirements of the IPS, and offer participants investment education so they have the background to make informed investment options.

Carosa: Under what circumstances can 401(k) plans offer only three equity funds and still comply with 404(c)?

Rosenbaum: They have to be different, internally diversified investment options with materially different risk and return characteristics.

Carosa: What does it mean to elect the "Safe Harbor" provision?

Rosenbaum: It means the plan sponsor of a 401(k) plan has elected to make mandatory full vesting contributions in order to automatically pass the Top Heavy, Actual Deferral Percentage, and Actual Contribution tests. The "Safe Harbor" provision is usually elected when plans have failed discrimination tests in the past or are on the verge of failing.

Carosa: In what started as individual states passing their own Prudent Investor Acts, we now have a Uniform Prudent Investor Act. What is the nature and purpose of the Uniform Prudent Investor Act?

Rosenbaum: The Act allows fiduciaries to utilize modern portfolio theory to guide investment decisions and requires risk versus return analysis. So a fiduciary's performance is measured on the performance of the entire portfolio, rather than just individual investments.

Carosa: The Prudent Investor Act allows plan sponsors, among others, to reduce their personal fiduciary liability by hiring an investment professional. Explain to what extent this reduces fiduciary liability and whether anything can be done to fully eliminate fiduciary liability?

Rosenbaum: You can never fully eliminate fiduciary liability — you can only minimize it. The most important way to minimize liability (other than liability insurance) is to hire an investment adviser for the plan who can help guide the plan sponsor and assist in the management of the fiduciary process. An ERISA 3(38) fiduciary can further minimize liability because, unlike a regular investment adviser, the 3(38) fiduciary has the discretionary authority over the plan, which means they assume the bulk of the liability.

Carosa: If a plan sponsor hires a bank as a full discretionary trustee, will this fully remove the plan sponsor's fiduciary liability?

Rosenbaum: Absolutely not. A discretionary trustee is effective when no individual from the plan sponsors wants to serve as trustee or the plan wants to qualify for a limited scope audit (if it requires an audit). It, however, does not eliminate the plan sponsor's liability.

Carosa: What is the nature and purpose of the 2006 Pension Protection Act (PPA)?

Rosenbaum: This legislation requires companies that have underfunded their pension plans to pay higher premiums to the PBGC and extends the requirement of providing extra funding to the pension systems of companies that terminate their pension plans. It also provides statutory authority for employers to enroll workers in 401(k) plans automatically; formerly, the authority came from DOL rulemaking. The PPA helped establish safe harbor investments, also known as Qualified Default Investment Alternatives (QDIAs), to protect employers from liability of losses suffered by automatically enrolled employees. It also allowed for service providers to offer investment advice to plan participants (although the DOL just finalized these rules in December, 2011).

Carosa: What is the most misunderstood aspect of the 2006 PPA?

Rosenbaum: It actually had the effect of employers mothballing their pension plans. In addition, the QDIA and automatic enrollment rules only added to the plan sponsor's burden.

Carosa: How are 401(k) plan sponsors most likely to make a mistake under the 2006 PPA?

Rosenbaum: They are unaware of their obligations, so they may not offer a QDIA that can help minimize their liability.

Carosa: In December of 2011, the DOL issued its final guidelines for individual participant advice as allowed in the PPA. What does this new rule allow 401(k) plans to do that they weren't able to do before?

Rosenbaum: It allows their plan provider to provide investment advice, as long as they meet the obligations of the regulations and get audited annually. Previously, plan providers could only offer general investment education.

Carosa: Why should or should not an ERISA plan have an Investment Policy Statement?

Rosenbaum: They should have one because it's an important cog of the fiduciary process and helps minimize liability.

Carosa: Besides the plan document, summary and an Investment Policy Statement, can you provide some examples of what good documentation might look like?

Rosenbaum: Minutes of any meetings where decisions concerning the plan are made as well as a review of plan providers for cost and adequacy of services. Also, every six to 12 months, there needs to be an investment review to make sure the plan still meets the IPS. In addition, every one to three years, the plan should have a review of their plan terms, administration, and cost as a check-up of the plan's overall health.

Carosa: What are the legal guidelines as they pertain to employee communications?

Rosenbaum: Participants need a copy of the summary plan description and a quarterly (if plan is daily valued) or annual statements of benefits. They must also be informed of any plan amendments to decisions to curtail benefits or plan termination.

Carosa: What are the three biggest obstacles you've seen that can hinder a plan sponsor's ability to fully comply with all relevant retirement plan laws?

Rosenbaum: 1) Employer's lack of sophistication in handling their role as plan sponsor and total reliance on their plan providers; 2) Lack of independence among their plan providers; and, 3) Lack of experience or competence among plan providers.

Carosa: Where do you see the greatest need for ERISA attorneys in today's retirement plan environment?

Rosenbaum: The greatest need is for small to medium-sized employers who are paying too much in fees and have plans that are out of compliance.

Carosa: Regarding the future regulatory environment, what should plan sponsors expect to see in the next year or so?

Rosenbaum: Within the next twelve months, plan sponsors should expect to see more competitive plan administration fees as well as more litigation for plan sponsors who don't handle their responsibilities competently.

I want to thank Ary for offering very thorough explanations of these sometimes complex and confusing regulatory areas. As always, it's a pleasure talking with him. I hope you found his comments as perceptive and enlightening as I did.

4 ESSENTIAL ELEMENTS THE DOL REQUIRES OF EVERY RETIREMENT PLAN

The United States Department of Labor (DOL) has issued a booklet entitled "Meeting Your Fiduciary Responsibilities." The DOL created this publication to help Employee Retirement Income Security Act (ERISA) plan fiduciaries better understand their duties and obligations. The DOL provides the following four "essential elements" of all retirement plans:

1. A written plan that describes the benefit structure and guides day-to-day operations;
2. A trust fund to hold the plan's assets (unless it's set up as an insurance contract);
3. A recordkeeping system to track the flow of monies going to and from the retirement plan; and
4. Documents to provide plan information to employees participating in the plan and to the government.

The DOL does not require the plan fiduciary to personally conduct each of these tasks. Rather, the DOL understands the fiduciary may (and should) often desire to delegate these duties to professional third party service providers. The act of hiring a vendor, however, is itself a fiduciary act. This process should therefore be well documented and prudent. Without proper documentation, it's more difficult for the fiduciary to prove due diligence during a DOL audit.

5 IMPORTANT DUTIES EVERY ERISA FIDUCIARY MUST FULFILL

An employee places much trust in an ERISA fiduciary. Because they have the responsibility to act on behalf of retirement plan beneficiaries, plan fiduciaries are held by the DOL to certain standards of conduct. The DOL has specified the following duties for all ERISA fiduciaries (the following points are quoted directly from DOL materials):

1. Acting solely in the interest of plan participants and their beneficiaries and with the exclusive purpose of providing benefits to them;
2. Carrying out their duties prudently;
3. Following the plan documents (unless inconsistent with ERISA);
4. Diversifying plan investments; and
5. Paying only reasonable plan expenses.

The list can easily intimidate the typical plan sponsor, trustee or executive. The DOL, however, understands the plan fiduciary cannot always have expertise in such a diverse variety of areas. In such a case, the fiduciary may limit fiduciary liability by hiring knowledgeable professionals to handle specific duties. The DOL focuses not on the end result, but on the due diligence process exhibited by plan fiduciaries. The DOL looks for prudence and considers it "wise" to document procedures and the decision-making process, including any meaningful comparisons used when selecting vendors, investments or any other choice the plan fiduciary faces.

The plan fiduciary conducts this prudent due diligence by closely adhering to the terms and procedures of the plan document. If a fiduciary relies on a vendor to provide plan documents, then the fiduciary will especially want to regularly review such documentation to ensure it reflects any changes in or specifics of the plan.

Finally, prudence maintains that the fiduciary must undertake diversification, especially when it comes to investment options. Such diversification helps mitigate investment losses over the plan's entire portfolio. As before, this is a process that should be documented — ideally through an investment policy statement — and periodically reviewed.

Everything an ERISA/401(k) Fiduciary Needs to Know About DOL Audits to Reduce Fiduciary Liability

What most often triggers a DOL audit? What liability exposure does the ERISA/401(k) fiduciary typically face as a result of a DOL audit? Can a retirement plan fiduciary face criminal charges? What does the DOL auditor expect from the ERISA/401(k) fiduciary? What are the four critical keys the plan fiduciary should focus on during a DOL audit? Does the DOL have an ideal "Wish List of Materials" they expect an ERISA/401(k) fiduciary to provide during a DOL audit?

I was fortunate to share the dais at a fiduciary seminar with Paul Holloway, an employee benefits attorney and partner at Harter Secrest & Emery LLP of Rochester, New York. We spoke of strategies the ERISA/401(k) fiduciary can employ to reduce fiduciary liability. To be honest, most of the plan fiduciaries wanted to talk about investment due diligence, but Paul brought up some very good points about what to do after the horse has left the barn — i.e., once you've been informed the DOL has decided to audit your plan.

One common misconception Paul mentioned dealt with the triggering mechanism for the typical DOL audit. According to Paul, unlike the IRS, the DOL generally does not select targets at random. Rather, the DOL relies on three primary factors when it comes to deciding whom to audit: 1) participant complaints; 2) Form 5500 issues; and 3) media reports. If you think about it, the astute retirement plan trustee can certainly take measures to reduce the likelihood of activating these triggers.

And why would a fiduciary want to do everything to avoid a DOL audit? Well, for one thing, the DOL indicates that 75% of the cases result in monetary penalties. Worse, in 2008 alone, the DOL closed over 200 criminal cases. In other words, once the government comes knocking at your door, there's a real good chance they'll leave with another trophy to place on their mantle.

So, should you just pack it in and order new pinstripes (wink, wink) from your tailor the moment the DOL calls? Of course not! The DOL is even kind enough to offer three "key" suggestions when time comes for an audit: 1) Be organized; 2) Be cooperative; and 3) Be helpful. Holloway, perhaps a bit wary of any government promise, counters with his own list of four real imperatives for the fiduciary facing a DOL audit: 1) Try to ascertain what triggered the audit; 2) Prepare materials in advance; 3) Review with counsel; and, 4) Have counsel present or available (i.e., know when to call counsel). I'll add a fifth key: Make sure you have thoroughly-documented processes and thoroughly-documented reports showing you're following those processes.

Finally, Holloway shared what he called the DOL's "Wish List of Materials" every ERISA/401(k) plan fiduciary ought to be prepared to provide during an audit:

- Plan and Trust (make sure it's signed)
- Forms 5500 (with attachments) for the last three years
- Summary Plan Description
- Fiduciary Liability Policy
- Fidelity Bond
- Trust statements for the last three years
- Meeting minutes
- Benefit statements
- Asset records
- Payroll contribution records

This top ten list might not make *The Letterman Show*, but it does provide a good guideline for the average ERISA/401(k) fiduciary. Certainly, you wouldn't want to wait until the DOL calls before assembling these materials. In fact, if you pay strict attention to the processes inherent in this list, the DOL may never call at all.

FOR THE 401(K) FIDUCIARY LOOKING TO REDUCE FIDUCIARY LIABILITY: WHO IS AND WHO ISN'T A REGISTERED INVESTMENT ADVISER?

The 401(k) fiduciary typically searches for ways to reduce fiduciary liability. This can be done by hiring what the United States Department of Labor (DOL) terms "prudent experts," particularly in the area of investments. The DOL permits a fiduciary to appoint, among others, a registered investment adviser to reduce personal fiduciary liability.

In the DOL booklet *Meeting Your Fiduciary Responsibilities*, the DOL explains how ERISA/401(k) fiduciaries can reduce their fiduciary liability:

> *"A fiduciary can also hire a service provider or providers to handle fiduciary functions, setting up the agreement so that the person or entity then assumes liability for those functions selected. If an employer appoints an investment manager that is a bank, insurance company, or registered investment adviser, the employer is responsible for the selection of the manager, but is not liable for the individual investment decisions of that manager."*

It's pretty clear what a bank or insurance company is (I hope), but it's not unusual for the fiduciary to be confused as to who is and who isn't a registered investment adviser.

First, let's explain what a registered investment adviser (RIA) is. An RIA is registered with the United States Securities and Exchange Commission (SEC) under the

Investment Advisers Act of 1940 (40 Act). Several years ago, the SEC no longer required certain smaller RIAs to register under the 40 Act. Instead, those smaller RIAs could register at the state level. Many states exempt certain smaller investment advisers from registering, so it's possible a firm offering investment adviser services may not be registered.

How can the plan fiduciary tell if an investment adviser is an RIA? That's pretty simple. The SEC requires all RIAs to provide prospective clients with a Form ADV Part II (or similar brochure). In addition, any RIAs registered with the SEC must file an electronic Form ADV Part I. The ERISA/401(k) fiduciary can then search for the particular RIA at the SEC's Investment Adviser Public Disclosure search site. It's a little bit more difficult for state-registered RIAs since every state has its own rules. While there's no need to outright eliminate state-registered RIAs, the prudent fiduciary may want to investigate if a state-registered RIA is appropriate.

There are two common misconceptions the ERISA/401(k) fiduciary often has regarding who is an RIA.

Mutual Funds — Although mutual funds, or Registered Investment Companies, are registered with the SEC under the Investment Company Act of 1940 (this can be perplexing — mutual funds have their own "40 Act"), mutual funds are technically securities. So, selecting a mutual fund is similar to selecting IBM public stock — something that's obviously not an investment adviser.

Brokers — Any number of types of individuals and firms can be brokers, including insurance companies, (remember, the DOL allows plan fiduciaries to use insurance companies to legitimately reduce fiduciary liability). These firms most frequently include broker/dealers and financial planners. A simple rule of thumb is if the individual you're dealing with has a securities license, then they're probably a broker. This doesn't mean they're not also an RIA, but, again, you can verify this by checking the SEC Investment Adviser Public Disclosure search site to be sure. Of course, even if they are an RIA, the fact that they're also a broker means the ERISA/401(k) fiduciary must undertake suitable due diligence regarding payment terms to ensure the relationship does not create a self-dealing conflict of interest problem (but this is the subject for a different chapter).

Even though the DOL permits plan fiduciaries to reduce their personal fiduciary liability by hiring a registered investment adviser, bank or insurance company, it's good to keep in mind the following warning offered by the DOL:

> *"However, an employer is required to monitor the manager periodically to assure that it is handling the plan's investments prudently and in accordance with the appointment."*

THE DOL'S NEW INVESTMENT ADVICE RULE: MORE (OR LESS?) TROUBLE FOR THE 401(K) FIDUCIARY

In early 2010, the Department of Labor released its proposed new Investment Advice Rule (*Fact Sheet: Proposed Regulation to Increase Workers' Access to High Quality Investment Advice*, U.S. Department of Labor, February 26, 2010). By October 2011, the DOL had issued the guidelines of this new rule, which became effective in December of 2011. The department estimates that two million workers and 13 million IRA holders would benefit from this rule to the tune of $6 billion. At the time of its original release in 2010, the question on the mind of every 401(k) fiduciary was: Will the DOL's proposed rule increase my personal fiduciary liability?

In a press release issued prior to the 2010 press conference announcing this rule, U.S. Deputy Secretary of Labor Seth Harris said, "These rules will strengthen America's private retirement system by ensuring workers get good, objective information. When that happens, workers make the kind of decisions that are good for their families and the nation as the whole." The release focused on three primary safeguards the DOL will put in place to prevent investment advisers from engaging in any conflict of interest.

First, the investment adviser cannot benefit financially from any recommended investments. Will this prevent advisers from any form of self-dealing, even if it's disclosed and even if it's revenue neutral? At a press conference on this issue, Phyllis C. Borzi, Assistant Secretary of the Employee Benefits Security Administration, a unit of the Labor Department, told reporters the proposed rule contains a fee level provision that says a person giving advice cannot be compensated directly or indirectly. This exclusion pertains to advisers, their employees and their firms. Borzi explained the rule is designed to eliminate conflicts of interest. She said the DOL wants to make sure advisers can't steer participants towards "higher fee investment options."

Second, advisers would be required to disclose their fees. According to the DOL's 2010 Fact Sheet, advice given must be on a "level-fee" basis (i.e., "fees do not vary based on investments selected by the participant"). However, in the text of its original Investment Advice Rule, the DOL acknowledges "several of these commenters argued that the class exemption contained in the final rule permits financial interests that would cause a fiduciary adviser, and individuals providing investment advice on behalf of a fiduciary adviser, to have conflicts of interest, but does not contain conditions that would adequately mitigate such conflicts."

Third, if an adviser uses a computer model to offer advice, those computer models would have to be certified as objective and unbiased. Borzi said this is one area where the new rule differs from the original Bush rules issued in 2009. She said the earlier rule permitted a lot more flexibility for advisers and, in addition to not having a level fee rule, allowed for using a computer model in a different manner, which failed to prevent advisers from steering participants to more lucrative investments.

The new rule does not address whether the investment adviser will act as a fiduciary or be judged by the fiduciary standard. In addition, the 2010 wording of the rule suggested any certification of a computer model emphasize fee and avoid historic performance. When asked about this and the possibility the DOL might be inadvertently giving index funds an advantage over actively managed funds, (see "Does the 'Lost Decade' Signal the End of Passive Investing?" *FiduciaryNews.com*, January 5, 2010) Borzi agreed there's a difference of opinion on this issue. She also said the DOL does not want to offer investment advice. At the time, she encouraged people to comment on it if the rule appears to do that.

In fact, true to her word, when the final guidelines came out in December 2011, the DOL went out of its way to say fees should not be the only area to consider and that other factors may be just as or even more important. The Final Rule, issued on October 25, 2011 states the Rule:

> *"...requires that any investment advice must be based on generally accepted investment theories that take into account historic returns of different asset classes over defined periods of time, but also notes that generally accepted investment theories that take into account additional considerations are not precluded."*

Still, the Rule does bring up many fiduciary questions. If you're a 401(k) plan sponsor, you might want to visit the next three chapters to find out if your most important questions are answered.

3 Pointed Questions Determine If the DOL Investment Advice Rule Increases Your Fiduciary Liability

As the previous chapter explained, after nearly two years of delays, in October of 2011 the Department of Labor finally issued the official guidelines to the so-called "Investment-Advice" Rule originally promulgated during the waning days of the Bush administration. Unfortunately, many 401(k) plan sponsors either: (a) didn't know individual advice was prohibited in the first place; or, (b) have no idea whether individual investment advice is a good thing or a bad thing.

First, a bit of history. The DOL doesn't have a stellar track record when it comes to making rules that involve investments. Nearly a decade ago, it embraced and today continues to display a Modern Portfolio Theory bias in a behavioral finance world. Just two years ago it officially blessed the then new concept of target date funds as one of the three pre-approved default investments for 401(k) plans. We know where that got us.

In January of 2009, the DOL introduced the Investment-Advice Rule. This edict gave brokers the ability to offer direct one-on-one investment advice to 401(k) participants. House Education and Labor Committee Chairman George Miller, D-Calif. led the charge against this, with the support of the Obama administration, because he felt it failed to adequately address the conflict of interest issue. Indeed, just recently, the DOL's Phyllis C. Borzi suggested continuance of the rule would lead to "biased" advice (see "Labor Department nixes Bush OK to let brokers advise 401(k) plans," *Investment News*, September 14, 2009).

Of course, it doesn't leave the 401(k) fiduciary much comfort knowing the DOL had several times deferred implementation of the Investment-Advice Rule before effectively killing it. Worse, the administration gave Congress and the SEC first dibs on redefining the "Fiduciary Standard" and possibly eliminating the "broker-dealer exemption" (see "The Fiduciary Standard Debate," *sweet-bun.info*, October 27, 2009). The worst fears weren't realized as the DOL, as promised, delivered the new Investment Advice Rule before the issue of the Fiduciary Standard was settled, even though the definition of "Fiduciary" (as in, "Who is?" and "Who isn't") has a tremendous bearing on the implementation of the new Investment Advice Rule.

So, while Washington fiddles with the Fiduciary Standard, here are three vital questions every 401(k) fiduciary must answer to determine if the new DOL ruling increases personal fiduciary liability:

1. **When was the last time you conducted a comprehensive 401(k) plan diagnostic review?** Such a review examines not merely regulatory compliance but also fiduciary liability exposure. Specifically, among the things to survey in a diagnostic include identifying all service vendors and all potential conflicts of interest. For a more complete description, see the chapter titled "5 Critical Components of a Plan Diagnostic Test" in Section VIII.

2. **Do any of your 401(k) plan's investment options pay commissions (including 12(b)-1 fees or revenue sharing fees)?** Few plans still buy traditional load (i.e., commission) based funds. Some continue to use funds that incur 12(b)-1 fees (although according to the ICI's most recent report, this trend is also going down). Many, however, have a soon-to-be revealed (once the new Fee Disclosure Rule becomes effective in July 2012)

exposure to hidden revenue-sharing fees. Fiduciary exposure increases when the 401(k) investment options include commissions, 12(b)-1 fees and revenue sharing fees.

3. **Who picks the 401(k) investment options?** Two potential liability exposures can occur here. First, the plan fiduciary might be choosing the funds directly in the mistaken belief that regulators treat mutual funds in the same manner they treat Registered Investment Advisers. To see the importance of this distinction, read the chapter titled "Broker or Registered Investment Adviser? What's Best for the ERISA/401(k) Fiduciary?" in the next Section. Secondly, many, especially smaller, plans have hired bundled service providers. The practical consequence of the original Investment Advice Rule encouraged this. While sometimes plan costs demand the use of bundled service providers, short of an outright discretionary trust relationship (where the bank becomes a named fiduciary of the plan), reliance on a single vendor may increase fiduciary liability.

It makes a lot of sense for 401(k) plan sponsors to answer these three questions before moving on to the next chapter, where we discover the benefits of the new Investment Advice Rule.

3 GREAT WAYS THE DOL INVESTMENT ADVICE RULE HELPS THE 401(K) FIDUCIARY

A re you breathing a sigh of relief? ERISA plan sponsors — the 401(k) fiduciary in particular — have now had time to digest the Department of Labor's new Investment Advice Rule. Commentators have coalesced around several key benefits of the Rule.

1. The Rule "bans" conflicts of interest — advisers can no longer direct plan participants to investments in which the adviser has a pecuniary interest ("New Rules on 401(k)s, IRAs Roil Advisers," Robert Powell, *MarketWatch*, March 2, 2010). Well, upon reading the fine print, it doesn't really ban conflicts of interest, but it does discourage them. The DOL will continue to offer an exemption on prohibited transactions by advisers if those advisers employ a fee-level arrangement and use a computer model — i.e., one regularly audited to ensure it contains no bias — to proffer advice.

2. The Rule requires all investment advisers to disclose their fees ("Proposed 401(k) Plan Regulations Aim For Enhanced Transparency," *Wall Street Journal*, February 26, 2010; "Suddenly, 401(k) Fee Disclosures Getting Plenty of Attention," *Investment News*, March 15, 2010). What can ensure the conflicted adviser does not direct the investor into funds that generate additional revenues to the adviser? We seem to live in the era of transparency, and, consistent with this, full, open fee disclosure will let the plan participant (and the plan's corporate fiduciaries) know with certainty if the adviser may be taking advantage of the plan in any way.

3. The Rule forbids brokers (i.e., non-fiduciaries) from giving investment advice — they may only provide education on investment options ("New Retirement Plan Rules Could Hurt Brokers," CNBC, March 26, 2010; "Rep or Fiduciary? Labor Department Says, 'Choose,'" *Investment News*, March 14, 2010). While generating controversy within the industry, this benefit may rise to become the most important for the 401(k) investor. The fiduciary requirement raises the level of responsibility for the financial service provider. Registered Investment Advisers already serve as plan fiduciaries, so this requirement changes nothing for them. Brokers, on the other hand, appear to be the service providers most impacted by this requirement. Transforming from the less rigorous "Suitability Standard" to the more stringent "Fiduciary Standard" can present problems for a typical broker's business model. It does, however, offer tremendous benefits for both plan participants and plan sponsors.

Alas, the Lord giveth and the Lord taketh away. It seems no matter how honest their intentions, with regulators, for every action there is an equal and opposite reaction. Be sure to read the next chapter to discover more.

3 TERRIBLE PROBLEMS THE DOL INVESTMENT ADVICE RULE POSES TO THE 401(K) FIDUCIARY

D id you know the Department of Labor's Investment Advice Rule may increase a 401(k) plan sponsor's fiduciary liability? If a plan enters into a prohibited relationship with a vendor — or if an existing relationship now becomes prohibited — fiduciary liability rises. (See "Talking Points: Investment Advice Regulations," *PLANSPONSOR Magazine* podcast from March 2010). Can the 401(k) fiduciary afford to ignore these critical issues?

1. The Rule makes it too difficult for brokers to maintain a viable business model in the absence of offering conflicted advice ("Will Participant Advice Rules Create Too Many Obstacles for Participants to Receive Advice?" *fi360 Blog*, March 29, 2010). No doubt many 401(k) plan sponsors, especially those of larger plans, were attracted by the apparent low cost of using brokers to deliver investment advice. The Rule now requires those brokers to change their business model or leave the business. In changing the way they do business, they may find it difficult to maintain the margins necessary to continue operating as they have been. While we must laud the DOL for forcing this issue, 401(k) fiduciaries must be prepared to find alternative vendors. While the market is large enough to provide for this, those plan sponsors may be disappointed to learn they may no longer be able to continue a long-standing relationship. Then again, that might be precisely the type of relationship the DOL frowns upon.

2. The Rule doesn't really overturn Frost. Recall, the DOL's Frost Opinion exempts fiduciaries from the prohibited transaction rule (see "Readers Select Top Fiduciary Stories of 2009: #7 The SEC's Statement on 12(b)-1 fees," *FiduciaryNews.com*, January 25, 2010). Rather than eliminating this obvious conflict, the DOL require advisers who use investments that generate fees for their firms to use "audited" computer models ("New 401(k) Transparency Rules Proposed," *Financial Advisor*, March 1, 2010). By requiring computer models, the DOL blesses only certain investment theories. If the history of trust law is any guide, codification of any investment theory is likely to lead to conflicts once those theories became outdated. (This most recently occurred in the early 2000's when the DOL and the Uniform Prudent Investor Act endorsed Modern Portfolio Theory just as it was breathing its last gasps.) Here's the conundrum for the 401(k) plan sponsor: when the theory goes stale, what should the fiduciary do — follow the law or do the right thing? It appears the computer model requirement materialized in order to continue to accommodate Frost. Here's a compelling idea: Why not simply revoke Frost over a set time period and give those fiduciaries and vendors continued liability exemption until that time period expires?

3. In its original proposal, by emphasizing fees to the exclusion of performance, the Rule gave an inappropriate advantage to index funds ("Labor Dept.'s 401(k) Proposal Could Rock Pension Advice Business," *Investment News*, February 26, 2010). Of all the problems with the proposed Rule, this appeared the most dangerous. Even the DOL, in a press conference on February 26, 2010, admitted it does not want to get into the investment advisory

business (one would presume the SEC would agree). Yet, by emphasizing fees and specifically prohibiting the use of historic performance, the DOL would have forced the fiduciary to select only low-cost mutual funds. We all know "low-cost" can easily translate to "index fund." The proposed Rule therefore encouraged plan fiduciaries to offer only (or mostly, or give undo preference to) index funds at a time when these funds are clearly under-performing their actively managed kin. In its final Rule, the DOL went out of its way to say fees are only one factor to use when selecting investments, but the cat might already have escaped the bag.

It's important we understand we cannot throw out the baby with the bathwater. The previous chapter outlines innovative ideas found in the rule that only those with a vested interest have complained about. We need some form of an Investment Advice Rule and what the DOL has offered has proven an excellent start. It has begun to create a framework that protects investors, but, as the above suggests, it hasn't gone far enough in one sense (keeping the Frost Opinion) but it has eliminated language that gives preference to Modern Portfolio Theory or low-cost mutual funds.

Exclusive Comments from Industry Insiders Suggest Fin-Reg's Fiduciary Standard May Impact 401(k) Plan Sponsors

The Congressional reconciliation committee compromise package for the proposed Financial Reform Act eventually became the Dodd Frank Act. (Before you start laughing at this irony, remember, this is a book about running 401(k) plans, not running the home mortgage industry into the ground. If you're interested in that, read my e-book *"Explaining the End of the World as We Know It: The Financial Crisis as of November 2008 — Why We Are Where We Are and Where We Might Go From Here"* available for free in the *FiduciaryNews.com* bookstore.) The law contains key provisions relating to steps necessary for the adoption of a broad fiduciary standard. While the law only asked the SEC to study and comment on the issue, many felt this legislation could have had a significant impact on the way brokers, financial planners, insurance sales agents, and other financial professionals ply their trade. (For a complete overview of the compromise, see fi360's article "Fiduciary duty for broker-dealers soon to be in the hands of the SEC" published June 28, 2010.) The implementation of a universal Fiduciary Standard may require 401(k) plan sponsors to revisit the vendors currently providing services to their plan and may even cause the removal of some of those providers.

That's the worst case. I spent several days speaking with industry leaders about this subject. To hear them tell it, this law may end up merely being much ado about nothing — or it could just change the world as we know it. (N.B.: Here I say "change it" not "end it."

David G. Tittsworth, Executive Director of the Investment Adviser Association (IAA), a not-for-profit organization representing the interests of SEC-registered investment adviser firms, would have preferred the statutory removal of the current broker exemption from the Investment Advisers Act of 1940. "Senator Dodd had that in his initial bill, but the Senate replaced it with a six-month study. Coming out of the reconciliation committee, the Securities and Exchange Commission (SEC) still had to conduct a study over the next six months, but the compromise changed the wording from 'the Commission shall' to 'the Commission may' enact rules following study."

Under the agreement, the SEC conducted a study to evaluate the effectiveness of existing standards, primarily in a retail arena. "Every member of our Association is an Investment Adviser registered with the SEC, and they all are subject to the Fiduciary Standard," Tittsworth says. "What we're talking about is extending the Standard to other people doing essentially the same thing. We think the fiduciary duty under the Investment Advisers Act is appropriate for both the investors as well as the professionals who offer the service."

Dan Barry, Director of Government Relations of the Financial Planning Association (FPA), said his organization has no official position on the matter. "We represent more than twenty-four thousand members and these individuals have different points of view. I haven't been able to discern a strong opinion or consensus of opinion."

Nonetheless, the FPA is on the record of supporting a Fiduciary Standard. "When Dodd first came out with the bill," said Barry, "we were part of a group that signed a letter that supported the proposal as an effective way to apply the Fiduciary Standard to brokers. There is an understanding there could be unintended consequences to any action. It was more about the fiduciary duty than specifically removing the broker exemption."

Barry does offer some practical implications should the SEC go forward with requiring all professionals offering investment advice to follow a Fiduciary Standard. "If it's just about execution, the Fiduciary Standard won't come into play. But, if the broker starts getting into advice, that's where the Standard kicks in. Once the SEC makes its rules, I would expect there to be greater clarification to make this clearer."

Still, Barry can see major changes coming from the adoption of a universal Fiduciary Standard. "The brokers are going to have to look at how they sell their products. If in the process of making sales transactions, they advise clients to make purchases, they're going to have to change that. You can envision something where there are greater disclosures about commissions, sales of proprietary products or principal transactions, disclosures about conflicts of interest, etc. I would expect that any final rules would emphasize greater disclosure, hopefully in simple words customers can understand."

Tittsworth remains more sanguine regarding the ultimate endgame. Consistent with this cautious approach, he says, "I think it could have been worse and it could have been better. As a first priority, we simply don't want to see Congress or the SEC water down the current requirements. Beyond that, we'd like to see a level playing field among professionals providing similar services."

He is quite clear on the IAA's next steps. "The battle now shifts from Capitol Hill to the SEC," said Tittsworth. "This final agreement represents a compromise. We're going to continue to support the Fiduciary Standard in the investment advice arena. We're going to provide the SEC with what they need to support adoption of a universal Fiduciary Standard. Chairman Schapiro has in the past made comments that broker dealers providing investment advice should be subject to a fiduciary duty. Ultimately, though, we have to wait and see what happens in the rule-making process."

Roger Wohlner, named by the *The Wall Street Journal* as the top financial blogger, best summarizes the view of many investment advisers when he says, "ANYBODY who recommends, sells, or otherwise facilitates a client moving into any investment vehicle owes that client a standard of care at the fiduciary level. The first consideration should be whether a financial product is in the client's best interest. To me, suitability is nonsense. But let me be clear, I am not talking about individuals who are do-it-yourselfers executing trades on their own. In this case, the TD Ameritrades, Schwabs, etc. do not, in my opinion, owe this Fiduciary Standard of care."

For the 401(k) Plan Sponsors, the adoption of a universal Fiduciary Standard may greatly impact how their plans operate. This will be especially true for plans currently receiving investment services from any entity not presently under a Fiduciary Standard. The action is now within the SEC arena, with an assist from the DOL. The SEC is already on record saying it wants to address the long festering 12(b)-1 issue. Wouldn't it be amazing if the SEC decided to kill two birds with one stone?

IS THE FIDUCIARY STANDARD ENOUGH? 3 CRITICAL FIDUCIARY DUTIES EVERY ERISA PLAN SPONSOR MUST KNOW

In mid-2010, Congress, regulators and the financial industry itself sat on the cusp of requiring all financial service providers that provide investment advice to adopt the Fiduciary Standard. This arcane debate has since become a partisan football. It's likely the DOL will broaden its definition of fiduciary and there's an even chance the SEC will adopt the Fiduciary Standard, if only because it levels what is now an unfair playing field between brokers and registered investment advisers. All 401(k) fiduciaries must familiarize themselves with the nature of fiduciary duties. The change in the law may expose these fine folks to a fiduciary liability they might not have anticipated.

"The duties ascribed to corporate trustees, especially the duty of loyalty, are often benchmark standards for other types of fiduciaries," wrote Janice J. Sackley, CLU, CFE in the March/April 2010 edition of *Currents*, a publication from the National Society of Compliance Professionals. She says many might be surprised to discover today's Fiduciary Standard debate in Washington derives from well-established trust law. A healthier appreciation of these traditional fiduciary duties may allow ERISA trustees, fiduciaries and plan sponsors to better assess their true liability risks. This awareness becomes more important if, in the future, Congress and/or regulators adopt the fiduciary standard across the board. Where fiduciary relationships already exist, a deeper understanding of these duties can help the plan fiduciary better evaluate whether their current advisers adhere to true fiduciary principles.

Among these and other critical points Sackley identifies, the following three trustee duties especially apply to ERISA fiduciaries:

1. Duty of Loyalty — The fiduciary must not engage in acts of self-dealing. This is perhaps the most fundamental duty.
2. Duty to Keep Property Separate and Maintain Adequate Records — Client property must be segregated from the property of the fiduciary and adequate records must be kept.
3. Duty of Prudent Investment — The fiduciary who manages investments has a duty to comply with the prudent investor rule unless otherwise agreed to with the client.

Sackley is a fiduciary consultant with Fiduciary Foresight, LLC, a firm that advises financial institutions on regulatory compliance and fiduciary risk management issues. These duties and others are discussed in the context of bank and thrift trustees in her original (and very well written) *Currents* article, "Duties of a Trustee and Other Fiduciaries; Will Trustees Set the Bar for the Fiduciary Standard?" The piece discusses the fact that regulations governing banks acting as investment managers are prescribed by the banking regulators and in some cases are more onerous than those currently stipulated by the SEC for registered investment advisers and by the Department of Labor for firms advising ERISA plans.

One wonders when regulators will ever go beyond the "Fiduciary Standard vs. Suitability Standard" debate and begin to address the real issue. Will Congress, the SEC and the DOL upgrade the current fiduciary standard to the trust model used by bank trust departments so successfully for more than a century? After all, unlike the mortgage derivative fiasco, when's the last time you heard of a bank scandal coming from the trust department?

SECTION FOUR:

– PROVIDER INDEPENDENCE –

HOW TO AVOID SERVICE VENDOR CONFLICTS OF INTEREST

408(B)(2) COMPLIANCE AND THE SERVICE PROVIDER LIST

In February 2012, the DOL issued a Fact Sheet outlining the final regulations of its Fee Disclosure Rule set to go effective on July 1, 2012. The DOL has added additional fiduciary duties to the every growing "to-do" list of 401(k) plan sponsors. Plan sponsors must now obtain fee disclosure information from, according to the Fact Sheet, "the following covered service providers:

> ➤ ERISA fiduciary service providers to a covered plan or to a 'plan asset' vehicle in which such plan invests;
> ➤ Investment advisers registered under Federal or State law;
> ➤ Record-keepers or brokers who make designated investment alternatives available to the covered plan (e.g., a 'platform provider');
> ➤ Providers of one or more of the following services to the covered plan who also receive 'indirect compensation' in connection with such services: Accounting, auditing, actuarial, banking, consulting, custodial, insurance, investment advisory, legal, recordkeeping, securities brokerage, third party administration, or valuation services."

Since many 401(k) plan sponsors receive these services from a single source, otherwise known as a bundled service provider, and since the new Fee Disclosure Rule now requires fees to be broken out by service, I thought it might be instructive to review the different types of service providers and their primary duties.

Corporate Trustee — Here we do not refer to the trustees of the plan, who are individuals named by the plan sponsor to safeguard and administer the plan. Instead, a Corporate Trustee, usually a bank trust company, provides "trust services" to the plan, including acting as a fiduciary to the plan. The Corporate Trustee may be directed by the plan sponsors or it may have discretionary powers. In neither case does a trustee relationship remove the fiduciary liability from the plan sponsor. As such, it is not expected for plans to have a Corporate Trustee. Most plans settle for a Plan Custodian and a Plan Investment Adviser.

Plan Counsel — This is the ERISA attorney who administers to the plan and who specializes in employee retirement benefit plan regulations and legal proceedings. Plans using customized plan documents generally require plan counsel. Plans using prototype documents can try to get by without one, but it makes sense for plan sponsors to have a good ERISA attorney in their Rolodex. Only a lawyer can answer legal questions.

Plan Accountant — Plans above a certain size require an annual independent audit; hence, the need for a plan accountant. Even plans below the required size should have an accountant on hand to answer any tax questions. Only a tax adviser like an accountant can answer tax questions.

Plan Custodian — This is the institution that actually holds the assets of the plan.

Plan Recordkeeper — The Plan Recordkeeper maintains all participant data and trade processing, including the disposition of salary deferrals from the Payroll Processor. The Plan Sponsor can also delegate to the Plan Recordkeeper, through a limited power of attorney, the authority to instruct the Plan Broker to initiate trades and the Paying Agent to make distributions. The Plan Recordkeeper may also provide TPA functions.

Plan Third Party Administrator (TPA) — The Plan TPA is involved in monitoring and testing the plan for ERISA compliance and for other administrative duties such as processing loans.

Plan Investment Adviser — The Plan Investment Adviser acts as a fiduciary to the plan, as required by the SEC (the DOL is currently reviewing its definition of fiduciary to determine whether it should be expanded to include other of the service providers listed here). The Plan Investment Adviser drafts the Plan's Investment Policy Statement, provides recommendations on the selection of investment options and performs periodic due diligence monitoring on behalf of the Plan Sponsor. A Corporate Trustee can also provide these same functions. Also, like the in situation of a Corporate Trustee, while hiring a Plan Investment Adviser does mitigate certain fiduciary liability (primarily under the Uniform Prudent Investor Acts), it does not fully remove fiduciary liability from the plan sponsor.

Plan Broker — A plan may use a Plan Broker in lieu of a Plan Investment Adviser. A Plan Broker currently does not have to act as a fiduciary to the plan. The Plan Broker may be a stockbroker or an insurance broker, or both.

Underlying Investment Options — These would include mutual funds, annuity contracts and other vehicles the plan may choose to invest in. Generally the plan does not pay direct fees to these entities, although, for example, mutual funds have operational expenses that generate an "expense ratio" that is disclosed in the fund's prospectus and financial reports.

Payroll Processor — Some plan sponsors contract their payroll processing duties to a third party. This is the Payroll

Processor. The Payroll Processor must work closely with both the Plan Sponsor and the Plan Recordkeeper to maintain the plan's data. In some cases, the Payroll Processor will take on the duties of the Plan Recordkeeper, although many Plan Sponsors prefer the functions be performed independently of one another so as to add another audit and control layer to the process of moving participant money.

Paying Agent — Usually the job of the Plan Custodian, this service includes disbursing any funds from the plan to any other party, including paying service fees and distributing assets to plan beneficiaries. In smaller plans, the Plan Sponsor may do this to save the plan money, but it's generally preferred to have an independent party performing this function.

These are the most often used service providers, although plans may hire consultants, actuaries or other vendors for tasks. The 2012 Fee Disclosure Guidelines require 401(k) plan sponsors to obtain fee information from any vendor receiving more than $1,000 and from any vendor receiving indirect compensation.

The DOL is particularly concerned with plan sponsors uncovering conflicts of interest as a result of fee disclosure. These conflicts of interest may occur in cases when certain services are bundled together or when preferential advice is given in return for payment. It is the intention of the Fee Disclosure Rule to reveal these conflicts of interest and for the plan sponsor to address them in an appropriate manner.

As such, it's a good idea for 401(k) plan sponsors to examine their list of service providers even more closely; otherwise, they might be surprised to find themselves among the poster boys of the next chapter.

STUDY SHOCKER: 9 OF 10 401(K) PLANS EXPOSED TO INCREASED CONFLICT OF INTEREST RISK

Just in time for the DOL's 2012 Fee Disclosure Rule, Deloitte Consulting LLP has completed a report for the Investment Company Institute (ICI). Issued in November 2011, *Inside the Structure of Defined Contribution/401(k) Plan Fees: A Study Assessing the Mechanics of the 'All-In' Fee*, offers some expected results, at least one shocking revelation not reported elsewhere in the media and, unfortunately, a typical misrepresentation that might just invalidate some of the most publicized conclusions.

One must keep in mind the relevant disclosures when reading the results of this survey. First, the results don't reflect the actual data, but a weighting of the actual data. Also, since some plan sponsors did not answer all questions, cross-tabulation between questions does become problematic, but that should be reflected in the associated statistics. Finally, while the survey collects quantitative fee data, it acknowledges it does not attempt to evaluate either the quality or value of the services associated with those fees. While measuring qualitative information is difficult, the DOL allows significant leeway with regard to paying higher fees for additional value.

Here are a few interesting tidbits about the survey sample. The vast bulk (i.e. 56%) of the respondents had less than $1 million in assets while only 7% of the respondents had greater than $1 billion in assets. As odd as that sounds, the actual DOL 401(k) plan universe exhibits an even greater skew. According to the DOL, 71% of the plan universe has assets of less than $1 million and a mere 0.1% has assets in excess of $1 billion. The survey sample is also skewed more to the Midwest and less to the South.

This new survey confirmed three key findings from the ICI's 2009 Fee Study, all of which would have been expected from anyone the least bit familiar with the 401(k) industry. First, there are many different types of fee structures and arrangements for the many different 401(k) plans. Second, the number of plan participants is inversely related to plan costs (i.e., the more participants, the lower the costs as a percentage of plan assets). Third, plans with bigger account balances also tend to have lower fees (again, based on a percentage of plan assets).

More interesting, however, are the results many would not have expected. The first is, two-thirds (67%) of the plans have not had a competitive review within the last three years. Roughly one in five plans between $10 million and $500 million have had a review within the last year. The most frequently shopped plans, however, were those with more than $1 billion, of which 30% have had a competitive review within the last twelve months. Strangely, plans between $500 million and $1 billion are the worst in terms of reviews, with the fewest number having reviews within the past year (6%) and the largest number of plans having had no reviews within the last five years (59%).

The survey surprisingly reports 91% of the respondents say they use the recordkeeper's proprietary investment options. We'll quote directly from the report: "ABC mutual fund company is the recordkeeper and the plan offers ABC mutual funds, ABC commingled trusts, or ABC separate accounts; DEF bank is the recordkeeper and the plan offers DEF mutual funds or DEF commingled trusts or DEF separate accounts; XYZ insurance company is the recordkeeper and the plan offers XYZ mutual funds or XYZ separate accounts or XYZ commingled trusts." Proprietary bundling like this would seem to offer the classic recipe for a conflict of interest problem, which would further seem to indicate there exists a greater potential for conflicts of interest in nine out of ten plans. Other reporters appear to have overlooked this particular fact, but it stands out as the most shocking aspect of this survey. It might also explain both the need for and the opposition to the DOL's new Fiduciary Rule.

Many plan sponsors would be interested to know the typical employee contributes 6% of their salary. The illustrative plan offers 14 investment options, with 96% of all plans using mutual funds, and 93% of all plans using equity investment options. In addition, only 23% of the respondents offer auto-enrollment, down from 45% in the 2009 Study. Deloitte says this reflects the greater portion of smaller plans responding to the latest survey, but it also calls into question weighting techniques used in either this survey or the 2009 Study.

Finally, here's the biggest problem with this survey: the "all-in" fee. The study's fee analysis is predicated on an aggregation of all fees. It does not break out its analysis by service provider category (unlike the *401(k) Averages Book*), which might have been more helpful to plan sponsors. By using the "all-in" fee, the survey inadvertently encourages a "bundled" service provider approach that other commentators have suggested might lead to higher fees. Worse, the methodology includes mutual fund expense ratios as part of the plan fees when these "expenses" are already (and more accurately) reflected in a fund's performance reporting. The DOL recently amended its Individual Participant Advice Rule to avoid emphasizing fund expense ratios without incorporating fund performance. Unfortunately, by including mutual fund expense ratios, the survey enables misrepresentations far too prevalent and may invalidate — or at least make meaningless — most of the results revolving around its "all-in" fee analysis.

Using the "all-in" methodology can lead one to conclude plans where assets are invested mostly in stable value options are "less expensive" compared to plans invested mostly in equity options. For a long time, policy-makers, plan sponsors and service providers felt plan investors were too conservative and needed to invest more in equities and less in stable income options. The 2006 Pension Protection Act addressed this concern specifically. By including expense ratios in "all-in" fees, analysts only encourage the continuation of this type of behavior. The study does provide average expense ratio data by asset class. In doing so, it indirectly admits the problem of including expense ratios in its analysis when it says a plan's asset allocation can impact its "all-in" fees.

The report, however, does not bring up the same point with regard to index funds. Plans using raw index funds appear "less expensive" than those offering actively managed or lifestyle funds. Despite periods of poorer performance, index funds may be fine for employees brave enough (and with the time to) determine their own asset allocation. Many employees, on the other hand, don't want to worry about making asset allocation decisions and would prefer the peace of mind of having professional management make these decisions. This, of course, brings us back to the question of the value one gets for the fees paid. In the case of investment products, that value — which can be different for everyone — cannot be measured with certainty, but its relevance sometimes trumps fees.

But, when it comes to the problems posed by revenue sharing, don't take it just from me. The expert I interview in the next chapter comes with impeccable credentials.

RON RHOADES ON REVENUE SHARING:
TWO HATS ARE WORSE THAN ONE

From time to time I feel it's important to make an effort to go beyond the quotes and sit down with thought leaders in the fiduciary arena in hopes of getting them to share some of their deeper thoughts. I was fortunate to catch up with Ron A. Rhoades, JD, CFP®, who shared the podium with me at an FPA Ethics Symposium in Buffalo, NY in September 2011. (It's always great to be in the Queen City when the Buffalo Bills are undefeated!)

Dr. Rhoades is an Assistant Professor and Program Chair for the Financial Planning Program at Alfred State College in Alfred, New York. He is also President of ScholarFi Inc., a fee-only RIA firm. Dr. Rhoades has written extensively on the fiduciary obligations of investment and financial advisors. He was the recipient of the 2011 Tamar Frankel Fiduciary of the Year Award, for "changing the nature of the fiduciary debate in Washington." He also was named one of the Top 25 Most Influential Persons in the advisory profession by Investment Advisor magazine for 2011. He currently serves on the National Board of NAPFA. Dr. Rhoades is the author of several books, and many published articles, and frequently contributes to comment letters to government agencies on issues affecting investment adviser compliance and fiduciary duties.

Carosa: Ron, first off, congratulations on your award. It's an honor to have this opportunity to talk to you on the topic of fiduciary liability and conflicts of interest. Let's start with revenue sharing, the popular industry practice where mutual funds pay the fees of broker-dealers, recordkeepers and other service providers in lieu of the plan sponsor paying those fees. Can you share your thoughts on revenue sharing, why it's a problem and how it can increase fiduciary liability for the plan sponsor?

Dr. Rhoades: The largest problem with revenue sharing payments, from the standpoint of the plan sponsor, is that they can vary the compensation paid to the investment adviser. The amount of revenue sharing varies from fund company to fund company, and it can also vary based upon either the new assets brought by the broker-dealer to the fund or the assets maintained in the fund, or both. This leads to an inherent conflict of interest — one so severe that a true fiduciary cannot effectively manage the conflict. In essence, the fiduciary advisor could receive greater compensation by recommending one fund over another. Essentially, the broker-dealer would be wearing two hats — a circumstance the "sole interests" ERISA fiduciary standard and the prohibited transaction rules (as originally written, without exemptions) were designed to avoid.

Carosa: You bring up a good point when you say "as originally written." The reality is the DOL has now carved out exemptions to the prohibited transaction rules all trustees must abide by. Short of re-establishing a pure fiduciary standard and reinstating these prohibitions, how can plan sponsors best maintain the fiduciary premise in the current regulatory environment?

Dr. Rhoades: In a true fiduciary environment, the compensation of the advisor is established in advance of any recommendations. This ensures the compensation of the fiduciary will not vary based upon the recommendations made. The fiduciary acts as the sole representative of the plan sponsor, and is prohibited from wearing two hats. If compensation of any form is then received by the fiduciary from anyone other than the client, then that compensation so received should be credited (in full) against the fiduciary's agreed-upon fee.

Carosa: OK, that's how to deal with the current regulatory environment. But we all know the DOL wants to broaden the definition of "Fiduciary" under ERISA. Do you think this new DOL proposal will fix the current problem?

Dr. Rhoades: While the plain language of ERISA adopts the "sole interests" fiduciary standard — a tougher standard than the "best interests" standard applicable to registered investment advisers — and hence outlaws conflicts of interest, the DOL has provided numerous exemptions from the definition of fiduciary. Hopefully the new rulemaking in this area will rectify this situation, with very few exemptions and with a full implementation of the "sole interests" fiduciary standard of conduct.

Carosa: Of course, some rather large and entrenched players in the financial services industry have fought the DOL, as well as the SEC, on the issue of the fiduciary standard. Even politicians, many of whom have expressed concerns about regulations hampering business in a slow economy, have asked the regulators to restrain themselves. Do you believe it's possible for regulators to create a fiduciary framework consistent with the traditional duties of fiduciaries (i.e., the "fiduciary standard") that allows existing business models to continue?

Dr. Rhoades: There have been numerous calls by the broker-dealer industry for the DOL to adopt a "compensation-neutral" or "business model-neutral" fiduciary scheme. In reality, however, fiduciary standards act as a restraint on various forms of conduct, and compel certain other types of actions (e.g., extensive due diligence on both overall investment strategy and investment product selection). Hopefully the DOL will force the securities industry to adapt to the fiduciary standard of conduct — it can so adapt, by changing its compensation practices and eliminating revenue-sharing arrangements. Ideally the fiduciary standard of conduct will not be diminished by seeking to adapt it to the business practices of an industry that remains largely composed of "manufacturer's representatives." Many a jurist has warned that, in the end, a true fiduciary cannot wear two hats.

Carosa: Well, we've been talking pretty theoretically up to this point. That's the professor side of you. Speaking of two hats, let me allow you to don your other hat and speak to the practical side of things. Many plan sponsors would rather focus on improving their business and don't have a lot of time set aside to address issues important to their 401(k). They would rest comfortably, though, if an expert such as yourself gave a few quick-and-easy rules of thumb to abide by. With that in mind, what advice would give 401(k) plan sponsors that they could act upon right now?

Dr. Rhoades: Plan sponsors should not wait for the DOL to act. The DOL's rules do not necessarily provide "safe harbors" for plan sponsors. Hence, I would advise plan sponsors to avoid any revenue-sharing arrangements, of any type, between the advisors and other vendors of the plan. This includes not only payment for shelf space, but also soft dollar compensation and other "back-channel" payments. Establish the compensation of the investment adviser in advance — before any investment recommendations are made — either as a flat fee, hourly fee, or percentage of assets (or some combination thereof). If revenue-sharing payments are in place, demand that they be credited, in full, against any fees paid to the broker-dealer firm acting as the fiduciary to the plan.

Carosa: Moving from the issue of revenue sharing, let's talk about 12(b)-1 fees. If revenue sharing is sort of a back-door way for plan vendors to "hide" compensation, then 12(b)-1 fees are the front door. There's no question there are much broader concern with 12(b)-1 fees. Indeed, for a time it appeared the SEC was on the verge of outlawing them. Recent studies by the ICI show the use of 12(b)-1 fees has tailed off considerably among 401(k) plans. Still, some plans continue to offer funds with 12(b)-1 fees. Do you have any straightforward rules plan sponsors should adopt regarding 12(b)-1 fees?

Dr. Rhoades: If 12(b)-1 fees exist and are paid out to the broker-dealer firm, those should be credited (in full) against the amount of the agreed-upon compensation with the broker-dealer firm. If 12(b)-1 fees exist and are not fully paid out to the broker-dealer firm (to be credited), then the plan sponsor should avoid the fund. There is no reason to pay 12(b)-1 fees to a mutual fund since 12(b)-1 fees were originally designed to assist in the retail marketing of a fund, where there is no benefit to the plan sponsor.

Carosa: Wow, you're pretty blunt. But that's probably the kind of advice 401(k) plan sponsors most desire. Are there any other skeletons hiding in the conflict of interest closets plan sponsors need to be aware of?

Dr. Rhoades: In addition, if the broker-dealer is chosen by a fund company to execute a large amount of trades for the fund (which can be, even without payment of soft dollar compensation, a questionable practice, given the outlawing of directed brokerage and the rise of electronic trading platforms at very low fees), this is a "red flag" that highlights the need for greater scrutiny as to whether the investment adviser is truly acting on behalf of the plan sponsor, and not its own. Is directed brokerage, which was outlawed by the SEC several years ago, still a problem? A simple statistical analysis of the relationships between many mutual fund complexes and broker-dealer firms, relative to those of other fund complexes, would show that directed brokerage remains an insidious problem in many segments of the broker-dealer industry.

Carosa: That's one many plan sponsors have probably never even heard of. It might be enough to have them question their existing relationships. With that in mind, what guidelines do you suggest 401(k) plan sponsors should require of their investment adviser?

Dr. Rhoades: When selecting an investment adviser, plan sponsors should focus on: (1) the amount of compensation paid to the investment adviser, because fees directly impact participants' returns; (2) the quality of adherence to the duty of due care by the adviser — as to due diligence in overall investment strategies utilized, plus individual fund due diligence; (3) whether the investment adviser possesses any limits as to the funds which could be offered (because why would a plan sponsor choose an investment adviser who cannot recommend the entire universe of mutual funds and ETFs — including the very best offerings out there — to execute the strategies adopted); and (4) expertise on all matters relating to the selection of other vendors, the education of plan participants, and the fiduciary duties of plan sponsors. A failing in any one of these areas could subject the plan sponsor to unintended consequences — including potential liability for breach of the plan sponsor's own fiduciary obligations.

It was an honor speaking with Dr. Rhoades, as his comments attest to his broad experience. As he suggests, others share his sentiments. We'll discover some of these folks in the next chapter.

SHOULD 401(K) PLAN SPONSORS SELL THEIR SOULS FOR ONE-STOP-SHOPPING?

We face these decisions each day of our lives in many different ways. You've just quenched your car's empty gas tank, but standing in the heat of the sun urges you to satisfy your own thirst. Rather than drive down the street to the grocery market, you decide the convenience of the service station's cooler far outweighs the higher cost of the ice-cold beverages it holds. But price and convenience can go both ways. Low-priced merchandise stores have recently added low-cost groceries to their inventory. In these cases, often the convenience of one-stop-shopping trumps the lesser quality of, in particular, those lower-cost dairy and produce items.

Is it a surprise, then, to discover the 401(k) world mimics this very same retail environment? From banks to insurance companies, from payroll processors to mutual fund families, the appeal of convenience often lures the 401(k) plan sponsor to these bundled service providers. But are the purported lower fees of bundling real, or are they a figment of some marketing department's imagination? Worse, do bundled providers act as a fiduciary trap given the very real conflicts of interest embedded within them?

Despite a growing consensus, which we'll reveal in a moment, the debate rages on.

"Bundled service providers can be good for smaller plans. I like the unbundled model for mid-size and larger plans. However, it is the type of bundled service provider that small employers should take the time to choose. There are many good bundled independent TPA/recordkeepers that provide open architecture, fee-transparent services along with robust 3(21) and 3(38) fiduciary services," says Sarah Simoneaux, a retirement services consultant from the greater New Orleans area and a Past President of the

American Society of Pension Professionals & Actuaries. "I think small and mid-size plan sponsors sometimes go for the 'name' providers because they think it is safer, when in fact, it frequently is not," she adds. "A Cogent study said plan sponsors cared more about service than about 'name' in 401(k) providers. The name just got you in the door."

Michael Spraul agrees. Spraul, a financial services professional from the Cincinnati area who spent nearly twenty years working for Fidelity, says, "I agree not all bundled service providers are great, [but] employers should work with the format that suits them best. If you go with a bundled platform, you are working with one company. If you un-bundle, you increase administration because you are working with multiple providers. That increase in administration will take time, and that time and expense should not be ignored."

Indeed, we recognize this last statement as the essential "one-stop-shopping" benefit of bundled service providers. In general, many cite the benefits of bundling to include a single point of contact for resolution of issues; depth and scale to deliver services; and, economies of scale that permit cost-effective service delivery.

However, there is less of a consensus on that last point. It's not clear if bundling offers convenience at a higher cost or at a lower cost with a lower quality product. Many feel the downside of bundling — the possibility for conflicts of interest with investment management objectives — represents a fiduciary trap with far more serious ramifications than saving a few bucks or making one's life easier.

Craig Freedman, Managing Director at 401(k) Certified Independent Investment Advisors, LLC in Boca Raton, Florida, says, "For some, the bundled product is a timesaver. But all plan sponsors still have an obligation to the plan to ensure the services to the plan are reasonable and in the best interest of the participants. The problem isn't that plan sponsors aren't able to get the same efficiencies at a reasonable cost on an à la carte basis. The problem lies in the ability of bundled plans to hide fees and gouge participants at the fee register."

Clearly, there's a growing consensus away from bundled service providers and towards an unbundled environment. "In a study published last year," says Chuck Miller, a consultant in financial services communications from the Chicago Area, "it was found that one of the hallmarks of an 'ideal' 401(k) was an unbundled plan, because it allows plan sponsors to have 'best of breed' services."

We now have more empirical data to support this consensus. Mike Alfred, Co-Founder and CEO of BrightScope, the 401(k) rating firm located in San Diego, says, "Large plans are almost always unbundled and typically lower-cost due to economies of scale. I don't think bundling is necessarily ever 'better' for anyone other than the service provider. There is a reason why the best mega plans in the country, like IBM and Lockheed Martin, are unbundled."

But by no means should one assume the benefits of unbundling accrue only to the "best mega plans in the country." "Technology and investment flexibility now make it possible for small and medium-size plans to obtain on an à la carte basis the same efficiencies once only found in a fully bundled product," says Freedman. "Recordkeepers, administrators, plan advisors and participant level fiduciary advisers can all now come together on an à la carte basis giving a plan sponsor the freedom to pick and choose the best provider for each function and replace only that provider who is not performing adequately, without sacrificing the other areas of service. I don't believe any one service provider can be all things to all people and do them all well."

Unlike large plans, however, smaller plans can't afford to dedicate specific personnel to manage their HR department, let alone corral a herd of 401(k) service providers. In the end, the temptation of making one's job easier may be too great for the "theory" of fiduciary liability to overcome. Perhaps Freedman sums it up best when he concludes, "Hopefully plan fiduciaries will recognize that what impacts the plan as a whole also impacts them as a participant and their families as well."

After all, spoiled milk and rotten vegetables aren't good no matter how conveniently available and no matter how low the price.

And if you think this issue is intricate, just wait until you see what we have in store next.

BROKER OR REGISTERED INVESTMENT ADVISER? WHAT'S BEST FOR THE 401(K) FIDUCIARY?

Here's an issue that can perplex even the most experienced ERISA/401(k) fiduciary: What's the difference between a broker and a Registered Investment Adviser? More importantly, does the difference significantly raise the fiduciary liability for the typical fiduciary? Two articles ("Industry Groups Differ On Fiduciary Standard," *Financial Advisor*, October 6, 2009 and "Broker-Dealer Standards Must Be Harmonized, Regulators Say," Sarah Borchersen-Keto, *CCH Financial Crisis News Center*, October 6, 2009) discussed the debate in Congress over the issue in 2009. Every ERISA/401(k) fiduciary must understand the implications of this debate.

At issue here lies the legal definition of "fiduciary" as it pertains to professionals offering investment advice. Why does this ongoing legislative battle remain critically important to ERISA/401(k) fiduciaries? Often, a retirement plan fiduciary will try to reduce personal fiduciary liability by hiring a professional investment adviser to act as a co-fiduciary.

Under the terms of both ERISA and the SEC, a registered investment adviser ("RIA") automatically becomes a fiduciary of the retirement plan as soon as the plan sponsor inks the adviser agreement. While the Investment Advisers Act of 1940 ("40 Act") clearly defines what type of entity qualifies as a fiduciary, the 40 Act explicitly exempts broker/dealers who provide investment advice "incidental" to their brokerage business. As a result, the SEC does not require broker/dealers to register as investment advisers; hence, broker/dealers do not fall under the definition of fiduciary.

Broker/dealers register under the Securities Exchange Act of 1934 ("34 Act") and fall under the regulation of

FINRA, a self-regulatory body. Rather than being held to the more rigorous fiduciary standard of care, they merely need to consistently practice their service under what's called the "suitability standard." The suitability standard only requires the broker/dealer to make recommendations appropriate for the client given the specific circumstances of the client.

Incidentally, I'm leaving banks out of this discussion because, while Dodd-Frank ostensibly "addressed" the banking crisis, it also institutionalized the conceptual confusion between broker/dealers and RIAs. Banks, while not regulated by the SEC, do offer fiduciary services (they're called "trust companies" or "trust departments") but may also offer brokerage services. So, just because a retirement plan fiduciary receives service from a bank does not necessarily guarantee that bank acts as a fiduciary. It all depends on which banking department provides the service.

Whether ERISA/401(k) fiduciaries reduce their personal fiduciary liability or actually increase it might well depend on whether those fiduciaries hire RIAs or broker/dealers. While the former clearly serve as a fiduciary, the latter does not. There can be instances, therefore, where plan fiduciaries firmly believe they have delegated investment decision-making to a professional fiduciary, but, in reality, they have merely agreed to place certain trades through a broker. If the fiduciary places the trades — in other words, picks the specific investments — then that fiduciary assumes the full liability risk. Because in this case the ERISA/401(k) fiduciary uses no intermediary to act as fiduciary, no other agent exists to absorb the fiduciary liability.

Worse, broker/dealers tend to receive compensation based on investment products sold (ERISA prohibits a fiduciary from receiving self-dealing compensation, with some worrisome exemptions, unfortunately). Such payment arrangements could leave the plan vulnerable to conflicts of interest. So, not only do 401(k) fiduciaries fail to reduce their liability when using a broker/dealer in lieu of a professional fiduciary, they may actually increase their fiduciary liability.

That being said, the DOL doesn't leave the plan sponsor flapping in the wind. Would you believe it actually provides valuable guidance on this matter? If not, read on.

10 QUESTIONS THE DOL WANTS 401(K) PLAN SPONSORS TO ASK THEIR INVESTMENT CONSULTANT

Are too many 401(k) investment consultants shrouding their true face? If you're a 401(k) plan sponsor interested in discovering the answer to this question, it only makes sense to turn to the Department of Labor (DOL) to see if it offers any insights. Indeed, the DOL offers many tools to 401(k) Plan Sponsors. Their Fact Sheet *Selecting And Monitoring Pension Consultants — Tips For Plan Fiduciaries* appears at first to be very useful for the typical plan fiduciary. Unfortunately it also appears to have a little problem. Right off the bat, according to its opening paragraph, the material is based on a May 2005 report published by the Securities and Exchange Commission (SEC). While this may make the Fact Sheet seem outdated, the lessons learned from that report are very much relevant today. This SEC report uncovered a major concern every 401(k) plan sponsor must address when it concluded: "The business alliances among pension consultants and money managers can give rise to serious potential conflicts of interest under the Advisers Act that need to be monitored and disclosed to plan fiduciaries."

As a result of this SEC revelation, the DOL put together a list of 10 questions to help the plan fiduciary determine if a conflict of interest may exist. I'll review these questions and add my comments, including how things have changed in the intervening years since the DOL first published them.

Are you registered with the SEC or a state securities regulator as an investment adviser? If so, have you provided me with all the disclosures required under those laws (including Part II of Form ADV)?

This is now a moving target, and things have changed dramatically in the last few years. While you can go to the SEC site to find disclosures about Registered Investment Advisers (RIAs), fewer of them have been permitted to register with the SEC. Currently, investment advisers with 100 million in assets can register with the SEC, but the asset threshold for retirement plan consultants increases to 200 million. All those beneath that target will have to register at the state level. On the up side, today, you can look up both Part 1 and Part 2 of ADV on the SEC site. N.B.: This is not a typo — the SEC has new Parts to Form ADV. The old ones (referenced in the original question) contain Roman Numerals while the new Parts use Arabic numbers.

Do you or a related company have relationships with money managers that you recommend, consider for recommendation, or otherwise mention to the plan? If so, describe those relationships.

This is the key question and it gets more problematic starting in 2012 with mandated fee disclosures. A plan sponsor will have to know, understand and potentially share this fee data with participants. Some bundled providers do not willingly share this information without being asked.

Do you or a related company receive any payments from money managers you recommend, consider for recommendation, or otherwise mention to the plan for our consideration? If so, what is the extent of these payments in relation to your other income (revenue)?

This question defines conflict of interests. While it's not clear what impact the DOL's new fiduciary rule (expected by the fall of 2012) will have on the current exemption of certain conflicts of interest, we do know the new Advice Rule seeks to eliminate this specific conflict of interest. Let's repeat this since it's potentially confusing: Right now, plan consultants are allowed to engage in certain conflicts of interest while participant advisers cannot.

Do you have any policies or procedures to address conflicts of interest or to prevent these payments or relationships from being a factor when you provide advice to your clients?

This is a disclosure question. 401(k) plan sponsors will need to first answer this question themselves: Is it appropriate to allow a conflict of interest just because a vendor admits to having one?

If you allow plans to pay your consulting fees using the plan's brokerage commissions, do you monitor the amount of commissions paid and alert plans when consulting fees have been paid in full? If not, how can a plan make sure it does not over-pay its consulting fees?

This question has faded to near-irrelevancy as soft-dollar commissions have been rigorously regulated (if not eliminated) over the past several years. In addition, these hidden fees will be exposed with the new fee disclosure mandate.

If you allow plans to pay your consulting fees using the plan's brokerage commissions, what steps do you take to ensure that the plan receives best execution for its securities trades?

Again, this question comes from an era when 401(k) plans were managed like traditional profit sharing and pension plans and in an era when soft dollars were considered an acceptable business practice. Today, most 401(k) plans use mutual funds, obviating the need to ask this question.

Do you have any arrangements with broker-dealers under which you or a related company will benefit if money managers place trades for their clients with such broker-dealers?

Although SEC regulations make it more difficult for mutual funds to engage in soft dollar practices, some funds may still employ this archaic method. It therefore makes sense to ask this question. By the way, this is a standard question the SEC poses to an investment adviser during an SEC audit. The SEC expects the adviser to always say brokers are chosen for best execution (see the above question).

If you are hired, will you acknowledge in writing that you have a fiduciary obligation as an investment adviser to the plan while providing the consulting services we are seeking?

Don't just ask them, demand they acknowledge, in writing, they have a fiduciary obligation. While the DOL still permits a fiduciary to engage in certain prohibited transactions, if it ever changes its tune, the 401(k) plan sponsor will want to have the investment adviser follow suit.

Do you consider yourself a fiduciary under ERISA with respect to the recommendations you provide the plan?

As with the previous question, the answer should be "yes." Otherwise, move on to the next candidate. Why is this question so critical? As stated above, a fiduciary has a higher standard — a duty to the client — that currently requires, at a bare minimum, at least disclosure of any conflicts of interest.

What percentage of your plan clients utilize money managers, investment funds, brokerage services or other service providers from whom you receive fees?

In the end, the consultant can provide all the right answers above, but if most of their revenues derive from non-fiduciary products, that might tell the 401(k) plan sponsor much more than any other answer (see the previous chapters on the issue of conflicts of interest).

As with any other resource on the Internet, it's important to identify who wrote it and when they published it. Sometimes stale information can be just as useless as no information at all. As of this writing, the Fact Sheet remains in a prominent position on the DOL's website, so many 401(k) plan sponsors may still use it. That's OK, but use it wisely.

And speaking of stale, let's take a look at what the SEC has been doing the past couple of years.

SEC's 12(b)-1 Proposal: Does It Actually Increase 401(k) Fiduciary Liability?

D id the SEC 12(b)-1 proposal offered in the summer of 2010 doom ERISA plan sponsors of 401(k) plans of less than $10 million? This possibility isn't as unbelievable as it first appears. Even the SEC questions the continued viability of the mutual fund distribution model designed specifically for these plans. Furthermore, does the SEC proposal — and the fiduciary standard it implies — expose some 401(k) plan sponsors to increased fiduciary liability? Or, will the fiduciaries embrace an obviously simple solution?

I talked to a spokesman for one of the largest industry groups in the financial services sector. On the condition of anonymity, he shared a shocking point in the SEC 12(b)-1 proposal that, given its potential impact, has, to date, failed to receive the media coverage one might expect.

To be fair, the issue pertains only to 401(k) plans — and small 401(k) plans at that. The Investment Company Institute (ICI) estimates 36 percent of all long-term mutual fund assets were held in retirement plans as of the end of 2009 (*2010 Investment Company Fact Book*, ICI, 2010). However, only 20% of all 401(k) plans still use mutual funds that assess 12(b)-1 fees of 25 basis points or more. So, we're talking about a little more than 7% of total mutual fund assets. That's why this matter doesn't get much media play.

On the other hand, if you're a 401(k) fiduciary or plan sponsor, this small, "oh, by the way" problem could greatly affect your business, your livelihood and even your lifestyle. SEC Chairman Mary L. Schapiro says, "Our proposals would replace rule 12(b)-1 with new rules designed to enhance clarity, fairness and competition when investors buy mutual funds." What she doesn't say, but the

SEC proposal states, is using mutual funds as investment options "may not be a viable option for retirement plans" under $10 million.

Which funds does this warning pertain to and which 401(k) plans are vulnerable? The SEC specifically cites mutual funds using R shares as those most at risk. According to *Forbes*, "The R is supposed to mean retirement and is geared toward investments parked in 401(k) and small corporate retirement plans, those with less than $10 million of assets." ("R Shares, Competitive–But For Whom?" *Forbes*, August 13, 2003). R shares are often used by these smaller 401(k) plans to pay service providers.

This explains the big concern in the retirement arena, but the revenue sharing concern is a real issue for all funds. Our anonymous source told me the potential impact on revenue sharing may result in a broker, under a 22(d) exemption, cutting prices to attract clients and then expecting the mutual fund to make up the difference. This could be problematic for smaller funds. In addition, adjusting for per-account costs will disproportionately impact smaller funds. This could make them less likely to enter the 401(k) market.

"Using a 12(b)-1 fee as direct compensation to the advisor in the ERISA world just doesn't make sense anymore," says Jim Sampson, Managing Principal of Cornerstone Retirement Advisors, LLC. Will brokers move to other investments to make up for loss of 12(b)-1? For example, sub-transfer agents are exempt and brokers may opt to become transfer agents. The bigger issue is for smaller retirement plans relying on 1% 12(b)-1 fees, but this is primarily a concern within the broker distribution model, and may accelerate a transition to fee-based (investment adviser) distribution models. This would appear to be the obvious and easy solution. Harold Evensky of Evensky & Katz, a Miami RIA, believes the "restriction or elimination of 12(b)-1 fees should in no way prevent providers from servicing the same client base and being compensated at the same level. Instead of earning a 1% 12(b)-1 fee, the advisor can simply charge a 1% advisory fee."

Under the current SEC proposal, the migration from the 12(b)-1 distribution model to the fee-based model may become the predominant strategy for this simple reason: Even if some distribution system incorporating a new "12b-2" model emerges, 401(k) plans will have to change their recordkeeping systems to account for individual lots. This accounting method — which may represent a costly change — is currently not done for retirement plans.

The SEC is quite blunt regarding this increased cost. Here's the language from their proposal:

> "…our proposal may require intermediaries such as retirement plan administrators or other omnibus account record keepers to begin tracking share lots and managing share conversions. This change may require these intermediaries to invest in new systems or enhance their current record-keeping and back office systems. If a retirement plan offers fund classes that deduct an ongoing sales charge, the proposal would require such shares purchased by plan participants to eventually be converted to a class that does not deduct an ongoing sales charge. This conversion requirement would create costs for retirement plan record-keepers because we understand that currently, most record-keepers do not maintain individual participant share histories. Record-keepers for plans that offer shares classes with an ongoing sales charge would need to begin tracking the date of

purchase of each share lot for each participant, and tie that share history to the appropriate conversion date. In addition, plans currently usually only have a single class of shares for each fund offered within the plan. If our proposal is adopted, however, if the single class that is offered within the plan deducts an ongoing sales charge, a second class of shares for each fund (i.e. a target class for converted shares) would have to be added to the record-keeper's systems, effectively adding more complexity and costs to their operations."

Jan Sackley, CFE, Fiduciary Risk and Regulatory Compliance Consultant at Fiduciary Foresight, LLC, feels "It would be much simpler if a transfer of shares out of a qualified retirement plan triggered an automatic conversion to the most favorable class available to the receiving account. Why force recordkeepers to create a new infrastructure to accommodate something that may be infrequent?"

Still, the proposal may force smaller plans unwilling to convert to a fee-based structure to reconsider the very existence of their plan. "Transparency has its consequences," says Ron Rhoades, winner of the 2011 Tamar Frankel Fiduciary of the Year Award. "Once very small 401(k) plan sponsors understand how much their service providers get paid," he continues, "they may opt to terminate their plans, and revert back to SIMPLE IRA plans (for less than 100 employees), or even to automatic payroll deductions into self-directed traditional or Roth IRA accounts. Indeed, given all the costs to maintain small plans under ERISA (TPA/record-keeping costs including tax filing, custodial fees, and other costs), one must ask why SIMPLE IRA plans and/or auto deduction to individual IRA accounts are not utilized more often, thereby avoiding costs resulting from ERISA's requirements."

As the SEC tackles the contentious 12(b)-1 fee issue, it remains cognizant the problems may differ for taxable investors compared to non-taxable investors. Indeed, as the stronger argument to retain 12(b)-1 resides on the taxable side not on the retirement plan side, the SEC freely discloses it expects other regulators, especially the Department of Labor, to hold far greater sway on the use of 12(b)-1 in retirement plans. But the 401(k) fiduciary cannot escape the fact the SEC may have let the cat out of the bag in so aggressively targeting R shares. Perhaps ERISA Accredited Investment Fiduciary Mark Levin best reflects the consensus. He says, "All fees should be disclosed and the clients will see the value or move on. Fully transparent programs will benefit all."

Just whether and how plan sponsors might benefit is the subject of our next chapter.

As Industry Takes Sides in SEC 12(b)-1 Debate, Will 401(k) Plan Sponsors Benefit?

In the weeks following the SEC issuance of its July 21, 2010 press release on 12(b)-1 fees, the financial services industry began lining up in a predictable fashion, each side preparing for the coming fight. What can 401(k) plan sponsors learn from the ensuing debate within the industry?

At the time, I asked industry insiders what they thought about the new proposal. Some of what they said may surprise you.

Joe Gordon, Managing Member at Gordon Asset Management, LLC, feels "12(b)1 fees are a notion that has outlived its usefulness. Fund companies do not need to charge these to distribute shares and collect assets. But, if the fees were fully disclosed, transparent, and flashing like a red light, then buyers would not be so easily duped."

Non-adviser providers like recordkeepers have also expressed concern. Lowell Smith, President of InspiraFS, Inc., says, "This will fundamentally change the way recordkeepers, including IRA recordkeepers like Inspira, price retirement plans and partner with distribution channels. In the retirement plan marketplace, this type of change without subsequent changes to systems, contracts and fee schedules will cost firms a lot of money and potentially be an extreme hardship financially during a period of already hard financial times. My hope is that enough time is given to implement such changes."

Still, investment advisers who don't use 12(b)-1 fees, express an often stark view of their use, but remain wary of government intervention. Tim Wood, Corporate Retirement Plan Fiduciary at Deschutes Investment Advisors, says "I think 12(b)-1 fees, when introduced in an ERISA environment, are not consistent with best practice because they can lead to disparate treatment: those participants that invest in the funds that levy 12(b)-1 fees are disproportionately paying the freight of the plan. I would like to see 12(b)-1 fees done away with entirely. However, I would prefer the industry do it on its own rather than through legislative fiat."

Despite evidence from the ICI showing the use of 12(b)-1 fees on the decline, many service providers, however, continue to use them. Elmer Rich III, Principal at Rich and Co., wonders "How will plan and participant services be paid for?" He expresses concern that "anything the industry tries to do is immediately 'tagged' as self-serving and 'dishonest.'" He prefers we continue to research the clues offered by other models, specifically how countries like India, Australia and Britain have experienced these matters. Rich suggests these models "were not successful."

Jeanine Broderick, CFIRS, FLMI, AIRC, ACS, Director of Compliance and Risk at Capitol Wealth, feels the attention paid to individual fees can mislead. She likens it to buying a house or a car. "When I buy a car, I don't know how much the salesperson is making or how much the dealer is making nor do I know how much the person who installed the steering wheel (a very important aspect of my vehicle) made for performing that task." She sees the role of regulators as more important, similar to the role of building inspectors when buying a house. She explains, "When I buy a house I don't know how much the electrician made. Goodness, what if he was underpaid and took a shortcut? My family could be at risk of a fire. Shouldn't I know if he was compensated adequately for doing a good job? How do I judge whether the electrician did what he should have done? What about the plumber? If the plumber was not paid enough he could try to make up for it by using shoddy materials, which could result in costly repairs. Oh, we have building inspectors. Yes, I see.

Don't we also have the DOL, IRS, SEC, FINRA and state regulators watching investments? Are county building inspectors so much better at their jobs than the DOL, IRS, SEC, FINRA, and state regulatory employees?"

Broderick sees investments and retirement accounts as being like homes and cars. She acknowledges that "a way to compare how much it costs me to have my investments in my employer plan vs. an IRA would be helpful to me. If I am not receiving a match and not saving more than I am allowed in an IRA this would allow me to make a better decision. I do not think I need to know how much person A, person B, Firm A and Firm B ad infinitum make. I think it clutters an already complicated area for many participants."

Furthermore, she sees the potential new 12(b)-1 rule as increasing the burden on plan sponsors, who "need a way to make good decisions about which plan provider they decide to utilize. Cost and expenses are one of those factors. I am not confident that requirements that increase costs because of mandated disclosures are the right path. It seems that a simple disclosure of total flat and variable costs would be adequate for the comparison."

Wood counters this argument by saying, "I find that in the current 401(k) environment, information is so scarce, it is difficult for the average person to be able to correctly analyze their own situation to assess if the value of what they are receiving justifies the cost."

It remains unclear if the SEC's proposal will address any of these concerns, as the SEC's concern deals with the entire mutual fund industry, not just the retirement plan environment. Indeed, the issues within the taxable/retail side of 12(b)-1 may outweigh those of the retirement industry. What has become clear, however, are the predictable sides industry players took. At the very least, this has shed some light on the inner workings of plan service providers, which may, in the end, provide the greatest benefit to 401(k) plan sponsors.

What else has this industry fissure revealed?

WILL 401(K) PLAN SPONSORS WONDER: DOTH THE 12(B)-1 INDUSTRY PROTEST TOO MUCH?

The SEC 12(b)-1 comment period officially ended in November 2010 with a flurry of high profile letters from large industry associations. The overwhelming response from these groups: change hurts, keep the status quo.

Oddly, the common thread among these disparate groups involves the use of 12(b)-1 fees in retirement plans. The Investment Company Institute claims, "The current use of 12(b)-1 fees in the retirement plan context is clearly not the functional equivalent of a front-end sales charge." The American Society of Pension Professionals & Actuaries (ASPPA) warned the SEC to "not undermine the success that servicing and administration arrangements have fostered for participant-directed retirement plans." Additionally, both the Council of Independent Recordkeepers (CIKR) and the brokerage industry's Spark Institute came out against the proposal. Again citing "non-distribution costs" in retirement plans, the Spark Institute asked the SEC to raise its proposed limit from 25 basis points to 75 basis points.

The clamor over how one squeezes the toothpaste of retirement plan fees might cause the typical 401(k) fiduciary to wonder if the industry might be protesting too much. For example, even the ICI's own September 2010 report *The Economics of Providing 401(k) Plans: Services, Fees, and Expenses, 2009* shows 73% of plan assets do not use 12(b)-1 plans and only 8% of the plan assets have 12(b)-1 fees in excess of the proposed 25 basis points. The ICI does not point to this fresh report in their SEC comment letter, but rather cites this quote from a then year-and-a-half old report it commissioned from Deloitte Consulting, *Defined Contribution/401(k) Fee Study* (Spring

2009): "While the median plan's 'all-in' fee was 0.72% of assets, median fees among plans with less than $1 million in assets were 1.89% of plan assets and for plans with more than $500 million in assets, the median 'all-in' fee was less than 0.50%." The ICI even referenced the following fact from the U. S. Department of Labor's Employee Benefits Security Administration, *Private Pension Plan Bulletin, Abstract of 2007 Form 5500 Annual Reports*, (June, 2010): "It is important to remember that small plans represent the majority of 401(k)-type plans and more than 8 million people actively participate in these small plans." While neither of the references cited in the ICI's comment letter spoke specifically to 12(b)-1 fees, the more recent (and omitted) report did.

Ed Ferrigno, Vice-President (Washington) of the Profit Sharing/401(k) Council of America, told me that although the 12(b)-1 issue affects only a small amount of total assets, it remains unknown how many of the smaller plans — and how many total employees — might be affected by 12(b)-1 fees.

Mike Alfred, BrightScope's CEO, is not surprised to hear industry groups are questioning the SEC's proposal. "These groups are just trying to defend the underlying economics of their members' businesses," he says. Alfred also supports Ferrigno, and points out "large plan sponsors with any sophistication are completely out of this [12(b)-1] game already. They're not interested in carrying unnecessary fiduciary risk."

And fiduciary risk is really what it's all about to the 401(k) plan sponsor and fiduciary. Blaine F. Aikin, CEO of Fiduciary360, offer three significant concerns all plan sponsors and fiduciaries must mull over if involved in a potential 12(b)-1 fee situation. "With respect to the receipt of 12(b)-1 fees by a service provider to an ERISA plan, there are a number of important considerations. First, if the service provider is serving in a fiduciary capacity, the fiduciary (under ERISA Section 406(a)(1)) must not engage in a transaction that 'constitutes a direct or indirect…furnishing of goods, services, or facilities between the plan and a party in interest, such as an investment advisor; [or] transfer to, or use by or for the benefit of, a party in interest or any assets of the plan.' Thus, a fiduciary must exercise extreme caution to avoid a prohibited transaction if they receive 12(b)-1 fees. The Frost Letter provides an example of how this can be done as it addressed a situation where the fees were used entirely to offset expenses that would have otherwise been incurred by the plan and no extra compensation flowed to the fiduciary."

"Second," says Aikin, "plan sponsors have a duty to understand (1) whether service providers are receiving compensation from such sources as 12(b)(1) fees, (2) the amount of such compensation, and (3) to ensure that the total compensation paid to each of the service providers is fair and reasonable for the services provided."

"Finally, non-fiduciary service providers are generally permitted to have conflicts of interest, often without proactive disclosure. This places a special burden on plan sponsors to be especially vigilant in investigating and evaluating fees paid to non-fiduciaries in order to meet the duty described in the second consideration above."

Readers might wish to reference the *Prudent Practices for Investment Stewards and Prudent Practices for Investment Advisors* handbooks published by fi360, paying particular attention to Practice 4.5.

Although a few groups like fi360 did submit a comment letter in support of the SEC's proposal, Alfred expresses concern about the general lack of groups or organizations supporting investors that might counter the service providers. "There are a handful of organizations you would expect to do more in this area. In general, investors are not well represented in Washington, D.C. There are, however, a number of investor advocates working in both the Education & Labor committee in the House and the Aging Committee in the Senate," he said.

The question remains (and in keeping with our Shakespearean motif), is the 401(k) defense of 12(b)-1 fees much ado about nothing? "It probably has been eight years since I came across a plan with 12(b)-1 funds in it," said Terrance Power, President of American Pension Services of Clearwater, Florida. His firm manages $350 million in qualified (50-1,000 life) plan funds, including multiple-employer plans. Power's firm bills directly and he sees many TPA firms doing the same. He acknowledges 12(b)-1 fees might be an issue for very small plans.

Ferrigno says, "If the rule goes through, it's clear the fee collection methodologies for some plans will have to change. The question is 'What will the impact be?'" Roger Wohlner, the financial advisor with Asset Strategy Consultants in Arlington Heights, Illinois, echoes this. "At the end of the day, it is the overall fund/plan expenses that matter most. I hope that if the 12(b)-1 fees are eliminated it doesn't lead to some sort of solution that is worse and less transparent to sponsors, participants, and consultants."

Still, other regulatory actions may force 12(b)-1 fees — and any similar alternative — out into the open. The DOL is now requiring per account expense reporting. Both the DOL and the SEC are in the process of redefining "fiduciary." It's not clear if the Frost Opinion will stand in light of the DOL's proposed new definition of fiduciary. I placed a call with the DOL for comments on this matter but the department did not want to speak on the record.

One thing is clear: Many providers are able to serve the 401(k) market with direct-billed asset based fees. Whether fees are direct billed or via 12(b)-1, they are still asset-based fees. Some people feel portions of the 401(k) service industry want to retain 12(b)-1 fees because such fees make it easier for those providers to hide their compensation.

These people feel daylighting such fees might actually drive 401(k) expenses lower by exposing a fiduciary risk some 401(k) plan sponsors have, to date, remained unaware of.

Alfred bluntly sums up this feeling. He says, "It just takes time for the rest of the marketplace to catch up."

While all the talk in the last three chapters may appear academic, it was an academic study that, for the first time, empirically showed how broker-sold funds, such as those incurring 12(b)-1 fees, have experienced poorer performance versus direct-bought funds. The next chapter describes this study and its important implications in the fiduciary standard debate.

Does NBER Study Seal the Deal
for Fiduciary Standard — or Just
Warn Plan Sponsors?

Will a study, published in 2010 as part of the National Bureau of Economic Research (NBER) Working Paper Series, be the final straw that forces regulators to adopt a universal fiduciary standard? The research, reaffirming a 2009 study published in *The Review of Financial Studies*, appears to provide empirical evidence showing broker-sold mutual funds significantly underperform direct-sold mutual funds. Most importantly, this underperformance exceeds the cost of broker's fees, meaning the underlying performance of broker-sold funds — before one even takes fees into account — substantially underperforms their direct-sold competitors. The implications for plan sponsors, however, may outweigh whatever the regulators determine.

Could this be the Holy Grail of all studies? Not only does it suggest a monetary advantage for the fiduciary standard over the suitability standard, but it also may explain the common (and widely reported) misperception regarding active versus passive forms of management.

Kerry Pechter first broke this story in his article "Are Direct-Sold Funds a Better Value?" (*Retirement Income Journal*, January 13, 2011). I contacted Mr. Pechter and he suggested I speak directly to the authors of the study.

The working paper, "Broker Incentives and Mutual Fund Market Segmentation," (*NEBR*, August 2010), was written by Diane Del Guercio (Lundquist College of Business), Jonahan Reuter (Carroll School of Management at Boston College) and Paula A. Tkac (Federal Reserve Bank of Atlanta). I spoke with Jon Reuter, Assistant Professor of Finance in the Carroll School of Management at Boston College, who explained the primary purpose of the paper was to try to uncover an economic purpose for the use of certain distribution models within the mutual fund industry. The researchers, after using investment return data from 1996-2002 to compare investment returns of broker-sold mutual funds with the returns of direct-sold funds, conclude that "within the full sample of actively managed domestic equity funds in CRSP, we also find robust evidence that funds distributed through the direct channel outperform comparable funds distributed through other channels by 1% per year."

Professor Reuter pointed out their paper "extended the analysis (along several dimensions)" of a 2009 study "Assessing the Costs and Benefits of Brokers in the Mutual Fund Industry" by Daniel Bergstresser (Harvard Business School), John M. R. Chalmers (Lundquist College of Business, University of Oregon) and Peter Tufano (Harvard Business School and NBER), which was published on May 21, 2009 in *The Review of Financial Studies*. Reuter credits this study as the first to "document before-fee performance differences between direct-sold and broker-sold funds." The NEBR paper confirms these results and then some.

But before we get into that, I thought you might be interested in this fascinating (and topical) tidbit from the 2009 study: "Financial advisors are fiduciaries, owing clients even higher duties; in theory, they must put their clients' interest ahead of their own. The extent to which investment professionals can be held to strict fiduciary standards presents complex legal issues, and investors may not appreciate distinctions between brokers and advisors. Nevertheless, if brokers' self-interested actions were to explain our results, it would call into question the nature of the relationships between consumers and those who serve them."

The 2009 study, however, did not include institutional funds in its analysis. Reuter's paper does — and that can have far-reaching implications for plan sponsors, along with the adoption of a universal fiduciary standard. While the NEBR study barely addresses the fiduciary standard debate, in a nutshell, the paper concludes direct-sold mutual funds (including institutional funds) outperform broker-sold mutual funds by 1%. Professor Reuter agrees "it is reasonable to conclude" 401(k) plan sponsors — and the participants of their plans — on average will tend to benefit from hiring a fiduciary charging an asset-based fee of less than 1% compared to buying funds through a broker.

And, unlike the analysis that proposes the existence of unidentifiable intangible benefits to retail investors using brokers (e.g., "one-on-one personal attention, or broker incentives to recommend certain funds"), no such non-performance benefit accrues to the participants of 401(k) plans (and might lead to a prohibited transaction if such non-performance benefit accrues to the plan sponsor).

The NEBR paper does a very good job explaining why direct-sold mutual funds outperform broker-sold funds using common sense economic theory. First, it "proves" the dichotomy of the two channels by showing very few funds (3.3%) attempt to market themselves both directly and through brokers. Second, by focusing on the educational pedigree of the portfolio managers from funds in each group, the study finds direct-sold funds are more likely to hire more expensive talent. In general, since performance is a key attribute in the direct-sold distribution channel, those funds tend to invest more in performance enhancing activities. On the other hand, broker-sold funds tend to invest more in marketing and distribution activities.

Oddly and perhaps counter intuitively, although they perform more poorly, broker-sold funds experience less turnover than their direct-sold counterparts. According to the study, "The relative lack of sensitivity to after-fee performance in the broker-sold channels is consistent with other factors driving flows in these channels (e.g., one-on-one personal attention, or broker incentives to recommend certain funds). It is worth noting that, unlike in traditional brokerage accounts where broker compensation depends on the number of trades their clients make, brokers selling mutual funds have less incentive to churn; broker-sold mutual funds compensate brokers for selling their funds and, through the use of trailing loads (12(b)-1 fees), for keeping clients invested in these same funds."

The paper concludes, compared to direct-sold funds, with broker-sold funds "there is little to no benefit to being a top performer and relatively little punishment for posting bad performance." The study ends with this prediction: "If payments to brokers for advice increasingly come directly from investors rather than via mutual fund families, the universe of funds that brokers are willing to recommend will likely expand, and competition is likely to focus more on after-fee returns."

There you have it. In short, this one paper, perhaps not as well read as it should be, almost accidentally seals the deal for the fiduciary standard, exposes the conflict of interest created by 12(b)-1 fees and, dare we say, touches the forbidden third rail of all investment research: it shows that — within the direct-sold fund channel — index funds have no inherent advantage over actively managed funds (and suggests past studies may have reached opposite conclusions by overweighting the impact of broker-sold funds); thus, adding another nail to the coffin in the all-too-often repeated misconception that passive consistently outperforms active.

FIDUCIARY STANDARD: BACKDOOR SOLUTION TO 401(K) PLAN SPONSORS' 12(B)-1 PROBLEM?

The previous chapter highlighted a research paper where one of the lead researchers said "it is reasonable to conclude" 401(k) plan sponsors — and the participants of their plans — on average will tend to benefit from hiring a fiduciary charging an asset-based fee of less than 1% compared to buying funds through a broker. There, I specifically cited 12(b)-1 fees as one of the attributes of broker sold products. Comments from April 2011 — both public and private — reveal one possible strategy for addressing the 12(b)-1 dilemma.

On April 8, 2011 in Dallas, Texas, SEC Chairman Mary L. Schapiro, in her remarks before the Society of American Business Editors and Writers, said the following of the Fiduciary Standard study released the preceding January:

> "The report noted that few investors are aware of or understand the difference between the fiduciary standard required of investment advisers and the less strict 'suitability' standard observed by broker-dealers. As I have long advocated, the report recommended the establishment of a uniform fiduciary standard of conduct for all financial professionals when they provide personalized investment advice about securities to retail investors. I believe that investment professionals' first duty must be to their clients, and I look forward to beginning work soon to codify the report's recommendations."

But just days earlier she had told the Securities Industry and Financial Markets Association that "budget and resource constraints meant some issues, like changes to 12(b)-1 mutual fund fees paid to brokers, would not be addressed until 2012 at the earliest," according to John Taft, chairman of SIFMA.

Given the research study cited in the lead paragraph, are these two statements — putting clients first vs. delaying changes to 12(b)-1 fees — incongruous? Or is the fiduciary standard a potential backdoor solution to the dilemma posed by 12(b)-1 fees?

Marcia S. Wagner, an ERISA attorney at the Wagner Law Group, wrote, given the proposed changes in the fiduciary standard by the SEC and the new definition of fiduciary offered by the DOL, brokers would "undoubtedly need to change their service model and redefine their role as plan advisers" ("Brace for Impact," *planadviser Magazine*, January/February 2011 issue) Wagner suggests it would be very difficult for non-fiduciary brokers to continue to accept 12(b)-1 fees since doing so "would trigger a non-exempt prohibited transaction under the Employee Retirement Income Security Act (ERISA)."

Rich Lynch, Chief Operating Officer of fi360, agrees with the 12(b)-1 fee problem cited by Wagner. He says, "These fees create conflicts for advisers and fund company directors, and they complicate the comparison and control of costs across funds." It's possible moving forward with these fiduciary changes would automatically remove the conflict of interest issue of 12(b)-1 fees, at least in the ERISA realm. Still, others see 12(b)-1 fees remaining — despite the acknowledged conflict of interest and the study showing they're likely not in the best interests of the client — simply by disclosing their limitations.

Ron Butt, Senior Partner at the ARGI Financial Group, feels the issue deals less with the actual 12(b)-1 fee and more with both disclosure and the nature and structure of brokerage firms. Butt says, "How a financial professional is compensated is not important to the public. It is the non-disclosure of how and the amount that will make the difference." He believes transparency might prove a problem for brokers providing little or no service. "Once the public finds out they have been paying for something they have not received," says Butt, "they will request refunds or, worse, file lawsuits or arbitrations. The brokerage firms are more concerned about the latter than the former." As to the structure of brokerage firms, Butt says, "They are set up to sell products and raise capital. It is only when these activities are not in the clients' best interest and/or are not disclosed that the problem occurs."

Not everyone, however, believes the industry can get by merely with more disclosure. T. Henry Yoshida, Principal at The Maresh Yoshida 401(k) Group, says, "If the SEC adopts a Fiduciary Standard, there will be no need to rule on 12(b)-1 fees since brokers/advisers will not be able to be compensated for managing a plan at all." He says the reason for this is "a provision of the Fiduciary Standard that states that the RIA or ERISA appointed Fiduciary must avoid conflicts of interest."

Lynch is concerned disclosure won't meet the objectives of the SEC. He says, "If the SEC does not move forward on its current 12(b)-1 proposal, even with disclosure and transparency of fees, investors still may not understand what those fees are."

The fiduciary standard might be a backdoor solution, but the truth is we don't know what's behind that door.

Perhaps we should leave the last word to Chicago-based financial planner Roger Wohlner, who says, "If the 12(b)-1 goes away (and it probably should) my fear is what will replace it. Will the cure be worse than the disease?"

More importantly, just what is the "fiduciary standard" and why should plan sponsors care about it. We'll tackle this conundrum next.

WHY SHOULD 401(K) PLAN SPONSORS CARE WHAT OTHERS THINK ABOUT THE FIDUCIARY STANDARD?

Confirming earlier studies, J.D. Power & Associates released their 2011 study on investor satisfaction and found retail investors have no awareness of the difference between the fiduciary standard and the suitability standard. This lack of awareness on the part of investors stood out as one of the cornerstone reasons why the SEC recommended the adoption of a uniform fiduciary standard. Although the J.D. Power survey measured only retail investors, its results might just jar 401(k) plan sponsors who think merely hiring a fiduciary represents the extent of what they have to do.

It's often difficult to tell the difference between a card shark and an honest dealer. According to the press release issued by J.D. Power that accompanied the survey results, "85% of full-service investors either have not heard of or do not understand the difference between a suitability standard and a fiduciary standard." It gets scarier. Again per the press release, "Among those full-service investors who are currently in a fiduciary relationship, 57 percent state that this increases their comfort level with their adviser, while 42 percent state that it decreases their comfort level." Said another way, it's very possible that for every five employees, two of them might react with concern upon finding their 401(k) plan sponsor has just hired a fiduciary.

Ironically, in a previous chapter we chronicled the result of an NEBR research paper whose lead researcher concluded 401(k) investors will tend to benefit from hiring a fiduciary charging an asset based fee of less than 1% compared to buying funds through a broker, (see "Does NEBR Study Seal the Deal for Fiduciary Standard — or

Just Warn Plan Sponsors?" on page 142). Yet, the J.D. Power survey shows investors not only can't conceive of the benefit of the fiduciary standard, but almost half of them aren't comfortable with it. Face it, when you're in the casino, you think everyone has an extra ace up their sleeve.

Let's first consider this question: Do 401(k) plan sponsors act more like the fiduciaries they're supposed to be, or do they act more like retail investors? The J.D. Power survey doesn't answer that question, but the experience of industry experts might provide some anecdotal evidence. "Most plan sponsors we talk to are exactly like that, they look at us as if we are crazy and making this stuff up to sell snake oil," says Mark Levin, an Accredited Investment Fiduciary (AIF) from Florida. He adds, "It's very frustrating, but eventually, over the next 20 years the DOL will somehow get the message out. They have a great website, but I don't think any HR people or business owners ever look at it."

Courtenay Shipley, CRPS, AIF of Nashville, Tennessee says, "If 'ERISA fiduciary' or 'fiduciary responsibility' doesn't have resonance with the plan sponsor and it's not on their radar to even ask about, any broker and any product will do. Hopefully the fight continues simply for media attention to raise awareness, especially in the small to medium-size business marketplace. Don't forget we live in a world where 401(k) plans are marketed by payroll and business solutions companies as though it were synonymous with 'Would you like fries with that?'"

But not all advisers have experienced this level of frustration. Sean McGarry, VP and Retirement Plan Service Manager at Rockland Trust in Massachusetts, says, "I am finding that more and more business owners are asking me the question, 'Will you become a fiduciary to the retirement plan?' Sometimes they don't know why they're asking it, but they seem to know it's an important question to ask upfront. In the last few months, I've even been asked, "Will you be a fiduciary under Section 3(21) or 3(38) of ERISA?" As a result, we have recently modified our Service Agreement in order to make this distinction."

Once a fiduciary adviser gets over the hurdle of finding a 401(k) plan sponsor that understands the importance of operating under the fiduciary standard rather than the suitability standard, the work doesn't stop there — for either party. The 401(k) plan sponsor, in appreciating the significance of the J.D. Power results, will need the diligence to adopt education programs that address the lack of sophistication among many of their employees. The fiduciary adviser can (and should) assist in this effort — if not directly then by identifying appropriate resources.

With so many employees not trusting their 401(k) plans (see "Workers Unhappy with 401(k) Plans," *USNews.com*, June 17, 2011), simply stating the obvious fact of the benefits of the plan hiring a fiduciary adviser may not suffice. In addition, in all but the most extreme cases, waiting for the new fee disclosure rules to kick in won't help either. After all, since a fiduciary standard adviser represents a higher level of service compared to a suitability standard adviser, one would expect to pay for that higher level of service.

Which now brings us to the final dilemma: Does the government have the right to force investors (and people in general) to do what's best for themselves? (Along the same lines, does the government have the right to prevent you from smoking, drinking excessively, partaking in illegal narcotics? etc. Theoretically, whatever you answer, it will be consistently the same for all these issues since they all fall under the generic "does the government have a right to protect you from yourself" kind of question.

And if you answered "no" to the above question and assuming we all desire a level playing field where everyone in the industry can operate under the same rules, would you be more comfortable with the government removing all fiduciary regulations from RIAs or with the government requiring brokers, insurance companies, recordkeepers, TPAs, accountants, etc. to conduct their investment advisory business under the same constraints as RIAs?

Fundamentally, once you remove all the industry lobbyists, these are the questions the politicians need to answer.

As a fiduciary, you don't have to even consider this question. The answer is already provided in centuries of tradition and practice. It's as certain as the number of aces in a fair deck of cards. A fiduciary must always act in the best interests of the beneficiary, even if the beneficiary is not aware of those best interests.

Alas, life teaches some players don't heed the directions. Indeed, many a Ponzi scheme has, for a time at least, profited by ignoring such arcane practices as the fiduciary duty. What's a plan sponsor to do? Are there rules they could follow to uncover scam artists before it's too late.

Funny you should ask as I titled the next chapter...

5 RULES FOR THE 401(K) FIDUCIARY SEEKING TO AVOID THE NEXT MADOFF

If there's one thing we learned from the Bernie Madoff Ponzi scandal, it's that even the "sophisticated" rich investor can fall victim to relatively simple and easily preventable schemes. Madoff bilked not only common investors, but also some of the most affluent celebrities in America as well as many a fiduciary from some prominent employee retirement plans. Fortunately, we don't need more regulation to prevent future Madoffs, we just need common sense (and, perhaps, a tad bit more enforcement of existing regulations). Here are five straightforward rules any investor and/or fiduciary can follow to avoid a personal investment Waterloo:

Rule #1: If it's too good to be true, it probably is.
Madoff's entire thesis lay on the foundation of greed — not merely his own, but the greed of those investors and financial consultants he fooled. Face it, no investment book promising merely modest returns ever became a best seller. The *hoi polloi* — "sophisticated" or not — constantly searches for that free lunch. The masses mistakenly believe they alone will profit from a popular fad. Unfortunately, shady gimmicks involving investments often depend on "the greater fool" theory, i.e., there's always another sucker willing to fork over his life savings. It's only when the conniver runs out of fools (or, in the case of Madoff, the market crashes), that the subterfuge is exposed and naïve investors realize their *colossal misjudgment*. It's best to take steps to lower your vulnerability — and, in the case of the fiduciary, your fiduciary liability — to this temptation by adopting common sense procedures to protect yourself from both unscrupulous criminals (the Madoffs of the

world) and unsuspecting professionals (remember, Madoff tricked high-powered investment professionals, too).

Rule #2: Resist the temptation of chasing performance by regularly updating your investment goals and tying them directly to a tangible objective.

Have a plan, set goals and monitor your progress annually (the typical fiduciary will create an investment policy statement for this purpose). If I've said it once, I've said it a million times, no one wants "Here lies John Doe. He beat the S&P 500" on his tombstone. Since you can't take it with you, it's important to know what you need to live the life you want — to achieve your lifetime dream! Sometimes, if you plan properly through the years and you're very fortunate, you won't even have to worry about what the stock market does. But, if you get caught up in the cocktail party chatter of one-upmanship of investment performance, you'll eventually find you're merely setting yourself up as an easy mark for the next Madoff.

Rule #3: Turn aside the use of one "bundled" provider for everything by employing multiple independent service providers.

Madoff apparently manipulated his books and statements to reflect imaginary returns. One-stop-shopping might make sense for big box stores selling commodity items (i.e., where quality doesn't matter), but it certainly fails the smell test for your retirement and investment accounts. For individuals, this mean making sure your investment adviser does not hold custody of your assets and is truly independent from (i.e., not selected by) the custodian of your portfolio. This ensures you receive statements from two unaffiliated companies. To add a higher degree of safety, you might want to make sure you can trade with different brokers. For retirement plans, in addition to separate custodians and investment advisers, you'll also need to have an independent third-party administrator (a.k.a. recordkeeper) as well as an independent auditor (for plans large enough to meet this Department of Labor Requirement).

Rule #4: Family, friends and folks with impressive resumes require just as much, if not more, due diligence as anyone else.

The real sad part of Madoff's machination is that he took advantage of people close to him, many of whom relied on his notable credentials. This doesn't mean you can't or shouldn't use family and friends or that you should ignore a person's past experience. It does, however, suggest an investor should select an investment adviser through a thorough and consistent process — no matter what the relationship you have with the investment adviser and no matter how spectacular the biography of the investment adviser appears.

Rule #5: You can't depend on government regulators.

Madoff was regulated by the United States Securities and Exchange Commission (SEC). They failed to discover his ruse for a number of reasons, mostly because it was difficult to independently confirm Madoff's records (see Rule #3) and because, unlike mutual funds, there are no independent audits required for the private investment fund Madoff created. One thing we know for sure: more regulations would not have helped the SEC. Lamentably, Madoff violated existing regulations and the SEC just did not catch them. Still, if a diligent regulator can't find a problem, how is a regular investor supposed to unearth it? Simple, just follow common sense (and Rules 1 through 4).

There you have it, the lessons of the Madoff Scandal. Whether you're an individual investor or an ERISA/401(k) fiduciary, you'd be fortunate to have a supplier that doesn't insist you obtain all financial services under one roof, one that believes clients are best served by a team of independent service providers and one that keeps you focused on your real needs, not the distracting roller coaster of the markets.

"But, wait!" I hear some readers asking. (Yes, despite the distance, my ears are ringing.) "What about fees? Isn't that what it's all about? Isn't that the main issue with service providers?"

Well, yes and no. If you really want to get into a discussion of fees, I suggest you go directly to Section Six on Due Diligence (although you'll miss a ton of good stuff in Section Five about Investment Policy Statements).

Hmm, you're right. You really need to read Section Five. After all, it does explain the basic building block of every successful 401(k) plan. Therefore, if you just promise me you'll pay attention to the next chapter's conclusion, I'll whet your appetite regarding fees with the following little ditty: If you take away only one piece of advice from *401(k) Fiduciary Solutions*, it would be the last two sentences in that paragraph.

STUDY REVEALS FIVE FACTORS THAT HELP LOWER 401(K) FEES

Every 401(k) plan sponsor should want to step down to lower fees (without cutting out anything important, of course). What if lowering 401(k) fees was as simple as counting the fingers on one hand? In a study released over the summer of 2010, the Investment Company Institute analyzed the ins and outs of 401(k) plan fees and expenses (see *The Economics of Providing 401(k) Plans: Services, Fees and Expenses, 2010*, Investment Company Institute, June 2011). What the study reveals may be enough to make 401(k) plan sponsors smash the palm of their hands against their foreheads and yell "D'oh!"

Enough has been said about the negative long-term impact of higher fees on 401(k) investments. Clearly, if we can identify ways to lower costs and still ensure reasonable service, 401(k) investors will benefit. As we enter into full, per-participant fee disclosure beginning in 2012, 401(k) plan sponsors will find themselves under greater pressure to either reduce fees or justify higher expenses. The ICI identified five areas that help lower per-participant fees:

1. The competition among all investment products, including mutual funds, to offer 401(k) participants service and performance;
2. The decision of plan sponsors to pay for at least some portion of the costs of 401(k) plans, which allows them to select cheaper funds from unbundled platforms;
3. 401(k) plans have economies-of-scale advantages, permitting them to purchase lower cost share classes;

4. The proactive dedication of 401(k) plan sponsors to make cost-conscious and performance conscious decisions; and,

5. The fact 401(k) plans have greater allowance for a more limited role of professional investment advisers.

Now, there are several important caveats to these factors. The easiest way to lower expenses is to cut services and benefits. Take factor five, for example: Some studies suggest individual investment advice may help participants achieve superior investment performance. This advice doesn't come for free.

As I've stated in a review of the *401(k) Averages Book*, ("Great Info for Every 401(k) Plan Sponsor: Review of 401(k) Averages Book," *FiduciaryNews.com*, April 26, 2011), smaller plans will normally pay a greater percentage in fees than larger plans for the same service. This represents the downside of the economies-of-scale rule. If you're small, you'll find fewer attractive fee options, so 401(k) plan sponsors must make sure they compare their plans to similarly sized plans, not the average 401(k) plan.

Finally, certain methods of achieving lower fees may not be in the best interests of 401(k) investors. In 2006, Congress passed the Pension Protection Act in part to dissuade 401(k) investors from placing too great a percentage of their assets in low return vehicles. Here's the rub: low-return vehicles tend to have lower fees. This means if 401(k) plan sponsors and participants focus too much on fees, they may select inappropriate investments.

And this ironically leads to the ultimate liability exposure for the 401(k) plan fiduciary. When it comes to fees, sometimes you get what you pay for. And that's not necessarily a good thing.

SECTION FIVE:

– INVESTMENT POLICY STATEMENT –

THE BASIC BUILDING BLOCK TO A SUCCESSFUL 401(K) PLAN

WHAT'S MISSING FROM YOUR 401(K) INVESTMENT POLICY STATEMENT?

Before the Rise of the Registered Investment Adviser (ca. 1970), before the ascendency of the no-load mutual fund (ca. 1980), heck, even well before the pre-eminence of the portfolio manager, there was… the trust document. Coming to full prominence in the 19th century, the trust document was a well-crafted series of instructions enabling the trustee to flawlessly cater to the needs of the beneficiary. Whatever the beneficiary needed as defined by the trust document, the trustee had the duty to try to provide. Without the trust document, we would simply devolve to the days of King John (i.e., pre-*Magna Carta* Britain).

We know Congress birthed both investment advisers and investment companies (a.k.a. "mutual funds") in 1940 with, respectively, the Investment Advisers Act of 1940 and the Investment Company Act of 1940. Yet, it took decades for both these forms of entities to become significant players. Likewise, it took centuries for arguably the world's first modern trust document, the *Magna Carta*, to evolve into the customary trust document we're familiar with today. By the 1800's, case law had settled on a standard language lawyers who drafted them could use to enhance a trust document's ability to protect the interests of beneficiaries.

Alas, for all its best intentions, the 19th century trust document contained some spurious investment advice. Indeed, the legal precision of the device as it pertained to safeguarding the beneficiary could only be matched by the horrendous nature of any prescribed investment rules. Following the lead of relevant trust laws, some trust documents prohibited the investment in equities far into the 20th century. Indeed, some trust documents today still place an undo emphasis on income, much to the financial ruin of the beneficiaries.

With the advent of Graham-Dodd's *Security Analysis* in the middle of the 20th century came a meaningful way to measure the relative merits of individual securities and, eventually, the value of portfolio management itself. (Yes, I know this wouldn't have been possible without the Prudent Man Ruling — from the 1830 Massachusetts court decision in the *Harvard College v. Amory* case — but just because the court opened that particular door doesn't mean the consensus walked through it.) It then became incumbent for portfolio managers to match the quantifiable attributes of potential investments with some sort of quantifiable description of the beneficiary or, as they were more often becoming, the client.

This ultimately led to a list of seven traits — Risk Tolerance, Return Requirement, Liquidity Needs, Legal Constraints, Time Horizon, Taxes and Unique Needs — identified and promoted by the CFA Institute (nee AIMR) as part of the training and testing associated with their CFA® certification program. By the 1990's, these seven traits found themselves identified as the critical components of a traditional Investment Policy Statement (IPS). With the close of the 20th century, the IPS had supplanted the trust document as the governing document of choice when it came to investments. Even in actual trust accounts, it's not uncommon to see a separate IPS created for that specific trust portfolio. With ERISA plans, the IPS became the legal document outlining investment due diligence procedures.

Unlike traditional single portfolio retirement plans, using the traditional IPS for the 401(k) plan sponsor poses three significant problems.

First, the original seven traits were devised in the pre-401(k) era, when institutions often used a single portfolio to address the retirement needs of an entire universe of employees. Under a 404(c) safe harbor, a 401(k) plan will need a minimum of three portfolios specifically designed to offer materially unique investment objectives. The traditional IPS cannot brook this inconsistency. We get around this problem mostly by ignoring it.

Second, the original seven traits do not account for education, a critical component for any 401(k) and something that must be incorporated into its IPS. In fact, this is how we get around the aforementioned inconsistency. A 401(k) plan that offers a series of distinct and exclusive investment options does so under a defined due diligence system for defined reasons. Employee (and trustee) education must speak in terms compatible with this system and these reasons.

Third, the original seven traits initially appeared during the era of Modern Portfolio Theory (MPT). Worse, they were interpreted in terms of MPT. With recent research in behavioral finance specific to 401(k) plans calling significant aspects of MPT into question, does it make sense to continue to use this archaic language in IPS developed for a 401(k) plan?

Perhaps it's time to review that IPS you've faithfully filed in the "Legal" folder for your 401(k) plan. You might just find a few things missing. The next chapter goes beyond simple structure and discusses points every 401(k) IPS must cover. After this general overview, I'll introduce you to a more detailed analysis explaining why the traditional structure of the IPS fails in today's 401(k) environment.

5 FACTS THE FIDUCIARY MIGHT NOT KNOW ABOUT THE 401(K) PLAN INVESTMENT POLICY STATEMENT

Does creating an Investment Policy Statement (IPS) reduce fiduciary liability or increase it? There's no clear agreement on this matter. The United States Department of Labor (DOL) does not require the 401(k) plan fiduciary to create an IPS, and some lawyers believe putting something in writing only gives the DOL a longer rope to create the noose with which to hang the fiduciary. On the other hand, the DOL has long maintained it has greater concern for processes than for outcomes, and benefits attorneys often view memorializing the process through an IPS and documenting its successful implementation as the surest way to reduce fiduciary liability.

The November 2006 *Report Of The Working Group On Prudent Investment Process* contains the following instruction: (N.B.: This report, produced by the Advisory Council on Employee Welfare and Pension Benefit Plans, was created by ERISA to provide advice to the Secretary of Labor and the contents of this report do not necessarily represent the position of the DOL).

> "If an investment policy statement has been properly formulated and memorialized, all prudent procedures covered will fall into place. This is predicated upon the fact that liability usually occurs when the fiduciary has failed to act in this area as opposed to acting improperly."

Once a 401(k) fiduciary decides that creating an IPS can reduce fiduciary liability, there are five straightforward questions every IPS must answer:

1. **Is the IPS Tied to the Corporate Vision and Mission?** The IPS outlines the basic processes of the firm's 401(k) plan. Fundamental to this is insuring the plan stays consistent with the corporate vision and mission. Some questions to answer: How does the 401(k) plan support the corporate vision and mission? Is there anything in the corporate vision and mission that is inconsistent with the 401(k) plan?

2. **Does the IPS have Meaningful and Clear Objectives?** This is critical to any clearly delineated set of processes and procedures. In the case of a 401(k) IPS, this specifically addresses 404(c) investment options and the due diligence process used in the selection and monitoring of those options.

3. **Is the IPS Properly Communicated?** Creating an IPS is one thing, but it's useless unless it is communicated to all relevant parties, including, but not necessarily limited to, plan trustees and fiduciaries, employees and vendors.

4. **Is the IPS Measurable?** While the objectives might be meaningful and clear, if there's no way to measure them, then the IPS fails to achieve its purpose. Here's a hint: Start at the end by identifying what's measurable and work backward.

5. **Does the IPS Allow for Independent Due Diligence?** The most common mistake made by

inexperienced fiduciaries is to merely accept an IPS offered by a third-party investment provider. These generic statements often place the fiduciary in greater liability peril. It's best to avoid a standard IPS (frequently referred to as a "statement of investment objective") supplied by a vendor providing investment services.

If the DOL focuses on process, then the IPS can offer an easy way to comply. However, a poorly constructed IPS may actually increase fiduciary liability. The 401(k) plan fiduciary is better off working with an independent fiduciary consultant when crafting an IPS.

WHY THE TRADITIONAL STRUCTURE OF INVESTMENT POLICY STATEMENTS WON'T WORK FOR 401(K) PLAN SPONSORS

To find the traditional structure of an Investment Policy Statement (IPS), we looked to the CFA Institute. The CFA Institute offers the CFA® designation to portfolio managers and securities analysts. We choose the CFA curriculum rather than the CFP® curriculum because the CFA Institute has consistently promoted the concepts used in an IPS long before the industry consensus agreed to the term "Investment Policy Statement" (as far back as the 1980's, the term was not universally accepted and at least some investment advisers used the alternative name "Statement of Investment Objective").

Whatever its name, the criteria promoted by the CFA Institute has remained constant. Contrast that to the CFP® curriculum, which, being a broader field of study, promoted traditional investment goals instead of the IPS. In fact, as late as the 2001, *Personal Financial Planning Theory and Practice*, Second Edition (by Michael A. Dalton and James F. Dalton and published by Dalton Publishing, LLC) — a popular text for those teaching the CFP® curriculum — did not even have an entry for "Investment Policy Statement" in its index. The fact this text only refers to "investment goals" leads to another problem altogether, which I clarify in the next chapter.

Regardless of the evolution of the term, the industry has now adopted its use as a minimum standard. The CFA Institute expects CFA® candidates and designees acting as portfolio managers for individual and institutional clients to formally use such instruments. The *CFA® Program Curriculum Volume 1 — "Ethical and Professional Standards and Quantitative Methods" Level 1*, published by the CFA Institute in 2010, states, "When an advisory relationship exists, members and candidates must gather client information at the inception of the relationship." Furthermore, the text stipulates that "this information should be incorporated into a written investment policy statement (IPS)…" (page 61).

Unfortunately, this is where things get a little difficult. In outlining the traditional structure for an IPS, the CFA Institute retains language from the era preceding the dominance of 401(k) plans in the institutional realm. While this structure certainly continues to work well for private individuals and single portfolio institutions like endowments, traditional defined benefit/defined contribution plans (i.e., pension and profit sharing plans) and, yes, even split-interest trusts with multiple beneficiaries, it represents an awkward construct for 401(k) plans.

To best understand why, let's revisit the four general areas the CFA Institute requires (according to page 62 of the text) "in formulating an investment policy for the client, the member or candidate should take… into consideration." The first area is "client identification," by which the CFA Institute means the "type and nature of clients, the existence of separate beneficiaries and approximate portion of total client assets." For a 401(k) plan, this basic information is good, but we do need more information on the plan demographics and other service providers. The CFA Institute does address this latter need on page 61 when it says "The IPS also should identify and describe the roles and responsibilities of the parties to the advisory relationship and investment process, as well as schedules for review and evaluation."

The second area involves "investor objectives." Here, the Institute breaks things down in two sections. The first deals with "return objectives," specifically citing "income," "growth in principal" and "maintenance of purchasing power" (see our reference in the next chapter on outdated language). The next focuses on "risk tolerance," meaning, per the Institute, "suitability" and "stability of values." In both cases, incorporating these measures becomes more awkward for a 401(k) plan, which, under 404(c) must offer at least three distinct investment options that might be at odds with the consistency implied by the standard IPS structure. More significantly, there is the problem of placing too much importance on "risk tolerance" (see "7 Deadly Sins Every ERISA Fiduciary Must Avoid: The 2nd Deadly Sin — The Joy of 'Risk'," *FiduciaryNews.com*, August 16, 2011).

The CFA Institute calls the third area "investor constraints." These comprise six different categories, some of which are irrelevant and some of which are impractical to consider for 401(k) plans. The first category is "liquidity needs," including "expected cash flows (patterns of additions/withdrawals)" and "investable funds (assets and liabilities or other commitments)." Clearly "expected cash flows" pertains only to retirees in the distribution phase (for which 401(k) plans in general may not be appropriate). As for "investable funds," that seems an issue more pertinent to the employee and his recordkeeper or payroll processer than with any part of the 401(k) plan's IPS.

The second category is "time horizon." This phrase sounds like the stuff TDFs are made of and, as such, clearly is of potential relevance to the plan's IPS. The same can't be said of the third category, "tax considerations." This has no place in a tax-exempt plan. The fourth category is "regulatory and legal circumstances." This is relevant given the nature of 401(k) plans and ERISA, with or without the 404(c) Safe Harbor election. The fifth category is "investor preferences, prohibitions, circumstances and unique needs," which appears to apply mainly to personal issues, not 401(k) issues. The final category is "proxy-voting responsibilities and guidance," which falls into the domain of the underlying investment options and does not affect the plan itself.

The final area identified by the CFA Institute is "performance measurement benchmarks." This area is too large to devote to a mere paragraph within a single chapter. I'll address this topic in the next section (Due Diligence).

Note, too, what's not included. At no point does the CFA Institute reference anything related to education being part of the IPS. Education must address the needs of both the plan trustees as well as the plan participants. It's critical for any identified education program to be delivered in a manner consistent with the IPS.

The CFA Institute makes no mistake as to the importance of a written IPS. On page 62, it bluntly states, "to fulfill the basic provisions of Standard III (C), [Duties to Clients — Suitability] a member or candidate should put the needs and circumstances of each client and the client's investment objective into a written investment policy statement (IPS) for each client." **This is good advice every 401(k) plan sponsor should take.**

One final piece of advice offered by the CFA Institute (again on page 62) is this: "Annual review is reasonable unless business or other reasons, such as a major change in market conditions, dictate more frequent review." Within the domain of the 401(k) plan, the IPS can probably be reviewed less frequently, as plan demographics generally take several years to change.

Before I present a 21st Century template for a 401(k) plan IPS, I want to revisit an underreported issue concerning the IPS — outdated language, particularly as it pertains to investment goals.

401(K) PLAN SPONSORS: IS YOUR INVESTMENT POLICY STATEMENT STILL USING OUTDATED LANGUAGE?

ERISA attorneys seem to have two minds when it comes to the Retirement Plan IPS. Some tell the plan sponsor it's safer not to put anything in writing, as this would then produce a documented record that can be used against the plan sponsor. Others warn it's safer to have an IPS as it limits the definition of the plan sponsor's fiduciary liability. Of course, in a 2008 Interpretive Bulletin, the Department of Labor wrote, "The maintenance by an employee benefit plan of a statement of investment policy designed to further the purposes of the plan and its funding policy is consistent with the fiduciary obligations set forth in ERISA section 404(a)(1)(A) and (B)."

And if you followed this advice from the DOL? Congratulations, you've done your fiduciary duty and created an IPS for your ERISA plan. The trouble is, as the first group of attorneys says, you've just created a written record that could and might be used against you. In fact, the older your IPS is, the more likely it will contain outdated language that might just land you in a pile of you-know-what. What is this language and how can you avoid it?

It's beyond the scope of one small chapter to provide a comprehensive review of updating an IPS, (that would be the point of reading this entire section), so we'll concentrate on perhaps the sexiest part of the plan: The Three Fundamental Investment Goals.

If you're a plan sponsor of a 401(k) plan, you're no doubt familiar with the 404(c) provision that requires you to offer at least three separate and distinct investment options to employees in order to safe harbor the plan. A better way to read this is "at least three separate and distinct investment goals," since investment options can (and do) have similar goals.

Many bankers, brokers and even some investment advisers continue to discuss investment matters in terms of these three traditional investment goals:

1. **Safety of Capital.**
2. **Generation of Income.**
3. **Capital Appreciation.**

The traditional goals have several advantages. They make intuitive sense. They accurately reflect the historic investment environment. They've been accepted and used for a very long time. Most important, they're really easy to understand. Indeed, if you're a veteran broker, you might remember being taught to describe the relationship of these goals with a pitcher of orange juice and three (very large glasses). Each glass represents one of the traditional investment goals. The broker would ask the client to pour as much juice into each glass that would reflect the relative importance of each goal. A client could pour everything into one glass, split it between two glasses, or pour a little bit into all three glasses. In the end, the broker would use this exercise to explain the nature of investing as a zero sum game. You cannot add to one glass without taking away from another.

That, in a nutshell, represents one of the disadvantages of the traditional investment goals. They do not reflect today's actual investment environment. They're outdated and, if they're still reflected in the language of your IPS, well, that can present a problem. Think of it in terms of this metaphor: If you want to get somewhere, would you use an outdated road map or an up-to-date one? The biggest issue with the traditional goals is that all of them, by definition, conflict with each other. Again harkening to our metaphor, if you had to get somewhere, say, Tahiti, by land, air and sea, would you accept a proposal that lets you take either a car, a plane or a boat, but not all three?

For decades, investors have been taught — rightfully so — that these goals each conflict with one another. In other words, the more emphasis the investor places on one goal, the less likely he will achieve the other two goals. However, all these goals, in practice and in theory, fail to account for inflation. In addition, any goal that emphasizes income generation suffers against a mountain of evidence suggesting total investment return provides consistently higher returns for long-term investors. Fortunately, you can address this by using the following set of practical investment goals intended to better serve plan sponsors and their employee-investors.

Enter the Modern Investment Goals. Today, every well-read student of investment theory — whether practitioner or casual investor — uses these goals in one form or another:

1. **Wealth Accumulation** — Building and growing a portfolio for some future use.
2. **Wealth Preservation** — A portfolio that maintains one's current lifestyle (or other objective).
3. **Wealth Distribution** — Depleting an existing portfolio in a controlled manner for some set term.

These Modern Goals come with several advantages. They make intuitive sense — everybody can think in terms of accumulating wealth, preserving wealth and distributing wealth. They accurately reflect the modern investment environment — if everything goes according to plan, one will use each of these goals at least once in one's life. These investment goals help the 401(k) plan sponsor concentrate on the pragmatic matters of investment management. By using such practical terminology, plan sponsors can directly relate the strategy of the goal to an associated investment strategy (i.e., the investment option). More importantly, these goals work together rather than conflict with one another. Ultimately, this is the proof of the pudding: The Modern Goals work in the modern world.

For example, let's compare Safety of Capital with Wealth Preservation. Both seem to be saying the same thing, but they are different. Safety of Capital implies the preservation of the investment principal or an actual set dollar figure. Wealth Preservation implies preserving the lifestyle allowable at the current level of wealth. At the very least, Safety of Capital, in its traditional sense, has ignored the impact of inflation on principal. Wealth Preservation takes into account the impact of inflation. In practice, a portfolio of pure US government bonds would be adequate to meet the investment objective of Safety of Capital. In practice, a portfolio of pure US government bonds would virtually guarantee the failure of meeting the investment objective of Wealth Preservation. A Wealth Preservation portfolio, in order to meet the objective to maintain the current lifestyle, would naturally be a more conservative portfolio but it wouldn't be a static portfolio. It would require investments that would likely keep up with inflation. (N.B. For those sticklers, we're assuming the jury is still out on the effectiveness of inflation-indexed Treasuries.)

This is not to say the Modern Investment Goals don't possess some disadvantages. First and foremost, not everyone readily accepts them. Recalling our travel metaphor, if you go to a travel agent with plans to travel to Tahiti and your travel agent calmly says, "Can't get there from here," do you think that particular travel agent will be able to get you to Tahiti? Does it matter to you if the travel agent tries to convince you that St. Thomas is really where you should be going? Said another way, as an individual, you might not want to go to Tahiti, but one of your employees could want to. Plan sponsors can't ignore the Modern Investment Goals.

Even when folks accept these goals, they might not use them, preferring the traditional world they grew up in. How does this stack up to our "Tahiti Test"? Well, say the travel agent now accepts that you can get from here to Tahiti. Alas, what if the travel agent does not have any packages to Tahiti? Again, does it matter to you if the travel agent can provide you with a really terrific package to St. Thomas?

Finally, even if users accept and adopt the Modern Investment Goals, we still have the problem that everyone might not understand them. One last time (promise), we'll invoke our by now tired metaphor. OK, the travel agent both accepts the idea of going from here to Tahiti and actually offers a package to Tahiti. Unfortunately, the travel agent isn't sure what it costs, who you need to pay or how you're going to make the various connections you need to make in order to get to Tahiti. Does it sound like you should be going to a different travel agent?

Truth be told, the Modern Investment Goals really aren't so new. They first appeared in my 1999 book *Due Diligence: The Individual Trustee's Guide to Selecting and Monitoring a Professional Investment Adviser* (Ardman Regional). They've appeared elsewhere in articles since and, under several variations of their names, seem to be growing in acceptance.

If you're a 401(k) Plan Sponsor, take another look at your IPS. Are your investment goals updated to reflect the language of the modern investment environment, or is your IPS just a travel agent with no clue about Tahiti?

HOW SHOULD A 401(K) PLAN SPONSOR CONSTRUCT AN APPROPRIATE INVESTMENT POLICY STATEMENT?

W hat worries the ERISA fiduciary most? After achieving sustainable profitability for their business, 401(k) plan sponsors' greatest concern most likely centers on their liability exposure as a result of their responsibility for investing institutional funds. **Constructing an appropriate IPS — one that truly unites the corporate vision and mission with the investment objective — represents the best method to alleviate this concern.** An IPS is essential for the reduction of liability. The statement must document the plan's mission and investment objectives, as well as the justification for these objectives. Without a written statement in place, 401(k) plan sponsors will not be able to effectively evaluate their true fiduciary liability. Does your plan have all the elements of an appropriate Investment Policy Statement or do you only think you have all the elements?

What is an 'Appropriate' IPS?

There exists at least one codified framework legislated to provide individual trustees and fiduciaries with some liability protection. Many states began passing some form of the "Prudent Investor Act" in the mid-1990s. In addition to what is now known as the Uniform Prudent Investor Rules, corporate retirement plans fall under the jurisdiction of ERISA, regulated by the federal Department of Labor.

A written IPS can act as the cornerstone to regulatory and legal compliance. With this written IPS, the fiduciary has documented the justification of the appropriateness of the institution's mission and investment objectives. From this, the fiduciary can better evaluate and monitor the institutional fund's investment performance. Therefore, the objectives of an 'appropriate' IPS include:

- A reiteration of the institution's Vision and Mission statements
- An assurance the IPS is consistent with the institution's corporate goals
- A provision for the Plan's mission statement
- A listing of the specific methods used to avoid the most common mistakes of Modern Portfolio Theory
- A thoroughly documented structure with clearly written prose that can be understood by all interested parties
- An outline of measurable procedures for trustees' and participants' education
- An accommodation for all other interested parties (if any)
- A list of meaningful goals
- A proper accounting of real risks as they pertain to the plan's exact demographics
- A well laid out identification of the method of evaluation
- An explicit timeline to regularly review and updated the document

How to Create a Structure for the IPS

We can assimilate the above in an intuitive, easy-to-understand table of contents. We'll break these down and follow each with a brief explanation of how to create them. Bear in mind, this process involves a substantial degree of due diligence. The 401(k) plan sponsor who lacks experience in this area may wish to complete this process with the help of a qualified fiduciary consultant.

Part I. Objective of IPS — This can be as simple as incorporating some form of the above paragraph "What is an appropriate IPS" as modified to meet the needs of the specific institution. For example, if there are specific regulatory criteria the plan must address, it should be stated here.

Part II. Statement of Corporate Vision — The components of corporate vision fall into three categories. These refer to those elements that define the rigid parameters within which the company moves as it seeks to achieve success in its business. Fiduciaries must fully understand these rigid parameters before they can even begin to define the Plan's mission statement and its IPS. Typically, this section would include: 1) a brief paragraph describing the company; 2) a list of the company's core values and beliefs; 3) a statement as to the company's overall purpose (i.e., its ideal role in society); and, 4) a statement of the mission of the company (i.e., its tangible goal). The corporate vision statement is often completed as a task separate and distinct from matters pertaining to the company's retirement plan. Nonetheless, it remains important to incorporate this body of work into the IPS. The tangible goal(s) derived from the mission statement is (are) used to identify the Part V (Investment Objectives) and Part VI (Method of Due Diligence) below.

Part III. The Plan's Mission Statement — Unlike the Corporate Mission Statement, which usually identifies dollar-denominated financial goals and needs, the mission statement of the ERISA plan contains broader language as to the general intent of the plan and its investments.

Part IV. Summary of the Plan's Vital Information — As with individual investment portfolios, here we list all the key individuals, including trustees, advisers and service providers, of the institution. In the specific case of retirement plans, we'll also include plan demographics.

Part V. Outline of Investment Objectives — The IPS now begins to define the broader investment objectives that will permit the portfolio to accomplish its stated mission. First and foremost, the fiduciary must determine if a "Total Return" or "Assigned Asset" methodology will be used. The Total Return method utilizes the entire portfolio to meet a financial goal. The Assigned Asset method assigns a specific portion of the portfolio to meet a specific goal. This section then outlines meaningful investment objectives that seek to accommodate all constituencies. These broadly defined objectives must outline and address the issues identified above.

In general, the Investment Objectives will consist of differing weights of the following standard objectives (for a more comprehensive explanation of these Modern Investment Objectives, see the previous chapter):

1. **Wealth Accumulation** (usually receives a higher weighting) — This Investment Objective is appropriate for investors wishing to grow assets over time. It implies a long-term time horizon. As such, it places long-term growth at a higher priority than reducing short-term volatility.

2. **Wealth Preservation** (usually receives a lower weighting) — This Investment Objective is appropriate for investors wishing to begin using assets in the very near future. It implies a short-term time horizon. As such, it places a greater emphasis on reducing short-term volatility rather than long-term growth.

3. Wealth Distribution (commonly used in specific circumstances) — This Investment Objective is appropriate for investors who seek to implement an asset distribution plan over time. The time period may be short-term or long-term. As such, this goal typically incorporates elements of Wealth Preservation depending on the exact nature of the distribution plan.

Finally, the IPS should explicitly state how it plans to satisfy some of the more common negative issues surrounding Modern Portfolio Theory. Because much of the industry still commits these mistakes, the fiduciary should proactively address them through the IPS. For example, most academics now acknowledge that the use of standard deviation (or similar statistical models) as a measure of risk may no longer be appropriate.

One word of warning here: Although the DOL has specified Target Date Funds as "qualified" for auto-enrollment, establishing a "target date" may actually harm investors and could create liabilities for the 401(k) plan sponsor. Why? Quite simply, employees have their own unique circumstances. While the retirement dates of some employees may be the same, their return requirements may be different.

Part VI. Method of Due Diligence and Evaluation — The IPS must define the specific criteria used to determine specific qualifications and evaluation parameters of the investment options. The Corporate Mission will typically identify cash flow assumptions, including any potential matching in the company's 401(k) plan. The fiduciary, often with the help of the fiduciary consultant, uses this data to calculate each investment option's risk/return profile. Portfolio management (including that within chosen mutual funds) and evaluation must then be conducted to conform to this profile. The investment option's profile is often a much better evaluation benchmark than industry indices or averages, which too often rely too heavily on relative performance (as opposed to the absolute needs of the investor).

Part VII. Trustee's/Fiduciary's Education Plan — It is generally a good idea to formulate a plan to provide ongoing education to individual trustees and fiduciaries of the plan. A fiduciary consultant can provide this service. It's important for the 401(k) plan sponsor to be careful here to ensure the avoidance of any conflicts of interest between the investment provider and the educational program, (I discuss this more thoroughly in next section of this book). For example, if a non-fiduciary (like a broker or a mutual fund company) offers trustee education, they may omit certain views because those views are not represented in their product offerings.

Part VIII. Employee's Education Plan — The company has employees that will have educational needs. These needs are appropriately addressed in the IPS. Here it is of paramount importance that the education provider be independent of the investment adviser, including any related mutual funds. Despite the DOL's new participant Investment Advice Guidelines, which allow this, it's safer for plan sponsors to eliminate any conflict of interest. Such conflicts of interest will exist when the organization responsible for serving education needs possesses a vested interest in the investment of certain options over other options. An example here would be a broker or mutual fund family having the opportunity, through their "education" program, to funnel employees' investments into higher fee investment options which benefit the broker or mutual fund family. (N.B.: The Investment Advice Guidelines require only "fee neutral" advice, but, this has only been in effect since December 2011 and hasn't been fully tested). Be mindful, though. Because most employees will need to invest in long-term options, even an independent education provider will likely direct most employees towards equity options — and these tend to have higher fees than stable income options.

IX. Compliance Review Plan — Lastly, the IPS should delineate a Compliance Review Plan taking into consideration the specific circumstances of the particular institution for which it is written. This section will address three areas: 1) the Annual Review of the IPS; 2) a Provider Analysis; and, 3) a Compliance Review and Audit. The degree of specificity of each of these areas will depend on the nature of the company, the size of the plan and the regulatory environment in which the plan exists.

Summary and Conclusion

Creating an appropriate IPS should not intimidate any individual trustee or fiduciary. The process represents a structured methodology meant to comprehensively address the fiduciary concerns of an individual who may or may not be a financial expert. Indeed, the end result of the process leads to the delegation of that duty — and at least a portion of the fiduciary liability — to a professional specifically trained for such services.

3 Reasons Why the 401(k) Fiduciary Should Use Both Active and Passive Funds to Reduce Fiduciary Liability

Much to the delight of the befuddled 401(k) fiduciary, the active investing vs. passive investing argument has become passé. Despite many purists still lauding one style over the other, ("Managed Funds Offer Little Cover From the Bear," *Wall Street Journal*, April 5, 2009; "Active Versus Passive Debate Rages On," *Investment News*, July 2, 2009; "Passive Investment May Beat Active Growth Management, But Value Beats Them Both," *The Globe and Mail*, September 22, 2009), it appears the debate may have settled into a détente. In terms of reducing fiduciary liability, this uneasy harmony can offer an excellent guide to 401(k) fiduciaries for three important reasons:

1. With all the studies, it's clear any researcher can find data to support a hypothesis favoring either active investing or passive investing. Perhaps we can attribute this to the "Snapshot-in-Time" anomaly first identified in a 2005 study. This common sense discovery simply states the ending date of the period chosen in any comparative of investment performance can overweight near term results. Known as "recency" in behavioral psychology, this phenomenon may also be responsible for the seemingly conflicting results pertaining to active and passive research.

2. That the "Snapshot-in-Time" effect can create misleading studies might offer a clue to both possibly increasing as well as avoiding fiduciary liability. If the superiority of passive or active depends on the time period chosen, this implies (as

the evidence bears out) some periods exist when passive outperforms active while other periods exist when active outperforms passive. A 401(k) fiduciary who chooses only active or only passive options in the plan may assume an additional liability risk. On the other hand, fiduciaries who provide both active and passive options may delegate that risk to the plan's participants.

3. After all, picking an investment style should be the employee's responsibility, not the plan sponsor's. In the end, the best we can say about the active vs. passive debate is that it reflects differing investment styles, not any exclusive truth. So, as in matters of faith, fiduciaries can best serve themselves by remaining agnostic and allowing participants the freedom to choose.

In the generation prior to the dominance of mutual funds as the preferred investment vehicle (i.e., when most folks invested directly in individual company stocks), sophisticated investors debated the merits of "growth" or "value" arguments. While remnants of that dispute persist (see *The Globe and Mail* article above), today most professionals understand it's no longer a question of growth OR value, but of growth AND value. We now accept that diverse portfolios can, and maybe should, have both types of stocks. Perhaps we may be nearing a new consensus, where it's no longer active VERSUS passive, but active WITH passive. Most telling, according to the aforementioned *Wall Street Journal article*, even "Vanguard, a big seller and proponent of index funds, nonetheless sees a place for active funds, which the firm also offers."

HOW MANY INVESTMENT OPTIONS SHOULD 401(K) PLAN SPONSORS OFFER?

F ar too many 401(k) plan sponsors don't know how to answer this important question. Of greater concern for 401(k) investors, far too many 401(k) plan sponsors fail to even ask the question. Instead, they opt to trust the guidance of their service providers, which may have a pecuniary interest in maximizing the number of offerings. First, let's examine why this question represents one of the most critical fiduciary decisions a 401(k) plan sponsor must make when establishing and monitoring a 401(k) plan.

The clearest reason why this might be important deals with fees. No, not the fees associated with the underlying investments, but the infrastructural costs associated with the mere number of options. Recordkeepers, third-party administrators and custodians all may charge more for each individual investment option, although typically extra charges are not incurred until the 401(k) plan has exceeded a certain maximum number of investment options. In addition to these providers, accountants may charge more if their work entails auditing investment transactions. The sheer number of options may simply increase the hours necessary to audit the plan and that can increase costs.

Why are these costs significant? Unlike, say, an indirect fee such as a mutual fund expense ratio, none of these direct fees can offer a positive impact on investment performance. As the DOL states in its commentary on 401(k) plan fees, a "1% difference in fees and expenses would reduce your account balance at retirement by 28%." These administrative fees can add up, and adding more investment options can cause them to add up quickly.

But fees aren't the only reason why 401(k) plan sponsors might inadvertently hurt 401(k) plan investors by offering too many investment options. A decade ago, a study conducted by Shlomo Benartzi and Richard Thaler ("Naive Diversification Strategies in Defined Contribution Saving Plans," *American Economic Review*, March 2001, Vol. 91.1, pp. 79-98.) suggested 401(k) investors tend to use simple decision-making heuristics when picking 401(k) investment options. These unsophisticated approaches often lead employees to merely split their dollars equally among all investment options.

While Benartzi and Thaler focused on the asset allocation implications of this, a far more meaningful impact was the over-diversification caused by assembling a portfolio of too many mutual funds. These naïve investors, in seeking greater diversification, may have actually created a *de facto* index fund, even when the underlying investments were all actively managed funds. The problem arises when one looks at the aggregate expense ratio of all these actively managed funds. This expense ratio tends to be much higher than a comparable index fund and, since the de facto index fund will likely yield a return similar to that comparable index fund, this expense ratio difference can only hurt the 401(k) investor. This is not an "active vs. passive" argument; it is an argument between high-cost and low-cost index funds.

Benartzi and Thaler tangentially touched on the real issue concerning why it's important for 401(k) plan sponsors to consider the number of investment options to offer on their plan menu. In 2000, Sheena Iyengar and Mark Lepper published an article, "When choice is demotivating: Can one desire too much of a good thing?" (*Journal of Personality and Social Psychology*, 76, 995-1006). Iyengar and Lepper showed, despite the popular idea that the greater the number of choices the better, it turns out the opposite it true — the fewer the choices the better. Later studies, including those like Benartzi and Thaler addressing 401(k) choice specifically, reached similar conclusions. In 2004, Iyengar, Huberman, and Jiang, "How Much Choice is Too Much: Determinants of Individual Contributions in 401(k) Retirement Plans" and in O.S. Mitchell and S. Utkus, Editors, Pension Design and Structure: New Lessons from Behavioral Finance, (*Oxford University Press*, Oxford, pp. 83-95.), researchers found too much choice actually lowered participation rates.

But all these studies postulated that the problem dealt with financial illiteracy, not pure economic theory. If this hypothesis were true, a greater number of choices would be preferred when presented to an ideally educated work force. A working paper recently published by the Harvard Business School ("When Smaller Menus Are Better: Variability in Menu-Setting Ability," David Goldreich and Hanna Hałaburda, August 10, 2011) tested this idea. They discovered "in an important economic context of 401(k) pension plans — we find that larger menus are objectively worse than smaller menus" and concluded, "this results in a negative relation between menu size and menu quality: smaller menus are better than larger menus."

What is the real impact of offering too many choices? In another recent study, Iyengar and Emir Kamenica spell this answer out quite precisely. Their study, published in the *Journal of Public Economics*, looked at data from the Vanguard Center for Retirement Research, including over 500,000 employees in 638 firms. Iyengar and Kamenica concluded that for every 10 investment options, equity allocation decreases by 3.28% and there's a concurrent increase of 2.87% in the number of participants who will allocate nothing to equities. These results are consistent with earlier research that concluded too much choice leads to sub-optimal decisions.

While this latest research doesn't suggest an optimal number of investment options, it does imply the optimum number is likely less than ten options. It should be noted ERISA Section 404(c) provides a safe harbor to 401(k) plan sponsors that include at least three "diversified" investment options that have "materially different risk and return characteristics" among other things (29 C.F.R. § 2550.404c-1(b)(3)(i)(B)). Between academic research and government regulation, it would appear the ideal 401(k) plan would have anywhere from three to 10 investment options.

That seemed simple, didn't it? Unfortunately, an August 2011 court case seems to have complicated matters. In *Renfro v. Unisys Corp*, the U.S. Court of Appeals in Philadelphia ruled against plaintiffs suing for breach of fiduciary duty because the plan had high-cost retail Fidelity funds. The fees of the 73 options ranged from 0.1% to 1.21% and the court ruled the participants had sufficient low-cost choices to invalidate their claim. Nothing was said about there being too many funds in the plan. Of course, to be honest, the case really dealt with Fidelity's duty as a directed trustee, not the number of options in the plan. Still, a few other cases have involved plans with several dozen investment options and neither the courts nor the plaintiffs seemed to have treated this fact as relevant.

Yet.

PROFESSIONAL ADVISORS SOUND OFF ON IDEAL NUMBER OF 401(K) PLAN OPTIONS

We've earlier discussed the problem discovered by behavioral researchers when plan sponsors offer too many options on their 401(k) menu (see the previous chapter). In perusing the open LinkedIn groups dedicated to 401(k) fiduciary matters, it appears many professionals understand the impact of these studies and have begun to offer practical suggestions both for their own firms as well as the industry in general. Here are some of the highlights of what they've said.

Colin Fitzpatrick Smith, Director of Investments at The Retirement Company, LLC of Cleveland/Akron Ohio, summarized the problem concisely. He recalls a time when his firm reviewed a 401(k) plan "with 26 participants with 36 choices…there was little participation in many of the investment options given the overwhelming number of choices."

With both behavioral scientists and fiduciary practitioners confirming the existence of the problem of too many 401(k) options, who's most responsible for addressing it? Craig Freedman, Registered Fiduciary at 401(k) Certified Independent Investment Advisors, LLC in West Palm Beach, Florida, says, "The one thing I strongly believe is that the change in a participant's investment behavior rests on the shoulders of those in a position to affect behavioral change, i.e., the plan adviser and/or a participant level fiduciary adviser."

The gauntlet laid down, the question is thus put to the advisors. John O'Reilly of Comprehensive Financial Advice in the greater San Diego area says, "The problem is: Are we talking about a typical mainstream (i.e., flawed) 401(k) plan that allows folks to build their own portfolios with individual funds, or a more sound, sane plan that provides only professionally designed portfolios spanning a risk continuum? If it's the latter, I suggest 5 is a good number, but 3-8 works fine."

Brian Douglas, Retirement Sales Consultant at Commonwealth Financial Network in Boston agrees with O'Reilly. "I think the ideal number is somewhere around 10; ideally I think 6, but, politically, 12 to 15 is probably more realistic," says Douglas.

Many of the professionals commenting on the LinkedIn groups concurred. They liked the idea of plans having fewer than ten (and closer to five) options, but conceded they're swimming upstream against a marketing current that encourages an almost unlimited choice. Still, they feel they can get their clients to accept "only" a dozen or so options.

Mark Griffith, CPC, AIFA, an independent fiduciary in the greater Boston area, had the most unique response. He says, "I believe the right answer is '1' (per participant). The only justifiable argument against this theory is which one. By '1' I mean a properly diversified portfolio, the construction of which is certainly debatable."

Sometimes the best things do come in the smallest packages. And '1' is as about as small as you can get.

AVOIDING DECISION PARALYSIS: HOW TO CREATE THE IDEAL 401(K) PLAN OPTION MENU

Maybe there's a way to satisfy both the findings of academia and the practicalities of the real world. As we've discussed in the previous two chapters, researchers have found too many 401(k) plan options detrimental to the employee. Sophisticated industry experts agree with these findings, but must also deal with the "politics" of the marketplace.

Perhaps a compromise is in order. In the next few paragraphs, we'll lay out a novel way to construct a 401(k) plan option menu that may satisfy both the finance professors and the financial professionals.

Let's start with this basic premise: Too many options spoil the investor. The idea that "choice" is bad seems counterintuitive, especially for any red-blooded American raised on the idea of the freedom of wide-open spaces. In fact, in 2005 psychology researcher Barry Schwartz wrote a popular book entitled *The Paradox of Choice: Why More Is Less* explaining this very phenomenon. In it, he states:

> "Freedom and autonomy are critical to our well-being, and choice is critical to freedom and autonomy. Nonetheless, though modern Americans have more choice than any group of people ever has before, and thus, presumably, more freedom and autonomy, we don't seem to be benefiting from it psychologically."

How could this be? One of the most cited papers on this subject is "When Choice is Demotivating: Can One Desire Too Much of a Good Thing?" by Sheena S. Iyengar and Mark R. Lepper (*Journal of Personality and Social*

Psychology, Vol 79(6), Dec 2000, 995-1006). The third study in this paper presented three different scenarios. Two involved choice, one where subjects were given a limited choice of six chocolates and the other where subjects were give a wide array of 30 chocolates. In the third scenario, subjects had no choice but were simply given chocolates.

Not surprisingly, it took longer for the 30-chocolate subjects to decide what to select than it did for the six-chocolate subjects to make their decision. Somewhat surprisingly, though, the 30-chocolate subjects felt they had "too many choices" while the six-chocolate subjects felt their number of options were "about right." Oddly, the 30-chocolate subjects found their decision-making at once more exciting yet more frustrating compared to the subjects selecting from only six chocolates. Both groups of subjects ended up being confident in their ultimate decisions. Finally, in terms of "buyer's remorse," subjects choosing from six chocolates were more satisfied with their decision than subjects choosing from 30 chocolates. Interestingly, both choice groups were more satisfied than the no-choice group.

We can summarize this paper in the following manner: Subjects with fewer choices are more satisfied and less regretful and, as a result, are more willing to continue "playing the game." Subjects with too many choices ultimately suffer a "tyranny of choice," a fundamentally disheartening and demotivating phenomenon. With this ammunition, we can create a new kind of structure for a 401(k) plan option menu that addresses both fiduciary concerns and behavioral concerns. It involves the creation of categories (or "tiers" as presented in "How Much Choice is Too Much?: Contributions to 401(k) Retirement Plans" by Sheena S. Iyengar, Wei Jiang and Gur Huberman, *Pension Research Council Working Paper*, March, 2010).

At this point it also makes sense to mention the 2008 book *Nudge* by Richard Thaler and Cass Sunstein. In it, the authors describe the advantages of offering employees a no-action-required option to "nudge" them towards participating in the plan (as well as forcing them to make better investment decisions). Much research has shown the advantages of adopting an automatic enrollment opt-out policy. Madrian and Shea (2001) concludes 98% of employees were enrolled after three years in plans with automatic enrollment options as opposed to only 65% enrollment for plans with only an opt-in approach. Similarly, Choi et al. (2006) found there was only a nearly unnoticeable increase in opt-outs one year after enrollment in plans with automatic enrollment versus in plans without automatic enrollment.

Here are five steps to create this ideal menu:

1. Create four categories of options with each category having a limited number of options (1-5 funds);
2. For those employees preferring to do things themselves in lieu of professional management, place them in the "Do-It-Yourself Asset Allocation" category catering to both the Wealth Accumulation and the Wealth Preservation investment objectives (which ideally contains index funds across relevant "style" categories — e.g., large-cap, mid-cap, small-cap and international — as well as a stable value fund);
3. For those employees who prefer professional management but don't want to think about anything else, place them in the "No-Action Required" category catering to the Wealth Accumulation investment objective (which ideally contains only one diverse asset allocation fund appropriate for the overall demographics of the plan);
4. For those employees preferring professional management but willing to identify only their general risk preferences, place them in the

"Lifestyle" category catering to the Wealth Accumulation and possibly the Wealth Distribution investment objectives (which ideally contains 3-4 asset allocation funds ranging from "conservative" to "moderate" to "aggressive"); and,

5. For those employees preferring professional management and willing to identify their specific return requirement, place them in the "Traditional Long-Term Growth" category catering to the Wealth Accumulation investment objective (which ideally contains three multi-cap equity, funds each with distinct characteristics — e.g., a domestic "Value" fund, a domestic "Growth" fund and an international fund).

Obviously, nothing would prevent an employee from picking funds across categories, but that would be the employee's choice. Those employees willing to use the category structure will benefit from two decision steps, each with limited choices, satisfying the academic researchers. At the same time, the 401(k) plan as a whole can still contain roughly a dozen funds, satisfying the current marketing environment that suggests to plan sponsors this is a "safer" number.

Life may or may not be a box of chocolates, but what we learn from that box can help plan sponsors and the typical ERISA fiduciary build a better 401(k) plan.

3 Ways 401(k) Plan Sponsors Can Help Employees Make Better Investment Decisions

D o you think 401(k) plan sponsors would be interested if they could discover a simple way to help their employees make better 401(k) investment decisions? Would these same 401(k) plan sponsors be surprised to learn government regulations and industry standards actually encourage 401(k) employees to make inappropriate retirement choices? If a smart class-action attorney happened upon this information, whom do you think might be held responsible for the dissemination of this misleading information — the government or the 401(k) fiduciary?

In 1999, Shlomo Benartzi and Richard Thaler published a seminal paper in behavioral economics ("Risk Aversion or Myopia? Choices in Repeated Gambles and Retirement Investments," *Management Science*, Vol. 45, No. 3, March 1999). In the decade-plus since its publication, both the SEC and the DOL have commented on the mutual fund performance reporting standard, yet neither regulatory agency has adopted the conclusions of this paper. Worse, both agencies continue to require mutual funds to report performance in a manner contrary to the conclusions of the paper and in a way that might actually mislead investors into making incorrect investment decisions. Needless to say, the industry hasn't complained. The current mandatory performance reporting requirements actually allow providers to avoid the kind of comprehensive performance disclosure that might impinge on their traditional marketing campaigns.

Despite the general disregard for the fruits of this research on the part of regulators and the industry, a 401(k) plan fiduciary may be at risk for not framing its reports to plan participants in a manner consistent with the Benartzi/Thaler paper. After all, just because the SEC doesn't require mutual fund companies to make these disclosures and just because the DOL doesn't require 401(k) plan sponsors to report performance consistent with the Benartzi/Thaler findings doesn't mean some smart class action attorney can't build a convincing case that a plan sponsor should have incorporated techniques to avoid misleading plan investors.

What's the secret revealed in "Risk Aversion or Myopia? Choices in Repeated Gambles and Retirement Investments"? If you've read the paper, you'll find a long dissertation on a concept known as the "fallacy of large numbers." In disproving this concept, Benartzi/Thaler drive a stake into the heart of Modern Portfolio Theory's very foundation.

The fallacy of large numbers holds that a rational decision maker will make the same decision no matter how many times the decision maker is given the choice to make the same decision. Paul Samuelson explained this in his 1963 paper "Risk and Uncertainty: A Fallacy of Large Numbers." In the paper, Samuelson tells the story of a flippant offer he once made to a coworker, where he offered to give the coworker $200 if a coin flip turned up heads as long as his colleague would promise to give Samuelson $100 if the fair coin flip yielded tails. The mark declined Samuelson's offer.

But, said the colleague, he would accept the bet if Samuelson allowed him to take this one bet 100 consecutive times. This apparent contradiction inspired Samuelson to develop a theorem that logically proved a rational decision maker must decline the 100 consecutive bets if he declines the bet once.

Benartzi/Thaler show that the apparent contradiction is not irrational and that Samuelson's rational decision-making theory is not relevant in the real world. The two researchers had earlier (1995) developed the concept of "myopic loss aversion," where a decision maker weighs near-term losses more heavily than long-term gains. The rejection of a single coin — with its 50% chance of losing — is consistent with accepting a series of 100 such bets — where the risk of a loss is less than 1%.

Moreso, Benartzi and Thaler suggested the framing of the outcomes can also influence a decision maker. For example, by looking at the bet in isolation, the $100 stands out as a significant sum of money (especially in 1963). On the other hand, had the choice been framed in terms of the decision-makers total wealth (let's say it's $100,500), a head would have yielded $100,700 total wealth while a tail would have led to total wealth of $100,400. Expressed in this manner, the decision-maker may have been less risk averse.

Now, here's the significant part. Once the two scholars wrapped up their discussion of coin flipping, they performed a test on 401(k) type retirement investments. In this experiment they asked USC staff employees who were investing in the university's defined contribution plan to make an asset allocation decision based on two hypothetical funds. The respondents were not told, but one fund represented the average return of stocks and another fund represented the average return of bonds. Some of those surveyed were shown performance in one-year increments and the others were shown performance reflected in thirty-year increments.

The results proved astounding. Those shown the one-year charts allocated only 40% to stocks while those shown the thirty-year charts allocated 90% to stocks. Most financial planners would agree retirement assets should generally be weighted more heavily towards equity investments. Interestingly, a second experiment was conducting involving UC faculty. The faculty allocated 63% to stocks when seeing the one-year charts but 81% to stocks when viewing the 30-year charts. In real life, the faculty allocates 66% of their retirement money to stocks. In real life, the faculty generally sees one-year charts.

Finally, Benartzi and Thaler employed two different kinds of 30-year charts. In one type, they expressed performance in annual terms. In the other, they expressed performance as a percentage of meeting the respondent's retirement goal. The stock allocation choices derived from using these two different 30-year charts were not significantly different.

Benartzi and Thaler conclude, "The manner in which the information is provided will influence the choices the employees make." The paper suggests three ways 401(k) plan sponsors can help employees make better investment decisions.

1. Avoid showing short period returns (typically anything less than five years) for long-term objectives.
2. Show long period returns (typically at least in 5-year rolling increments) for long-term objectives.
3. Encourage employees to review 401(k) balances only once a year (yes, that means reconfiguring internet access and mailing participant statements no more frequently than required by law).

Plan Sponsors can easily include each of these items in their 401(k) plan's IPS as well as in their plan policies and in their vendor RFPs.

3 MORE WAYS 401(K) PLAN SPONSORS CAN HELP EMPLOYEES MAKE BETTER INVESTMENT DECISIONS

If a picture is worth a thousand words, how much more is a graph worth to a 401(k) investor? More pointedly, academic research shows there's a right way and a wrong way to communicate critical investment information. How many 401(k) plan sponsors have read this research? Has the typical fiduciary incorporated it into the plan's IPS, employee education programs and summary reports? But here's the scary question: Does ignorance of this knowledge increase fiduciary liability?

In the last chapter I told you how the 1999 Benartzi/Thaler research paper, "Risk Aversion or Myopia," first exposed the fallacy of certain industry-standard performance reporting techniques in retirement plans. Benartzi/Thaler showed how this reporting may lead to ineffective investment decisions by plan participants. The two researchers concluded that since the contributions to 401(k) plans will generally be invested for longer time periods, the data shown to plan participants must echo this fact, not distort or omit it.

Scholarly exploration did not end in 1999. A recent research paper out of the Australian School of Business at New South Wales ("Financial Competence, Risk Presentation and Retirement Portfolio Preferences," *Australian School of Business*, Bateman et al., July 3, 2011") gives insight as to how an employee's allocation decisions will vary whether given textual descriptions or graphical displays of performance data, and whether the emphasis is on event frequencies or return ranges. Experimenters gave survey participants three portfolio options to choose from: 1) a 100% bank account with a guaranteed real rate of return of 2%; 2) 50% bank account and 50% growth assets with a 3.25% return; and, 3) a 100% growth assets portfolio featuring a 4.5% return. The higher return in the growth portfolio is congruent with the higher long-term return of stock-dominated portfolios.

Three results of the Bateman paper stand out as informative to plan sponsors.

First, when shown the frequency of losing years (i.e., the number of years where a loss occurred divided by the total number of years in the time period), employees chose the conservative bank account more often. But when shown the frequency of positive years (i.e., the number of years where a gain occurred divided by the total number of years in the time period), they chose the growth portfolio more often. Obviously, the frequency of loss years reveals the frequency of positive years and vice-versa, so, technically, expressing one automatically expresses the other. However, in a manner consistent with the myopia phenomenon discovered by Benartzi/Thaler, investors appear biased by the context (or "framing" to use a behavioral term) posed by the presentation.

Second, in another restatement of the Benartzi/Thaler paper, the research of Bateman et al. indicated graphical displays of returns help participants better grasp actual performance data and encourage risk tolerance. When respondents viewed graphs of 90% probability ranges of returns, they chose the bank account less often than when viewing the identical information about risk and return via a textual description of the range presentations. Perhaps even more useful to 401(k) plan sponsors, Bateman also observed the number of people who switched to the growth option as a result of seeing the graphs was greater among people who scored lower in numeracy tests. (Numeracy measures the ability to use numbers and reason mathematically.) This correlation between numeracy and graphical representation implies the effectiveness of graphical displays on participants amongst all intellectual levels may overcome variations of mathematical literacy. This may therefore supersede the traditional reliance on 401(k) education programs.

Finally, the Bateman paper reveals the highest number of employees changed their choice after being given data about the probability of just one end of the loss-gain spectrum. Respondents were given information on only a single extreme (i.e., "1 in 20 chance of return above y%" or "1 in 20 chance of return below x%"). The researchers concluded, "Consumers do not infer that a high probability of losses also implies a high probability of gains or vice versa."

The authors point out factors other than presentation of performance data, such as wealth levels and optimism vs. pessimism, can also impact plan participant choices. Still, they deduce, "for a majority of consumers the risk information is significant and influential, but large changes in underlying risk do not change choice probabilities as much as changes in the way the risk is communicated." Knowing the tendencies of how employees make complex decisions regarding their retirement savings will help the plan sponsor to be cognizant of and thus help steer participants away from the common mistakes that cause many to be financially underprepared for their retirement.

The Bateman paper points to three ways 401(k) plan sponsors can help employees make better investment decisions.

1. When expressing returns in terms of frequency, use the word "gain" or a similar positive frame;
2. Use graphs when showing returns or probability ranges of returns; and,
3. Avoid one-sided measures since investors cannot infer that a high probability of losses also implies a high probability of gains and vice versa.

As with Benartzi/Thaler, Bateman et al. shows 401(k) plan participants can avoid making suboptimal allocation decisions when 401(k) plan sponsors and any other investment fiduciary provide information about investment options in a 'frame appropriate' context. Being frame appropriate in the case of retirement investments involves the creation of mental accounts that, although unique to each person, exhibit certain universal generalities. These frames would also include a schedule of financial needs. Taking these steps will aid the apportioning of savings to wealth preservation and wealth accumulation investment goals as appropriate. Unfortunately, without regulators imposing the relevant mandated disclosures and presentation requirements on the financial services industry, 401(k) plan sponsors are left to their own devices in delivering this very useful information to help employees make better investment decisions.

NEW STUDY EXPLAINS WHY
THE 401(K) MATCH FAILS

It's the dilemma of every 401(k) plan sponsor: How can I boost my 401(k) participation rate in order to satisfy IRS non-discrimination rules? Many feel offering an employee match and/or employee education represent no-brainer answers to this oft-heard question. But a new study from Yale and Harvard researchers suggests this stunning answer: People will walk right past free money — knowingly!

James J. Choi (Yale), David Laibson (Harvard) and Brigitte C. Madrian (Harvard) reveal startling results in their paper, "$100 Bills on the Sidewalk: Suboptimal Investment in 401(k) Plans." Just after *The Review of Economics and Statistics* accepted the paper for publication, I sat down and spoke to James Choi, who shared with me a pre-publication copy of the paper.

The researchers conducted several tiers of testing to arrive at their results. First, they looked at data from seven companies across a diverse group of industries including consumer products, electronics, health care, manufacturing, technology, transportation and utilities. They found the average worker older than 59 ½ lost 1.6% of their annual pay (or $507) by not taking full advantage of employer matches. The largest loss was $7,596, which represented 6% of the worker's salary.

Why focus on employees aged 59 ½ and above? Choi says it's because they're more acutely awareness of their impending retirement and the need that entails. In addition, these veteran workers are thought to have greater experience managing their own money. Finally, and with a mean tenure of 16 years in this particular study, they ought to have had enough time to become familiar with their firms' respective 401(k) plans.

After looking at the general data, the researchers took their experiment to the next level with the help of Hewitt Associates. In randomly assigning employees to receive one of two surveys, the authors sought to determine to what degree additional education could improve employee participation. After all, if the lure of an employer match doesn't light a fire under the employees, certainly better education will do the trick, or so says conventional wisdom.

Unfortunately, the evidence suggests reliance on education stands as more of a myth than reality. Any improvement proved statistically insignificant. In addition, while outside factors may have muddied previous studies, this work "has the advantage of being theoretically unambiguous and requiring few additional assumptions to identify." Indeed, by using a survey sample including only individuals older than 59 ½, the researchers dealt with employees who, if they failed to contribute up to the match, violated the no-arbitrage condition. In other words, the money could have been contributed, received the free company match and then immediately withdrawn without any negative impact on the employee.

Why? The authors found evidence employees who did not take full advantage of the match tended to procrastinate and were less financially literate. If free money and better education doesn't inspire these employees, what will? Co-author James Choi offers this thought: "Plan sponsors can encourage employee engagement by creating firm deadlines for action. Alternatively, sponsors can make action less onerous by simplifying choice menus. It's a lot less painful to consider two or three alternatives than to consider the thousands of possible choices that a typical 401(k) menu offers. The more painful it is to make a choice, the more likely it is that an employee will decide to push the decision off to another day."

HOW PLAN SPONSORS CAN HELP 401(K) INVESTORS AVOID OVER-DIVERSIFICATION

Orson Welles created *Citizen Kane*, believed by most cinephiles to be the greatest motion picture of all time. Only twenty-five years old when he made this masterpiece, Welles's reputation rose to that of a (then) modern Mark Twain. Such was the genius of Welles that his stature alone filled every scene he appeared in. Later, a markedly larger Welles filled the screen in other ways. The obviously obese Welles was left to lament, "Gluttony is not a secret vice."

Unfortunately the deadly sin of over-diversification too often lays hidden from the average 401(k) investor. Over-diversification, however, is no secret to the academic researcher and the well-informed investor. As long ago as 1997, *Better Investing* — a magazine for amateur investors — published the article "Don't Carry Diversification Too Far." That piece pointed out, "Depending on which research study is cited, students of investing generally agree that 12 to 16 carefully chosen stocks will bring most of the benefit of reduced risk that can come from portfolio diversification... There is only so much risk that can be diversified away. No matter how many additional stocks or industries are added, the risk inherent in equity investing will remain; and often the more stocks held, the harder it becomes to best the market averages."

Plan sponsors and 401(k) investors must pay attention to the article's summation: "There is a point at which diversification can move away from being a prudent action and become a limiting factor to further success." The two important phrases in this sentence are "prudent action" and "limiting factor." The DOL has repeatedly cited the need for 401(k) plan sponsors to act with prudence and to consider all factors. Over-diversification is one of those factors ERISA plan sponsors seeking to reduce fiduciary liability must consider.

Plan sponsors have two options to help 401(k) investors avoid this sin. The first remains wholly within their control. The second relies on the employee.

The first case puts the 401(k) plan sponsor squarely in the driver's seat so the plan sponsor can nip this sin in the bud. Ultimately, the plan sponsor is responsible for the options available in the plan. This includes the specific make-up of mutual fund choices. Here, the plan sponsor can instruct the investment adviser to focus on diversified funds containing fifty or fewer holdings. This doesn't mean limiting the plan to funds with only fifty holdings, but it does imply reducing the number of funds with hundreds of holdings. (Note: This only applies to actively managed funds as, by definition, index funds will have hundreds of stocks.)

As part of this effort, the plan sponsor must ensure there are only a limited number of options (at least three) and that each option represents a diversified portfolio. Diversification here refers to sector, industry and market capitalization. The objective is to permit the 401(k) investor to avoid selecting more than one mutual fund to achieve diversification. (We'll leave the subject of diversification among asset classes for a later book.)

For example, a "bare bones" plan could contain just three options: a stable value option; a 50-stock diversified "value" equity fund, and a 50-stock diversified "growth" equity fund. This way, even if the 401(k) investor succumbs to the "naïve diversification strategy" discovered by Benartzi and Thaler, there's little chance of overlap between the three options and, with only 100 stocks held between the two equity funds, there remains a reasonable possibility for the employee to do better than an index fund.

Bear in mind, this simple example could represent just one tier of the four-category plan we described earlier.

These three options would best fit in the category designed for employees seeking traditional long-term growth options. Of course, what's to prevent employees from tier hopping in a manner not intended by the plan sponsor or the plan's investment adviser?

This brings us to the plan sponsor's second tactic to help 401(k) investors avoid this sin. A well-articulated and easily understood education program offers a vital alternative for plan sponsors who want to reduce their fiduciary liability. These programs require plan sponsors to engage investment consultants who are familiar with over-diversification and how it manifests itself in the 401(k) investor's decision making process.

In addition, plan sponsors should demand that periodic reports summarizing plan options include the number of holdings and the percentage of top ten holdings for each fund. Since these reports are designed for and shared with employees, the inclusion of this data will give 401(k) investors the ability to quickly assess over-diversification. Does the fund have more than 50 stocks? Does the fund have hundreds of stocks? If the fund has less than 50 stocks, what percentage of the portfolio contains the 10 largest holdings of the fund? Ideally, the education program would walk through these questions and discuss the range of answers while emphasizing the ideal.

When Washington birthed 401(k) plans, the intention of providing three distinct investment options meant to address the then prevailing wisdom that, for all practical purposes, the world consisted of only three asset classes — stocks, bonds and cash. The idea was to diversify among asset classes (indeed, the remnants of that original language can still be found in some DOL publications). At first, it was thought each distinct option could be mapped to each asset class, but it didn't take long to realize "distinct" equity formats could occupy two of those slots (e.g., growth and value). Soon, financial rocket scientists invented ever more "distinct" equity formats and financial service providers were too glad to sell these products.

By 2006, it was determined the situation had evolved to the detriment of the 401(k) investor. For the most part, regulators felt 401(k) investors were being too cautious in too many ways (including by not even participating in the plan). The 2006 Pension Protection Act, in part, addressed this with default options designed to serve as a viable single fund option for the disinterested employee.

At the same time, the sin of over-diversification seeped into the decision making of the 401(k) plan investor. Naïve diversification strategies using too many options created a no-win situation for the 401(k) plan investor. Based on recent discussions on various 401(k) fiduciary-oriented LinkedIn Groups, it appears a growing number of investment advisers have concluded the best route for most 401(k) investors is to select a single diversified fund and plan to hold it for the long term.

If this sounds like plan sponsors should limit fund options to "target date funds," it's not intended to. Any single diversified fund with a limited number of underlying holdings will do (and also offers the possibility of an extended track record). In a sense, allowing 401(k) investors to select only one option with 50 or so stocks seems to fly in the face of conventional wisdom. That's because conventional wisdom only appears conventional because it's the result of decades of aggressive advertising. Alas, repeating an error, no matter how many times it's repeated, doesn't change its fundamental incorrectness or the results of academic studies showing focused portfolio managers tend to perform better. The idea of focusing your resources on a few well-researched ideas isn't new. While trying to climb out of his personal bankruptcy in 1893, Mark Twain, in *The Tragedy of Pudd'nhead Wilson*, wrote:

"Behold, the fool saith, 'Put not all thine eggs in the one basket' — which is but a manner of saying, 'Scatter your money and your attention'; but the wise man saith, 'Put all your eggs in the one basket and — watch that basket!'"

SECTION SIX:

– INVESTMENT DUE DILIGENCE –

IMPLEMENTATION WITHOUT DOCUMENTATION IS NOT IMPLEMENTATION

4 STEPS 401(K) PLAN SPONSORS MUST TAKE TO ENSURE A DOCUMENTED INVESTMENT DUE DILIGENCE PROCESS

Investment due diligence presents one of the most difficult tasks for 401(k) plan sponsors, but it doesn't have to be hard. The challenge stems from the often misunderstood nature of the fiduciary's duty regarding investment due diligence. Many 401(k) plan sponsors incorrectly assume they must design a process that picks the best investment options for their employees. While this is a laudable goal, the DOL is wise enough not to hold 401(k) plan sponsors to this impossible task. What the DOL desires, quite simply, is to see a clearly articulated process that the 401(k) plan sponsor faithfully implements and executes continuously. The DOL doesn't want to get in the middle of the active vs. passive debate or the value vs. growth argument. As long as 401(k) plan sponsors act consistently and conform to an established due diligence process, they have fulfilled at least this portion of their fiduciary duty.

Stripped down to its bare bones, the 401(k) Investment Due Diligence Process consists of these four steps, each of which should be incorporated directly in the plan's Investment Policy Statement (see the chapter "How Should a 401(k) Plan Sponsor Construct an Appropriate Investment Policy Statement?" on page 175):

1. **Documented Selection Process** — This process specifically defines and outlines the components used in initially selecting investment options. Since many 401(k) plans have multiple categories, this is usually the first level of the selection process. The second level details the key criteria the plan will use to select specific investment options within each

category. For example, we might only pick funds whose portfolio manager has at least five years of experience with that specific fund or whose portfolio consists of no more than 50 stocks.

2. **Documented Monitoring Process** — This portion of the process identifies the monitoring methods to be used by the 401(k) plan sponsor (or by the fiduciary adviser the plan sponsor chooses to delegate this duty to). Though it's likely the same key criteria above will be mentioned, here we'll expect to see how sensitive each individual criterion is to any specific variance. Again using the examples above, we might say we'll need to remove the fund if the experienced manager leaves, but we can continue holding a fund until its portfolio exceeds 60 stocks.

3. **Consistent Analysis and Comparisons** — This step is admittedly tricky. Well, at least part of it. The consistent portion represents the easy half. It is the decision as to what you should compare things to in a consistent fashion that poses the greatest struggle for the 401(k) plan sponsor. For example, although it's assumed a mutual fund should be benchmarked to an index, this isn't necessarily the best idea. For one, each mutual fund is required by the SEC to choose its own index benchmark (this is listed in the fund's prospectus). As a result, different funds in the same category might choose different indexes. It's better to choose a benchmark that can be evenly applied across funds in the same category.

4. **Periodic Documented Review** — Here's the easiest step, often made more difficult because of

this nasty tradition of viewing investments on a quarterly or monthly basis. On one hand, confirming the assets are in proper order is something that should be done monthly through the custodian statement. On the other hand, mutual funds are like aircraft carriers — they take a long time to turn. As such, 401(k) plan sponsors are probably better off conducting an investment due diligence review on a semi-annual basis.

It goes without saying the 401(k) plan sponsor must undertake the due diligence process in an unbiased fashion. That means any outside provider who assists in the due diligence process needs to be an independent provider, i.e., one having no connection to the investments chosen.

In the next chapter, we'll take a look at some key components 401(k) plan sponsors incorporate into the first two steps of their Due Diligence Process.

The Ten Commandments of 401(k) Investment Due Diligence

While the four steps to a well-documented 401(k) investment due diligence process just fell in our laps, getting into the nitty-gritty of the first two steps — the identifying the selection and monitoring processes — might prove a tad bit more laborious. There's another thing about this particular portion of the due diligence process I must warn you about. It's the part where the arguments start.

If you take any two investment advisers and ask them which specific characteristics one should focus on when selecting a mutual fund to be included among a 401(k) plan's investment options, you're likely to get vastly different answers. Fortunately, in speaking to different advisers, we've been able to whittle down their recommendations to very broad areas — wide enough for most advisers to swim comfortably within.

I.   **Company's Custom Statistics** — It all starts here, with specific data pertaining to the company's demographics. This data set will produce the major criteria 401(k) plan sponsors — or their advisers — will later use when determining appropriate fund options. Todd Reid, General Agent for Intermountain Financial Group in Salt Lake City, Utah, says this will indicate the "time horizon, liquidity, and true risk tolerance" of the plan's investors; hence, this data is a great starting point towards selecting funds.

II.   **Company's Goal-Oriented Target Analysis** — While company demographics might seem generic, it's important to recognize that even employees of the same age may have different return requirements. In order to best select relevant funds for the plan option, it's critical to know the range of target returns. This will come in handy during the later performance analysis of each candidate fund.

III.   **Key Characteristics of the Fund** — Before even getting into performance and costs, it's important to identify a set of key differentiators you'll review among all funds, whatever the investment objective. Boyd Wagstaff, 401(k) and Qualified Plan Specialist for Intermountain Financial Group, likes to focus in on the fund managers. He looks at years of tenure and style. "We want to make sure that fund or investment is true to its value," he says. "For example, if we are looking for a large-cap value stock, we want to make sure it does not change to some other style, but that it remains consistent with its original design."

IV.   **Peer Group Performance** — Manny Schiffres, Executive Editor, *Kiplinger's Personal Finance* in Washington, D.C., says, "We look at performance, specifically the consistency of performance. How has a fund done year by year against its peer group and an appropriate benchmark is far more important than cumulative results, which can be swayed by one outstanding year."

V.   **Rolling Long-Term Performance** — This approach to performance measurement is more consistent with the results of studies in behavioral finance as it dodges the dangers of short-term volatility and avoids the "snapshot-in-time" phenomenon Schiffres refers to. He says, "Analysis of the sort that says this or that fund has beaten its peers or an index over the past 1, 3, 5 and 10 years is bogus. As mentioned earlier, one outstanding (or awful) year totally distorts the numbers. Plus, because this sort of analysis can change depending on whether a fund is strong at the beginning or the end of the period, even if the results are essentially the same in either case, it is obviously a flawed approach to analyzing performance."

VI.   **Generic Fund Statistics** — All funds share common traits. Some of them may reveal characteristics the plan sponsor will want to shun or emphasize. These can include the number of holdings (addressed previously in the chapter titled "Over-diversification and the 401(k) Investor — Too Many Stocks Spoil the Portfolio" on page 204), the concentration of holdings, the fund's size and any unique costs associated with the fund. When it comes to a fund's size, Schiffres says, "The bigger the fund, the harder it is to manage. This is especially true when the fund focuses on less-liquid investments, stuff other than big-cap stocks and Treasury bonds. When you buy in big quantities, you tend to force up the price of the security you're buying. When you dump large quantities, you help push down the price. Neither is helpful to the manager." Regarding costs, besides the usual expense ratio, Reid also looks at the "sales charge in relation to the fund class, and available break points purchased. The different fund fees vary by Class A, B, and C. Some classes have front-end fees, while others do not. Service fees are also a piece of the fees needing to be considered and vary by manager, and length of deferred sales charge."

VII. **Proprietary Written Description of Fund's Investment Objective** — These next four Commandments have one thing in common. They all rely on written documentation beyond the fund's prospectus. While plan sponsors must read the prospectus, they must also remember the prospectus is inherently a sales tool. Getting a third party's opinion can often help the plan tune out the seemingly attractive pitch of an inappropriate fund. Sometimes this third-party view comes from an adviser, sometimes it comes from a publisher. Ideally, it will be proprietary in nature, aimed at the specific needs of the plan and not for the general mass market. The first detail the 401(k) plan sponsor will want to see is an objective description of the fund's investment objective. That's the basis of each of the next three items.

VIII. **Proprietary Written Analysis of Fund's Ability to Meet its Objective** — Did the fund meet its objective? Plan sponsors should not count on the fund to tell them. Select an unbiased party. Reid uses these sources to "review the history, performance of sector, and scrutinize any drifting that may have occurred." He says, "It is my duty to my clients to ensure them the funds stay true to their sector and that the allocations are relevant."

IX. **Proprietary Written Commentary on Fund Management** — According to Schiffres, "the manager is the person responsible for the record." He matter-of-factly says, "Past performance is not guaranteed. Expenses pretty much are baked into the cake. In other words, expenses are something you know in advance, so you want to keep them as low as possible. Of course, super-low expenses are the main justification for going with index funds. To recommend actively managed funds, you have to feel confident that you can identify managers you think are good enough to overcome their expense disadvantage."

X. **Proprietary Written Recommendation of Relative Appropriateness** — When all is said and done, a plan sponsor must always ask, "Is it time to replace this fund?" Here it's vitally important to have a wide variety of choices, since any limitations may expose the plan sponsor to greater fiduciary liability. Wagstaff says, "We use a variety of sources to compare and contrast. We use third-party resources and we look for balance. We don't want to load the platform up with one type of fund. We prefer a large number of funds to cherry pick and collect a platform for our clients that we believe is cost appropriate, diversified, and offers excellent returns."

We trust this represents a Decalogue possessing both credence and compatibility. Not only does it make sense to use, but the vast majority of plan sponsors can easily adopt each category of scrutiny.

You remain free to argue those particular nitty-gritties within each category. However, before you do so, you might find it useful to continue with the remainder of this section. It might just provide some of that fuel you've been looking for to add to your fire.

Let's begin with a summation of the ideal 401(k) investment due diligence process.

THE CHECKLIST FOR THE IDEAL 401(K) INVESTMENT DUE DILIGENCE PROCESS

When you look through the totality of *401(k) Fiduciary Solutions*, you start to see the due diligence process coming together in a structured manner. What at first appears as nothing more than a series of random dots gently flowing across the landscape coalesces into an intricate constellation that can stand for the ages (or at least until the 401(k) plan sponsor revises the plan's investment policy statement). It's a wonderful and peaceful sight to the eyes of many beleaguered 401(k) plan sponsors looking to reduce their fiduciary liability. Rather than ask you to read (or re-read) the entire corpus again, for your convenience, I've put together this checklist (and a short explanation of each item):

☑ **Documented Selection Process** — Every 401(k) plan sponsor needs to have a written selection process. One can't rely on a haphazard approach and still maintain compliance with one's fiduciary duties. Besides actually putting it in writing, the selection process should contain or utilize several elements, each of which we describe below.

☑ **Documented Monitoring Process** — Before the 401(k) plan sponsor can even add the first fund to the plan's menu of investment options, it will be wise to define in writing how all selections will be monitored. There's no sense in getting into a finger-pointing game when it's too late. State upfront how the plan sponsor will measure and assess the investment options.

☑ **Incorporate the Techniques of Behavioral Economics** — I can say this another way: "Avoid the Techniques of Modern Portfolio Theory" but, in doing so, we'll no doubt upset some apple carts. Still, it's critical the 401(k) plan sponsor understand the limitations of investment theories and not underestimate the psychology of plan investors. By incorporating the techniques of behavioral economics right in the selection process, the plan leaves investors with at least one less chance to trip themselves up.

☑ **Analyze at Least 10 Critical Parameters** — Once the 401(k) plan sponsor starts looking into specific mutual fund candidates, it's helpful to have enough data points for comparison in order to ensure a credible comparison. We'll say the minimum is ten, but it's not unusual for professionals to look at twenty or more parameters when analyzing mutual funds.

☑ **Options in Line with Objectives** — Here the 401(k) plan sponsor ties the due diligence process directly back to the investment policy statement. This is also where delegating to the wrong adviser can prove most damaging. Many advisers still utilize techniques derived from Modern Portfolio Theory (even if they don't know or admit it). A properly constructed investment policy statement will avoid these devices and instead rely on techniques derived from behavioral economics. If an adviser insists on using Modern Portfolio Theory in contradiction of the investment policy statement, then "Houston, we have a problem."

☑ **Options are Materially Unique** — This represents another difficult challenge. Many naïve 401(k) plan sponsors insist every investment option regularly yields high returns. In fact, this item, coming from the 404(c) Safe Harbor provision, practically demands options (and their underlying funds) exhibit non-covariant behavior. That means while some funds have spectacular returns, other funds must necessarily have less than spectacular returns (and vice-versa). If all the funds always move in the same direction to the same degree, they're probably not materially unique.

☑ **Review Options vs. Benchmarks** — It's one thing to define a monitoring process (see above), but it's another thing to execute that process. This item addresses execution. It goes a step further and implies the monitoring process should have already identified pertinent benchmarks. And by benchmarks, we don't necessarily mean indexes or even similar funds. Benchmarks might also include plan specific return targets, which leads right to the entry on the checklist...

☑ **Use Consistent Risk/Return Wording** — This is the cousin of "Options in Line with Objective" since this is another source of conflict between vendors, particularly those that continue to use Modern Portfolio Theory vs. behavioral economics techniques. When the plan's investment policy statement incorporates risk/return wording consistent with behavioral economics, the 401(k) plan sponsor should not be using an investment consultant that provides reams of statistical data on beta, Sharpe Ratio or any one of a multitude of mathematical artifacts from Modern Portfolio Theory.

☑ **Use Industry-Accepted Sources** — This doesn't mean not to use a vendor's proprietary system, it just means the vendor's proprietary system should be using data from industry-accepted sources. Unlike almost any other form of investment product, this is incredibly easy for mutual funds. Mutual funds provide their data to the government on a regular basis and there are firms that compile that data.

☑ **Documented Independent Evaluation** — This one goes without saying. Never ask someone selling the product to also evaluate it. Sure they'll do it anyway, but get a second opinion. Someone without a vested interest in a particular mutual fund family will be more likely to both see the warts and tell you about them. Lastly, if any 401(k) plan sponsors haven't grasped this concept yet, here it is: Document everything. It's the only proof they'll be able to provide the DOL when the auditing regulator comes knocking at the plan sponsor's door.

So there you have it. Thousands and thousands of words based on dozens and dozens of interviews summarized into a ten-item checklist. But, here's the best part. Due diligence is like a river. It's constantly moving; hence, constantly changing. Fifteen years ago it was written in the language of Modern Portfolio Theory. Today it is written in the language of behavioral economics. Fifteen years from now…

…well, you get the idea. In the meantime, since you've gone through all the trouble of actually paying for this book, let's delve a little deeper into some of the aspects I've just described. But, *caveat emptor*, some of the following many not be suitable for those with weaker stomachs (or, at least, minds still stuck in the 1980's).

401(K) PLAN SPONSOR PRIMER —
THE RISK-RETURN TRADEOFF

One of the more significant investment models developed by the academic industry goes by the name "Modern Portfolio Theory" (MPT). It attempts to provide a theoretical basis for why people invest in the various things they invest in. The theory is not causal. In its most pure form, it does not try to predict an outcome in the manner of theoretical physics (although financial alchemists often try to make it do such a thing). Many practitioners believe MPT died a decade or so ago. If that's true, it retains a very vibrant ghost.

Alive or dead, the notions of "risk" and "return" — the fundamental elements of MPT — will remain a common sense cornerstone to any prevailing investment theory. Of the two, the average person understands the latter a lot better. The "return" represents the amount of money made (or lost) on a particular investment (not including what you originally paid for the investment).

Here's a simple example: Suppose you opened up a savings account by putting $100 in it. After exactly one year, you close the account and the bank gives you $101 back. Your return is $1 (since we don't include the original $100 used to open the account). In this case, because we had the bank account for exactly one year, we calculate the "annual rate of return" by dividing the original investment ($100) into the return ($1) to come up with 1%.

To pound home the thought, we'll try one more example. Say we bought 100 shares of XYZ Corp. for $10 a share and sold the stock one year later for $8 a share. We would have paid $1,000 for the stock and received $800 when we sold it. Our return would be -$200 (i.e., we lost $200 on the investment), yielding an annual rate of return of -20%.

Pretty straight-forward stuff compared to how we define risk. In strict theoretical terms, MPT suggests the risk associated with an investment depends on the volatility of returns. Wow. A mouthful.

Said another way, let's take two investments — your savings account and XYZ Corp. stock. Since the bank promises to pay you a certain amount (in this case, 1%), you are nearly certain to get that return on your money (and if your savings account is less than $250,000, the U.S. Government, through the FDIC, guarantees you get that money — at least through December 31, 2013). XYZ Corp. stock, on the other hand, makes no guarantees. It doesn't even have to pay a dividend. We therefore have a wide variety of possible returns. The annual rate of return of XYZ Corp. can range from -100% (you lose all your money) to infinity (you make loads of money).

Risk measures how certain an investor is of getting a return. The investor can depend on the bank paying interest on the money in the savings account. The investor cannot, with equal certainty, predict the return of XYZ Corp; thus, XYZ Corp. stock is riskier than a savings account. In fact, because the investor is virtually certain to get the return on the money placed in the savings account, we might be tempted to call this a "riskless" investment.

Now, despite our example, one shouldn't conclude the wisest thing is to always keep one's money safely stashed in a savings account. The terms "safe" and "risk" are linked — something which is "less risky" is said to be "safer."

Recall the savings account will only yield an annual return of 1%. XYZ Corp., on the other hand, can produce a return much more than this. In order to decide what to invest in, says MPT, one must consider both the risk and the return associated with the particular investment.

The "risk-return tradeoff," simply stated, implies one will expect a greater return from a riskier asset. For example, would you pay more for an old lotto ticket that has already won $100 or a new lotto ticket that only has a 50% chance of winning $100? In the purely mathematical world of game theory, you would pay no more than $100 for the winning ticket and no more than $50 for the risky ticket. (The $50 is determined by calculating the average of the two possible — and equally likely — returns, namely $0 and $100, the average of which being $50.) Since the first ticket is known to be a winner, you get back 100% of your original ($100) investment on the "sure thing" ticker. If the second ticket is a winner, this risky ticket pays back 200% of your original ($50) investment (i.e., you get 100% of your original investment back plus that same amount again in winnings).

More risk, more return. The price you pay for an investment is directly related to the return you expect that asset to yield. Please note the above does not imply higher absolute prices always mean lower risk. The price we refer to is the relative price. For example, to change the lottery example a bit, suppose the old lotto ticket only won $25, but you still have a 50% chance of winning $100 on the new ticket. You would therefore pay at most $25 for the riskless ticket (it's riskless because it's already won the $25) and still no more than $50 for the risky ticket. In this case, the safer ticket costs less in absolute terms than the riskier ticket.

For the investor, less risk means less expected return. Savings accounts rarely outperform, say, the best start-up company stocks. Of course, on the flip side, a savings account would almost never underperform the worst start-up company stocks (which all tend to lose money). So, according to the theory, whether or not you invest in savings accounts or start-up company stocks depends on how much of a loss you can stomach.

So, how exactly can we measure risk? Well, that's an age-old question the sages in their ivy-covered towers continue to debate. Perhaps we'll tackle that at a later date.

DO MUTUAL FUND FEES REALLY MATTER TO 401(K) INVESTORS AND FIDUCIARIES?

A mutual fund's expense ratio represents only one factor in analyzing the appropriateness of a mutual fund as an investment. For years, the Department of Labor (DOL) was on a foolish crusade. Under the banner of "protecting 401(k) investors," the DOL appeared more likely to merely — and arbitrarily — increase fiduciary liability. If a plan sponsor, trustee and any other ERISA fiduciary couldn't have seen how this campaign would increase their liability, then how could they have taken the proper actions to reduce their fiduciary liability?

Unfortunately for fiduciaries, Washington constantly falls victim to the behavioral fallacy known as "recency." For those not familiar with this academic realm (or our earlier mention of it), recency means overweighting the most recent event you've witnessed. It's why current players tend to overpopulate "greatest team" lists. It's also why sports Halls of Fame insist on waiting five years after retirement before a player becomes eligible for consideration. Worse, when applied to government, lies that awful corollary of recency: the knee-jerk reaction.

When markets fall (as they do periodically), hundreds of thousands of investors (read "voters") lose money. Rather than allowing time to heal this wound, our friends in the Capitol tend to prefer to act. Here's the problem: investment advice, like witchcraft, tends to be a little hard to pin down. So the bean-counters in the various constitutional branches focus on the most measurable factors.

Only two measurable factors exist in the world of investments: performance and price. Of course, we're all taught "past performance cannot guarantee future results." No administrator will want to risk losing the boss's reelection chances by relying on something that's not guaranteed. That leaves price, or, in the case of mutual funds, the extremely easily measurable expense ratio. A mutual fund expense ratio includes everything from the investment adviser fee, to the independent auditor fee, to all regulatory fees (just to name a few). Some advisers use the expense ratio as an exclusive criterion when assessing the appropriateness of recommending a particular mutual fund.

This is wrong. Even if the DOL demands it, focusing too much on a mutual fund's expense ratio may actually increase fiduciary liability and hurt 401(k) investors.

Why? Because a mutual fund's expense ratio represents only one factor in analyzing the appropriateness of a mutual fund as an investment. Other factors may in fact be more important (including, among other things, portfolio manager tenure, number of holdings, total net assets, investment objective and consistency of returns). For the fiduciary, a fund's expense ratio can become less relevant should the fund exhibit reliable high performance. Fund expenses, then, only rise to pertinence when all other factors are equal. Any fiduciary consultant can easily demonstrate this.

This explanation has the merit of being easy to understand as well as making perfect common sense. Why, then, do reporters, regulators and even some members of the financial industry chase the red herring of mutual fund expenses? It's simple. Of all the possible fees underlying 401(k) plans, mutual fund expenses are the easiest to measure with reliability. Unlike all other 401(k) plan service providers, mutual funds are required to disclose their financials — which include fee information — twice a year. Some vendors don't even need to disclose their fees! (Although the DOL has addressed this with the release of guidelines for its Fee Disclosure Rule.)

The mutual fund expense issue is perhaps one of the lower priorities when it comes to reducing 401(k) fiduciary liability. Indeed, the ICI report shows the average total expense ratio incurred by 401(k) investors in stock funds was 0.72%, exactly half of the average of all stock funds. The same is true for bond funds (0.52% versus the average 1.06%).

So, what should the 401(k) fiduciary focus on? I've already revealed some of our answer, but I encourage you to explore the remaining chapters of this section for more. In the meantime, I'll leave you with this:

> *It's not what you pay a man,*
> *but what he costs you that counts.*
> — Will Rogers

401(k) Fees That Shouldn't Matter

In this chapter we'll point out fees that get more press than they should. In the next chapter ("401(k) Fees That Matter") we'll profile real out-of-pocket fees. Out-of-pocket fees matter to the 401(k) fiduciary. ERISA plan sponsors can negotiate these direct fees and, if they choose to, pay them from company assets rather than plan assets. Paul Escobar, a retirement consultant with US Wealth Management, brings up an interesting dilemma when he says, "The focus these days is on 'fees,' and interestingly enough, on fees that largely, aren't negotiable. The average plan can't negotiate the expense ratios in a mutual fund or embedded in ETFs, can't negotiate the 12(b)-1, and can't negotiate any hidden fee. So, as a result of 'fees are everything' we will be legislating to ignore performance or any qualitative measures for investments as would be considered by an expert prudent man." Is Escobar on to something?

The DOL's original draft Investment Advice Rule (*Fact Sheet: Proposed Regulation to Increase Workers' Access to High Quality Investment Advice*) stated investment advice should emphasize fees over past investment performance. Unfortunately, the draft did not distinguish between fees that matter and fees that shouldn't matter. The previous chapter ("Do Mutual Fund Fees Really Matter to 401(k) Investors and Fiduciaries?") commented on the potential problem with this approach. This chapter will instead explore recent academic research that might be new to the average fiduciary.

Common sense would suggest, all other things being the same, that mutual fund fees will have a negative impact on fund performance. While this simple statement actually contains more complexity than would appear, a recently published research paper provides empirical support. In

2010, the *Review of Financial Studies* published "Why Does the Law of One Price Fail? An Experiment on Index Mutual Funds," by James Choi, David Laibson and Brigitte C. Madrian. The experiment asked 730 experimental subjects (all Harvard and Wharton staff and students) to each allocate a hypothetical $10,000 among four real front-end load S&P 500 index funds with a wide variety of fees and different inception dates.

The paper reveals that "despite eliminating non-portfolio services, we find that almost none of the subjects minimized fees." This was the circumstance even when, in the specific case of the MBA students, the subjects indicated fees were an important factor in making their decision. The researchers also found these sub-optimal decisions persisted despite subjects being given "cheat sheets" to better inform their decision-making. In the end, this research reveals two important conclusions: 1) Disclosure and education, while offering modest improvements, still do not lead to "optimal" decision-making; and 2) Investment performance (in this case based on inception date) may have more influence on decision-making than fees.

So, should these indirect fees matter? Co-author James J. Choi, Assistant Professor of Finance at the Yale School of Management, feels they should. Consistent with other research, Choi says, "While lower expense ratios predict better investment performance, expense comparisons are mostly useful among funds within the same asset class." Choi does, however, bring up a potential problem with the DOL's (strictly interpreted) original draft Investment Advice Rule when he adds, "Comparing expense ratios of bond funds to international equity funds, for example, would be like comparing apples to oranges."

D. Bruce Johnsen, George Mason University School of Law, has a different view. He wonders, like Escobar, if it makes sense focusing on these fees at all. Johnsen uses economic theory to support Escobar's practical reality. His paper "Myths About Mutual Fund Fees: Economic Insights on Jones v. Harris," *Journal of Corporation Law*), argues fees are irrelevant as a first approximation. Johnsen writes, "the more difficult it is for investors to monitor and assess management quality, the higher the fee necessary to assure quality. By paying the manager a premium fee, investors assure that the adviser has more to lose in the long run by deceptively lowering quality."

Johnsen feels investors may see fees as a proxy for "quality assurance." But, he warns, "Management quality is only partly a function of current or past returns. It may, for example, also have something to do with the procedural protections that go into assuring the adviser or his employees do not engage in self-dealing."

Choi's empirical research doesn't necessarily address Johnsen's theoretical claim because "quality assurance" was not one of the eleven decision-making factors included in Choi's survey. Still, Choi offers, "I think the more likely explanation is that people overlook expense ratios, which hit you only slowly over time and are never itemized on a statement, but manifest themselves only through a lower NAV. People are more sensitive to loads, which are quite salient."

So where does that leave us in determining the difference between those fees that really matter (direct fees) and those fees that shouldn't matter (indirect fees)? Academics may argue to varying degrees, but regulators will have the final say. Unfortunately, different definitions of fees only confound the ERISA fiduciary.

Service providers charge direct fees (called a "management fee" by the plan's investment adviser) over and above any mutual fund expense ratio. The DOL adds to the confusion by calling a portion of the fund's expense ratio a "management fee" (the other portion is called "other fees"). Although technically correct from the point of view of the Investment Company Act of 1940, the confusion arises when one considers the direct management fee mentioned above. The fund's expense ratio is similar to the expenses of a publicly traded company. They aren't fees paid by the shareholders of the fund, they represent expenses paid by the fund to conduct its business. For publicly traded companies, investors look at past performance (primarily through earnings). Likewise, it appears that for mutual funds, investors may place greater weight on past performance, despite what the SEC desires.

Perhaps Escobar sums up the feeling of many investment professionals frustrated by regulators' inability to address their clients' real concerns. "I cheered when the Supreme Court found that only 'egregious' fees could result in a breach of fiduciary duty," says Escobar. "I humbly suggest," he concludes, "that if it's a participant-directed plan, participants should be given the opportunity to choose for themselves on the matter."

401(k) Fees That Matter

The DOL wants 401(k) Plan Sponsors to look at fund fees. The average ERISA fiduciary accepts the definition of "fees" without much deliberation. Will this casual acceptance eventually sting the fiduciaries in their collective liability posterior?

In his book *You Are Here: A Portable History of the Universe*, Christopher Potter devotes an entire chapter to the dilemma of measurement. This quandary confronts and, ultimately, may confound even our smartest scientists. Why?

Unfortunately, no matter how hard we try, we tend to base measurements on arbitrary and often purely convenient references. So, while modern instrumentation allows us to measure with ever increasing preciseness, the relevancy — or, more aptly, the irrelevancy — of those measurements haunt the dark shadows of the brightest minds. Should we use a yard or a meter? Fahrenheit or Celsius? The solar year or the lunar year? Yes, researchers can justify the impertinence of such choices by citing the mere need to identify relationships and trends. "The choice of measurement units," they explain, "merely reflects a scalar translation."

If you know what that means you probably should be reading a book with more intellectual heft.

So, which 401(k) fees really matter? Where should the fiduciary focus to reduce liability? For the purposes of this chapter, we'll concentrate on those fees associated with investment options, not administrative costs. The DOL says investment fees are "by far the largest component of 401(k) plan fees and expenses." (For an excellent breakdown of all fees, see the DOL publication *A Look At 401(k) Plan Fees*.) To the extent the 401(k) plan sponsor uses a bundled service provider, the burden of justifying fees becomes more difficult not because of the raw size of the fee, but because it's very difficult to really identify what fee goes to what service.

Even by looking solely at the fees associated with investment choice, the fiduciary can land in a state of confusion. Investment choices have both direct fees and indirect fees. Worse, professionals, academics and regulators don't agree on how to reconcile the difference. Yes, a vested interest in certain investment vehicles may shade some points of view, but, for the most part, we most likely see what Potter describes in astrophysics occurring within the financial industry. If it's easy to see, we tend to use it as a measurement of fees. If it's inconvenient, we may neglect it, no matter how significantly it ultimately impacts long-term investment performance.

The typical 401(k) fiduciary will immediately recognize a direct fee. These fees offer the most convenient yardstick — plan sponsors must authorize their payment (either out of fund assets or by the plan sponsor's pocketbook). Examples include brokerage commissions paid to brokers who sell the investments to the plan fiduciary (the DOL calls these charges "Sales Charges") as well as investment management and fiduciary consulting fees paid to individuals and firms who select the investment choices on behalf of the plan fiduciary. These fees can (and should) remain consistent regardless of the type of investment chosen. Of course, too often, these fees become obscured and hidden by 12(b)-1 fees, but that's the subject of another article. The same goes for certain fees embedded within annuities and other brokerage products. The DOL is trying its best to shine daylight on these conflicts of interest (see the chapter "3 Great Ways the DOL Investment Advice Rule Helps the 401(k) Fiduciary" on page 89).

Notice what's missing: The expense ratio of the mutual funds that make up the investment choices. There's a good reason for that.

TIMELY STUDY REFUTES 4
MUTUAL FUND FEE MYTHS

Just as the Supreme Court was about to hear the celebrated mutual fund fee case *Jones v. Harris* in 2009, a new paper came out suggesting "muddled thinking in the scholarly literature, in the excessive fee case law, and in regulatory pronouncements" has encouraged the propagation of four false assumptions regarding the impact of mutual fund fees on investor returns. George Mason University Law professor D. Bruce Johnsen refutes these four popular myths in his paper "Myths About Mutual Fund Fees: Economic Insights on *Jones v. Harris*" (George Mason Law & Economics Research Paper No. 09-49, posted October 7, 2009).

Here are Johnsen's four myths:

1. **Fund Shareholders Own the Fund's Investment Returns** — It's commonly held that fund shareholders ought to reap any performance benefit once they buy shares of the fund. Economic theory, on the other hand, suggests any excessive performance will dissipate with the entry of rational shareholders. Because of incoming shareholders, current shareholders "have no exclusive claim to prospective investment returns resulting from superior manager skill."

2. **A Reduction of Advisory Fees Will Increase Investor Returns** — As with the first myth, the "rent" theory of economics suggests new entrants will capture any expected benefit from lower fees. As a result, low-fee funds tend to have larger total assets. "As a first approximation, the level of advisory fees is irrelevant to fund investors. Eliot Spitzer and others who have suggested that lower

advisory fees will increase investor returns dollar-for-dollar are simply mistaken."

3. **Fund Management is Subject to Declining Average Cost** — Johnsen cites the Wharton Report specifically as the perpetrator of the myth that economies of scale will decrease fund costs. This turns out to be an economic mixed metaphor of sorts. Economies of scale costs decrease as output rises due to demand. "But assets-under-management is not an output investors demand, nor is it an accurate characterization of what fund advisers produce."

4. **Mutual Fund Fees Should Match Pension Fund Fees** — Here Johnsen takes a more novel approach. Not only does he employ the well-understood "comparing-apples-and-oranges" argument, he goes one step further to explain the economic justification for the appearance of a price disparity. "The economics literature recognizes any number of models that show how market forces overcome the quality assurance problem where information is costly." In a nutshell, "pension plan sponsors and insurance companies face far lower costs assessing manager quality than do dispersed public mutual fund investors." As a result "lower fees are exactly what we should expect" for institutional clients.

Johnsen concludes that the very nature of the freedom mutual fund investors enjoy precludes them from extracting excessive returns in the guise of lower fees. Indeed, the myth-busting professor bluntly states, "Mandatory fee reductions are likely to injure fund shareholders." In other words, mutual fund shareholders can't have their cake and eat it, too.

INTERVIEW WITH MUTUAL FUND FEE MYTH-BUSTING PROFESSOR

Like many college students, D. Bruce Johnsen faced a summertime dilemma. Painting houses to earn money for school, a homeowner called him to do a difficult job. Johnsen looked at the house and realized it required stain — something he had never done before. He really needed the money, so he offered to do the job for $300. The owner looked at the young college student and frowned. Johnsen's heart sank. But the customer countered, "How about if I pay you $450?" The incredulous scholar asked, "Why? That's more than I'm asking." The wily owner only smiled and replied, "Sure, but I want you to do a good job."

Johnsen, now a professor at George Mason University School of Law, never forgot that story. The common sense "you get what you pay for" philosophy permeates his recent study, "Myths About Mutual Fund Fees: Economic Insights on *Jones v. Harris*" (George Mason School of Law, *Law & Economics Research Paper No. 09-49*, posted October 7, 2009) which we reviewed in the previous chapter. Professor Johnsen was kind enough to consent to an exclusive interview with me. His conversation revealed not only how some have abused common economic sense, but how — just maybe — the issue of mutual fund fees raises fiduciary liability only when the 401(k) fiduciary circumvents market forces by actively trying to address the issue.

Carosa: Professor Johnsen, can you summarize the main point of your paper?

Johnsen: The paper addressed an issue [then] facing the Supreme Court, *Jones v Harris*, which concerned the fees charged to mutual funds by the adviser managing the fund's portfolio. Although you wouldn't know this from reading the popular press, economic theory clearly suggests paying high fees is justified in a world where the average shareholder doesn't have the wherewithal to monitor the adviser to assess the quality of services. This is known as the *efficiency wage notion*. In other words, reducing fees entails an added cost that can be more than the savings. The paper describes and refutes what I call the four myths associated with the *Jones v Harris* case.

Carosa: What is the greatest danger to 401(k) fiduciaries posed by the proliferation of these myths?
Johnsen: Fiduciaries are on the hook for higher fees only if they have some negotiating leverage to bargain with. However, this is a calculus. As soon as a plan begins negotiating, the plan's monitoring costs increase. Unlike mutual fund fees, monitoring costs may not be readily measurable — that's one of the reasons why mutual fund fees get all the press but other 401(k) fees don't. So, it becomes a business decision to determine whether, as a 401(k) fiduciary, you want to act as a benign fiduciary — i.e., allow market forces to determine fees — or act in an active manner by not only negotiating fees lower, but also incurring the costs of monitoring those lower fees beyond what the market would do. Now, here's the cruel irony and the greatest danger posed by the myth of high mutual fund fees: by taking back some of the responsibility normally delegated to professional advisers, an active fiduciary may in reality take on a greater fiduciary liability. So, a 401(k) fiduciary might be better off just leaving well enough alone and let the market decide the optimal fee for any mutual fund the plan invests in. Indeed, there's no guarantee active fiduciaries will even meet their objective. For example, it's quite possible, even in the hypothetical case of a large pension plan that commingled its assets with public

investors who can come and go, that market forces will
ensure normal risk-adjusted returns.

Carosa: Which myth is most prominent as it pertains to
401(k) plans?

Johnsen: As you can guess from the above, I feel the myth
most relevant to 401(k) plans and their fiduciaries is the
one that states mutual fund fees should match pension fund
fees. High prices — in this case higher fees — might
ensure higher quality service, thereby relieving the
fiduciary from incurring monitoring cost. In other words,
higher fees "bond" the performance of the adviser. So, if
you're a small plan fiduciary, it might make more sense to
pay higher "investment advisory" fees than to incur even
higher monitoring costs elsewhere.

Carosa: What is the best thing 401(k) plan fiduciaries can
do right now to address these myths?

Johnsen: Well, the first thing they can do is simply relax.
No one can expect you to spend a dollar to save 50 cents —
and this is precisely the pragmatic result of being too
aggressive chasing lower fees. A fiduciary needs to
optimize across various dimensions of costs and benefits.
This is just not good economic calculus. It's a simple
business decision and should be protected by the business
judgment rule absent some kind of demonstrable
misconduct by the fiduciary such as self-dealing, gross
negligence, or bad faith.

Carosa: What is the one thing you hope most to achieve by
publishing this paper?

Johnsen: This goes right to what I do as a scholar. I'd like
to see the law be more careful about embracing economic
principles. For example, many critics of mutual fund fees
assert there are "economies of scale" in fund management
without any real understanding of what the term actually

means. They say that with fixed costs that do not increase with assets under management, average cost must decline. Such a statement has nothing to do with economies of scale, which occur when the average cost of producing a good investors want declines as more of it is produced. "Assets under management" is not a good, and it is not what investment advisers produce. In fact, any investor would be better off if he or she could restrict the growth in assets from other investors. I explain all this in the paper. In the end, to say that fees should decline as assets under management increase you must have some kind of theory about adviser compensation and incentives to say anything intelligent. As a first approximation, my paper makes the point that fees are irrelevant because money can flow in and out of mutual funds to equalize expected returns adjusted for risk. To assume high fees reduce returns dollar-for-dollar is simply wrong. Lower fees are not necessarily better where you cannot observe quality. You just need to look at basic economic theory to understand there's really nothing systemically malevolent going on here.

Carosa: Are there any final thoughts you'd like to leave us with?

Johnsen: There is something that has bothered me tangentially. For plan fiduciaries, legal risks arise under ERISA only if something bad happens and the lawyers have reason to start poking around. Success resulting from fund inflows breeds higher "total" fees, and ironically this leads to a more tempting target for excessive fee suits under Section 36(b) of the Investment Company Act (1940).

*   *   *   *   *

So it seems the notion that somehow fees reduce returns may not necessarily be true at all. Lower fees may not necessarily be better where the cost to monitor quality exceeds any anticipated savings. Indeed, just as a homeowner in need of a paint job felt many years ago, when it comes to high fees, sometimes you get what you pay for. And that reality often leaves investors smiling.

YALE/HARVARD STUDY REVEALS DISTURBING 401(K) FEE PARADOX

W ill a 401(k) investor choose a fund with lower fees or a fund with higher returns? The average fiduciary might think this a silly question, but its answer might just have revealed a hidden liability should the Department of Labor had made good on its Investment Advice Rule as originally proposed in 2010. Why? The DOL's first draft required fiduciaries to emphasize lower fees and not historic returns when selecting investment options for 401(k) plans. Despite this nudge away from past performance, 401(k) investors would have continued to see (SEC-mandated) performance disclosures.

In its final guidelines, the DOL reversed its position and allowed fiduciaries to incorporate criteria other than fees. Still, it's instructive to consider the ramifications if the DOL would had required the 401(k) plan fiduciary to ignore a fund's investment performance. Since the SEC would still have required funds to disclose that performance, the answer to our "silly question" rises to importance. If the original DOL language had gone through, one would have hoped 401(k) investors would have also ignored investment performance. But, what if they didn't? Who would have been left holding the liability bag?

A recent study ("Why Does the Law of One Price Fail? An Experiment on Index Mutual Funds," by James Choi [Yale], David Laibson [Harvard] and Brigitte C. Madrian [Harvard], April 2010, *Review of Financial Studies*) revealed this precise paradox. The three researchers conducted a series of experiments designed to remove the white noise found in the low/high fee debate. Here's how they did it:

White Noise #1: "You get what you pay for" (Part I)
— The ongoing active vs. passive debate — Index funds
tend to have lower fees than actively managed funds. This
makes sense given there's more work involved in actively
managed funds. The debate centers on whether active beats
passive or passive beats active. With this debate comes the
"you get what you pay for" counter-argument by active
managers; hence, the introduction of white noise in the
low-high fee debate. It's really difficult to compare apples
to oranges, so the Choi-Laibson-Madrian research team
ignored the debate altogether and compared only S&P 500
index funds (thus also avoiding the "which index is the best
index" question).

White Noise #2: "You get what you pay for" (Part II)
— The higher fees means higher service debate — Some in
the industry argue various "non-portfolio" services justify
higher fees, even among the S&P 500 index fund offerings.
The non-portfolio services argument suffers from
subjectivity. Choi et al. decided to steer clear of such
capricious data and only include funds without non-
portfolio services.

White Noise #3: The Rational Investor debate
— Theory suggests investors who make rational decisions
ought to pick lower cost funds, especially when White
Noise #1 and #2 have been stripped out. To make it even
more likely, the researchers selected subject pools more
likely to support the theory of the rational investor. The
largest subject group consisted of Harvard staff members.
These white-collar non-faculty employees have spent many
years managing their own finances and 60% of them have
some form of graduate school education. The next largest
subject group consisted of Wharton MBA students with an
average combined SAT score of 1453 (98th percentile).
The remaining subject group included Harvard students
with an average combined SAT score of 1499 (99th
percentile). The researchers found all three groups

possessed greater measurable financial literacy than the average American investor.

To summarize: The researchers picked four otherwise identical S&P 500 funds (they did have different fees and different inception dates). They picked very intelligent subjects. The funds only offered performance as no non-portfolio services were included. Despite all this, the study revealed a disturbing paradox. "Almost none of the subjects minimized fees" and paid a remarkable 1-2% more than they needed to. The staff and Harvard student groups admitted they paid little attention to fees in making their decision. Ironically, the Wharton students "claimed that fees were the most important decision factor for them, yet their portfolio fees were not statistically lower than college students' fees."

How could this be when all funds were the same portfolio? Since each fund represents the S&P 500 index, one would expect similar future investment performance. Although some minor tracking errors can exist, the "since inception" performance varies because all funds started on different dates.

Here's the important news: When it comes to making their investment decision, all three subject groups placed a high weighting on past returns. This suggests the common sense answer to our opening question: investors will choose higher returns over lower fees. Such a decision making process may have caused increased fiduciary liability for fiduciaries, who would have been required to ignore past performance, once we add the White Noise of higher cost actively managed portfolios which can produce better performance results than lower cost index funds.

Did the researchers offer any methods to solve this paradox? They tried three methods to help the subjects make the "right" decision (i.e., pick the lowest cost fund). In the first case, they distributed a one-page "cheat sheet" that summarized fund fees to the subjects. This was meant to highlight the fee differential between the funds. In the second case, they gave the subjects a one-page FAQ about S&P 500 index funds. Here, the researchers wanted to make sure the subjects knew none of the four funds had any investment advantage over the other and, indeed, should perform the same. In the final case, the researchers provided historical return information based on the inception date of each fund. This last case was meant to duplicate the sometimes misleading nature of mutual fund advertising.

"In sum, although better disclosure and financial education may be helpful, the evidence of this article and Beshears et al. indicates that their effect on portfolios is likely to be modest." On the bright side, Choi et al. conclude subjects who make suboptimal choices have less confidence in their decision. The researchers anticipate there's a greater chance these people might make better choices in response to professional investment advice. So, there may be hope that further research might be able to take advantage of this.

Unfortunately, it doesn't improve the position of the ERISA plan fiduciary, who might have been forced into a position of providing investment options counterintuitive to the decision making process of the typical 401(k) investor.

WHY FEES MAY BE LESS IMPORTANT
TO 401(K) PLAN SPONSORS

Stanford Professor Charles Lee finds evidence against market efficiency "liberating" and views behavioral theories "primarily as opportunities." A decade ago he suggested that a "naïve view of market efficiency, in which price is assumed to equal fundamental value, is an inadequate conceptual starting point for future market-related research." He has said the Efficient Market Hypothesis ("EMH") "is an over simplification that fails to capture the richness of market pricing dynamics and the process of price discovery." He points out its current use operates "with no reference to the original caveat." He feels "that moving from the mechanics of arbitrage to the EMH involves an enormous leap of faith. It is akin to believing that the ocean is flat, simply because we have observed the forces of gravity at work on a glass of water."

How does this impact the typical 401(k) plan sponsor? Reading between the lines, it appears Professor Lee's research exposes two myths commonly perpetrated by some in the financial services industry and seemingly taken as "accepted" or "standard" investment theory by regulators. When the DOL originally proposed its new rules for 401(k) fee disclosure, columnist Chuck Jaffe simplified the proposal to this simple maxim: "Low costs are good." In what might surprise many, Professor Lee maintains, "We should therefore expect the after-fee performance of active managers to approximately equal their benchmark." In one statement, he not only refutes the naïve oversimplification of fees, but also erodes the all-too-common lore regarding the "predominance" of index investing over active management. It's therefore critical 401(k) plan sponsors — indeed, any fiduciary for that matter — fully vet all the relevant research as part of their standard due diligence process.

I spoke with Professor Lee. Here's what he had to tell me:

Carosa: It seems like academic studies "proving" index investing trumps active investing get all the press. We know from real life (the 2010 "lost decade" article in *FiduciaryNews.com*, the 2005 "Emperor Exposed" research study in the *Journal for Financial Planning*) that sometimes active wins and sometimes passive wins. There is no clear "only" or "best" way to invest in terms of active or passive. So, why then is there this consensus that "passive beats active" is the only way to think?

Lee: I don't understand that either. Index funds are not a new invention. It is silly to argue that, almost 40 years after their invention, index funds remain, collectively, a "colossal bargain." If they are, then the size of the active management business (over one trillion dollars just in hedge funds) must be the biggest behavioral anomaly of all.

I am glad to see many well-run index funds are now available to retail investors at low costs. But there will always be active managers, because that is what the indexers are free riding off of. The social value of markets derives from this public good called "the approximately right price," which the active managers help produce and the passive managers (as well as all decentralized decision makers in a free economy) exploit. The question is whether this public good is being priced correctly (i.e. whether active managers as a whole are charging the right economic rent for their talents/efforts).

I think, on average, the typical active manager will beat the market before fees and look, well… AVERAGE, after fees. That is what competitive equilibrium looks like. That seems to be what the most recent academic evidence suggests.

As one of your earlier columns noted, people probably under-weight the effect of fees and over-weight past performance (alternatively, we might say they have a preference for "positive skewness," or the "lottery-like" attributes of certain asset classes, such as actively-managed funds). That, plus the over-confidence bias, might suggest that not enough people are indexing. However, the "passive beats active" mantra is definitely getting old.

Your readers might be interested in an article I wrote on market efficiency and behavioral finance ("Market Efficiency and Accounting Research: A Discussion of 'Capital Market Research in Accounting' by S.P. Kothari." *Journal of Accounting and Economics* ["JAE"] 31 [2001] 233–253). In this article, I offer a detailed treatise on the problems with a naïve faith in market efficiency, as well as the importance of behavioral finance. This is a carefully written piece that has been received well and withstood the test of time.

Carosa: It's been said Modern Portfolio Theory ("MPT") begat the Rational Investor which in turn begat the Efficient Markets Hypothesis ("EMH") which ultimately begat Index Investing. In what ways has Behavioral Economics ("BE") eroded some of the fundamental axioms of MPT and EMH?

Lee: I am not sure I agree with the causal chain. Modern economics, like all social sciences, begin with some assumptions about the Nature of Man. Thus the Savage axioms of rationality (assumptions we make about the "Rational Man," or "Rat" for short) is foundational. To these axioms, we add somewhat cavalier assumptions about costless arbitrage, and we get the EMH and the Capital Asset Pricing Model ("CAPM"). MPT is a latter-day derivation of the CAPM that has been adapted for use by many advocates of active management.

How is all this related to behavioral economics? BE strikes at the root of this causal chain. It states that the "Rat" is not always so predictable (or at least in casual observation, he seems to depart from the predictions of normative theory). If the basic agents are not fully rational, we cannot expect equilibrium results to be quite so stable as theory suggests. BE states that prices are constantly buffeted by waves of investor sentiment apart from fundamental values, and that only the constant vigilance and (constrained) resources of the arbitrageurs keep markets from going further astray.

Sections 2.2 and 2.3 in the JAE article discuss the nature of our faith in the EMH. Your readers might find the discussion on "The Limits of Arbitrage" (Sec 2.4) and "What's Wrong with the Traditional Model" (Sec 2.5) in the article useful as well.

As an aside, MPT, as practiced by many active managers today, is actually quite a useful bastardized version of a multi-factor CAPM or Arbitrage Pricing Theory ("APT"). It is bastardized because it does not actually preclude the existence of alpha (whatever is left unexplained by the factors is, if consistently positive, deemed alpha). Moreover, it does not use portfolio returns as risk factors, and does not use time-series betas as factor loadings. Finally, it actually builds in transaction costs and other costs of arbitraging a bet. So, all in all, MPT is not necessarily incompatible with behavioral investing. It can be a useful tool — like a tractor to a farmer — so a good risk model can help an equity portfolio manager zero in on a pure alpha (often behavioral) bet.

Some aspects of MPT are quite useful to investors as well. For example, it can help us separate Alpha from Beta. Beta is cheap and Alpha is scarce. Investors should not pay Alpha prices for Beta products. Just as scotch and soda should not be sold, by weight, like scotch neat. Today, we see increased user sophistication in this area, as people are

asking the right types of questions of active managers —
what is your expected correlation with the market, how
much of your returns is actually a Beta bet, how much
active risk are you taking to earn your active returns, etc. In
these portfolio management applications, MPT does not
require strong rationality assumptions. Risk models such as
BARRA simply measure and forecast asset co-movements,
and is agnostic as to the source of these co-movements.

Carosa: What do you see replacing the old "rational
investor" MPT as the preferred academic theory?
Lee: In Sec 3 of the JAE article, I describe a form of
"Rational Behavioral Model." I don't know whether these
models are replacing the old models, but in my view they
offer a promising direction.

Carosa: In seeking comment on the proposed revision to
the Advisor Rule, the DOL recently asked the industry to
comment on "standard investment theory." In the paper
you've referenced, you said, "The market knows better than
the government." What is the potential downside for the
government to decree a "standard investment theory" in its
rules and regulations?
Lee: Hmmm… I think it is useful to explain to most
individual investors the various descriptive characteristics
of the core asset classes, and the relative importance of
strategic asset allocation (vs. market timing and security
selection), in developing an investment plan. But I have a
hard time going beyond that in sketching the outlines of a
"standard investment theory."

Carosa: What do you see on the horizon regarding
behavioral investing?
Lee: The core of behavioral investing is identifying
attributes that investors tend to over- and underprice. The
former tend to be more salient but less reliable than the

latter. Boring accounting quality indicators, for example, tend to be under appreciated by investors. Sexy growth numbers and what (Burton) Malkiel calls "Castle in the air" stocks tend to be over-priced. The empirical proxies change, but the basic concepts do not.

Carosa: Do you feel, a la the Groucho Marx article, ("3 Reasons to Outlaw Index Investing Right Now [and One Selfish Reason Not To] in 5 Acts," *FiduciaryNews.com* May 12, 2012), index investing exposes a theoretical free rider problem that, taken to the extreme, could (also theoretically) destroy the capital market?
Lee: Absolutely. I make this argument in my article.

Carosa: Is there anything else you'd like to say?
Lee: People who really respect market efficiency study it; they do not assume it.

Carosa: Professor, thank you very much for sharing with me your thoughts on some of the misconceptions in the use and promotion of indexing and active management as well as your insights in the evolution of investment theory.

JUST A SUGAR PILL? DISCLOSURE'S "AH-HA!" MOMENT

On September 24th, 2010, The Committee for the Fiduciary Standard held the Fiduciary Forum. Knut A. Rostad, Chairman of the Committee said, "[Securities and Exchange Commission] Chairman Schapiro has stressed the investor protection mission of the SEC in her speeches and actions; the Fiduciary Forum 2010 focused attention on the very dramatic limitations of investors and consumers, raising huge questions as to the effectiveness of disclosures as a core investor protection tool. It was disclosures' 'ah ha' moment."

The star of the Forum may well have been Daylian M. Cain, Assistant Professor of Organizational Behavior at the Yale School of Management. Cain's groundbreaking research reveals disclosure may not help — and may actually hurt — investors, including ERISA plan sponsors. While he likes the idea of transparency, he feels disclosure can only become more effective when all parties understand its shortcoming. I was fortunate enough to obtain an exclusive interview with Cain shortly after the Forum.

Carosa: What first inspired you to look into the possibility disclosure might actually do more harm than good?
Cain: Back in the late 90's, I was sitting in on a Bioethics class, taught by Chris MacDonald at St. Mary's University in Nova Scotia, and we were discussing conflicts of interest. A classmate brought up disclosure as a remedy. It occurred to me that a disclosure by a doctor (e.g., he had some sort of financial ties, say, to the pharmaceutical industry) would be difficult for a patient to process; after all, should the doctor be trusted less because of a conflict of interest, or trusted more because of strong relations to

research? And, I worried that, even if a patient should be inclined to get a second opinion, doing so may involve taking another day off of work, and (in those remote Maritime towns) perhaps another four hour drive to see a second specialist. So, I wondered how alarming a disclosure would have to be before it inspired the patient to go through the hardship of getting a second opinion. The day I landed at Carnegie Mellon, where I did my Ph.D., I began researching these ideas with Don Moore (now at Berkeley) and George Loewenstein (CMU), who were working on conflicts of interest. We knew from Kahneman & Tversky's work on "Anchoring" (the process by which mental starting points "stick" to affect subsequent judgment) that even what the audience knows to be randomly generated suggestions can affect their judgment; if a random suggestion can affect judgment, then I worried that a mildly discredited suggestion would also likely affect judgment. So, in the beginning, I was merely worried that disclosure would fail to be of sufficient help. It turns out to be potentially worse than that… We have found that disclosure can have perverse effects — making advice worse, creating pressure to follow the advice (the "panhandler effect"), etc… Although in general I think disclosure is probably a good thing, just not a great thing, I still worry that the worst effect of disclosure is that it causes regulators to feel the problems of conflicts of interest are solved.

Carosa: Elaborate on the "pandhandler effect" you refer to — where might one see it and how can one avoid it?
Cain: This was inspired by work I do with Jason Dana (University of Pennsylvania) on charitable giving, and was researched by Sunita Sah (Duke), Loewenstein and myself. The idea is that people often feel pressured to give to someone who asks, like when a panhandler asks for money. When an advisor leans forward and informs the client he

has a financial stake in the client's decision, it puts pressure on the client to comply with that advice because it is now common knowledge that the advisor is helped by compliance. So, clients may trust the advice less but will feel more pressure to comply. We find this effect to be strongest in one-on-one social situations, where it is clear that the advisor will see how the client responds to the advice. We are currently researching the boundary conditions for when this effect is strong enough to sway behavior and when it is not.

Carosa: Your paper "The Dirt on Coming Clean: The Perverse Effects of Disclosing Conflicts of Interest" (with G. Loewenstein and D. A. Moore, *Journal of Legal Studies*, January, 1-25, 2005) suggests disclosure may work with sophisticated estimators, but not unsophisticated estimators. Has later research changed this?

Cain: We have tried several rounds of feedback, and disclosure still failed. Koch and Schmidt (U. Mannheim) found that MANY rounds of feedback do help clients; Church and Kuang (Georgia Tech) look at how sanctions for giving biased advice can help disclosure work better. This later research suggests hope for disclosure, especially for savvy, repeat players, like institutional investors. But, I think the jury is still out. First, while experience may help clients, it can also help advisors who are trying to manipulate them. And, anchoring (i.e., a biased suggestion impacting subsequent judgment) has been shown to be extremely robust to experience. That said, I am hopeful that we can learn how to make disclosure work, and experience with it is surely needed. Perhaps once people understand how big a problem conflicts of interest are — and that they are a problem even for well-meaning professionals who think they are being objective but who are being swayed by their own interests (something echoed in Bazerman, Loewenstein and Moore's, "Why Good Accountants Do

Bad Audits") — then disclosure of such conflicts might be more properly alarming. We have found that disclosures are not alarming enough, even after being burned by a conflict once or twice. And, after all, some of our biggest decisions are made but a few times in our lives. I am not against disclosure, and I am anxious to learn more about how to make it more effective. But right now, disclosure is often a boiler-plate afterthought, printed in fine-print legalese, not the sort of alarm-bell regulators assume it to be.

Carosa: You just said, "While experience may help clients, it can also help advisors who are trying to manipulate them." Give us an example of how this might help advisors manipulate clients. How can clients avoid this manipulation?

Cain: If clients learn to discount information more, advisors can learn to give even more manipulative advice. Now, one might think that biased advisors are already trying to be as manipulative as possible, but we don't find this to be the case. We find that even biased advisors feel a moral obligation to keep an eye on the truth. But, the less truth the client expects, the greater moral license the advisor feels to give increasingly biased advice. That said, I don't think experience is a bad thing. I think that once people learn (perhaps through experience, or perhaps through exposure to the research like this) that conflicts of interest are problems even for well-meaning advisors, then maybe disclosures will become sufficient warning devices. In fact, I am all for transparency, disclosure, experience, and such things. I just doubt that these things alone will solve the problem. Years of research from social science can tell us that once we let biased advice out of the bag, like an untrue but scandalous rumor, it is difficult to undo its effects.

Carosa: In the "Dirt" paper, it appears the conclusion is that the estimator's (i.e., the client) interests are best served in the case where the adviser has no conflict of interest. In practical terms, this would appear to suggest, rather than relying on disclosure, it may be more effective to simply remove the broker exclusion from the Investment Adviser Act. Is there anything in the subsequent papers that leads to a different conclusion?

Cain: To date, I still believe that the best solution to conflicts of interest is to avoid them, at least with more vigor than we currently apply. Christopher Robertson (Harvard) has also been writing on this: We need to encourage the production of unbiased advice. In a forthcoming paper with Loewenstein and Moore (Journal of Consumer Research), we show that the mere availability of unbiased advice is not enough, since clients often are not sufficiently motivated to seek it out when disclosures are made about the advice the clients are currently receiving. So, we may need to put unbiased advice alongside conflicted advice. Of course, unbiased advice may be hard to come by, and some conflicts of interest may be intractable, but I insist that we take a harder look at these conflicts.

Carosa: You mention practical problems with a "cooling off" period (giving the client some time after signing the paperwork before the service is actually delivered) in a recent review paper with Sah and Moore. For example, this "cooling off" period might cause the client to miss an investment opportunity. Do you still have those reservations?

Cain: I do not have research-based problems with a cooling off period. I just wonder about the full ramifications of such a hindrance to a fast transaction. There are costs and benefits that I am not in a position to weigh. Our research is too preliminary on this. Again, regulators will have to weigh the pros and cons of any change in legislation; I just want them to go in with a more skeptical eye when it comes to disclosure.

Carosa: What have you seen in the financial industry that makes you believe they understand and appreciate your research on disclosure?

Cain: Certainly the regulators are more sensitive to the idea that disclosure may not be a panacea, and there is lots of discussion around this very issue, especially since the last financial crisis. The regulated (doctors, big pharma, Wall Street, etc.) may prefer disclosure, rather than sever the ties that line their pockets; but most people are coming around to the idea that someone need not be intentionally corrupt to have difficulty in objectively navigating a conflict of interest.

Carosa: What have you seen among regulators that would lead you to believe they understand and appreciate your research on disclosure?

Cain: More and more, regulators are asking, "So, what should we do, then?" Well, for the last five years, my colleagues and I have been saying that the current treatment (disclosure) is not working. And, if all I do is inspire a sincere look at the problem, I will consider my job well done. But, of course, I appreciate the "what then?" question; it is what everyone, myself included, is working on. What I can say is that, in the past, we thought disclosure worked better than it did, we thought the clients could assimilate disclosure better than they could, and we assumed that conflicts of interest were only problems for the intentionally corrupt. Now, regulators are revisiting these issues with a more skeptical lens. We need to be more aggressive in eliminating conflicts of interest, more wary of those who have conflicts of interest, more energetic about getting second opinions, and more on the lookout for unbiased advice.

Carosa: What is the best possible solution — in your mind — that is consistent with your research?

Cain: I think of disclosure as half medicine, half sugar pill. If we throw a sugar pill at the cancer that is conflicts of interest, it may not cause direct harm (although, in some cases, it may), but we could be doing harm if that "treatment" replaces more effective measures. Sure, clients have the right to know what their advisors are up to. But even if disclosure does not make matters worse, disclosure often fails to correct from the biasing forces of conflicts of interest. So, what then? We should aim to eliminate conflicts of interest wherever feasible. Easier said than done. But, I say to regulators: Treat the world as if conflicts of interest are more dangerous than you thought, harder for even well-meaning professionals to objectively navigate, and treat disclosure as if it does not work as well as you'd like; then go from there. With Sah and Loewenstein, we are examining how to make disclosure work: cooling off periods, different types of disclosures, providing unbiased advice, etc. The research is still at the early stages. Certainly, we need to start giving hard consideration of measures to encourage getting unbiased advice out there. As said in "The Talking Cure," (Talk of the Town column, James Surowiecki, *The New Yorker*, December 6, 2002), "Transparency is well and good, but accuracy and objectivity are even better. Wall Street doesn't have to keep confessing its sins. It just has to stop committing them."

Carosa: Thank you, Daylian. It's been a delight to talk to you and learn from you. I'm sure our readers would agree.

A Fiduciary Test Drive of
the New DOL Fee Chart Using
Top 401(k) Funds

On October 14, 2010, the Department of Labor (DOL) issued a news release stating its final rule to "improve transparency of fees and expenses to workers with 401(k)–type retirement plans." Assistant Secretary of Labor for EBSA Phyllis C. Borzi said of the rule, "We are giving workers the tools they need to make the best possible decision about investing the nearly $3 trillion held in their 401(k)-type plans. Now they will have information about different investment options to help them make wise decisions." The DOL even provided an initial suggestion called a "Model Comparative Chart" for fiduciaries to download (via its home page), although this chart adds a "Since Inception" column not included in the DOL's accompanying fact sheet. They've since scrapped this version and promise to come out with a revised version sometime in mid-2012.

To give the 401(k) plan fiduciary a better sense for the original table, how to use it and what might have been wrong with it, I married the DOL's Model Comparative Chart with BrightScope's ranking of the top ten most widely held mutual funds in 401(k) plans. Before I even started, I had to make two decisions. First, I decided to ignore the "Since Inception" column in the Model Comparative Chart in deference to the DOL's fact sheet. From a practical standpoint, while inception data on individual funds is handily available (it's required in the fund's prospectus), finding since inception data on the associated benchmark is almost impossible without creating it by hand for every fund. In addition, it's not clear what the value of since inception data offers, but we're getting ahead of ourselves.

The second decision involved the choice of benchmark. The DOL has indicated the fiduciary can choose any appropriate benchmark, including, but not necessarily limited to, various indices, Lipper categories or Morningstar style boxes. We chose to use both indices and Lipper categories. The SEC requires funds to list a benchmark index in their prospectus, so it makes sense to believe some might prefer to measure a fund against an index. We didn't necessary choose the index selected by the particular fund, but an index generally accepted and recognized by both professional and retail investors (remember, this comparison chart is intended for use by employees who tend to behave more like retail investors rather than professionals). As you'll find out in the analysis, we found using only an index left too many questions, so we wanted to use a peer benchmark, too. We chose Lipper over Morningstar because the former contains more than nine "style" boxes, includes a more complete universe of funds and is readily available every day in the *Wall Street Journal*.

Finally, regarding the Model Comparative Chart, we'll focus only on Tables I and III, since only those two Tables are relevant to mutual funds. Following the list, we'll provide a review both of the Model Comparative Chart and a potential analysis of the top ten mutual funds based on both the Model Comparative Chart and our improved modifications to that chart. A word about the top ten mutual funds: We contacted BrightScope for specific tickers and the company told us they combined data for all share classes in their report. As a result, we'll show multiple class shares where relevant (and omit any classes not available to retirement plans). BrightScope's top ten ranking is parenthetically added in front of each fund.

DOL'S NEW PERFORMANCE REPORTING REQUIREMENTS: A BOON OR A RISK TO THE 401(K) FIDUCIARY?

In the Model Comparative Chart for its new 401(k) disclosure rule, the DOL broke its sample Model Comparative Chart into two parts. This chapter will focus on the first part — Performance Reporting — specifically, its suggested layout for Table 1. As we demonstrate the use of Table 1 via the top ten most widely held mutual funds in 401(k) plans as identified by BrightScope, some apparent issues immediately pop out. The 401(k) fiduciary just might find these new disclosure rules could increase fiduciary liability, as we'll explain.

First, here's the DOL's suggested wording for Part I: "Table 1 focuses on the performance of investment options that do not have a fixed or stated rate of return. Table 1 shows how these options have performed over time and allows you to compare them with an appropriate benchmark for the same time periods. Past performance does not guarantee how the investment option will perform in the future. Your investment in these options could lose money. Information about an option's principal risks is available on the Web site[s]."

What's immediately apparent from this comparison chart is its reliance on the same "snapshot-in-time" performance-reporting anomaly employed by the SEC in its mutual fund prospectus reporting requirements. William A. Noyes, CFA, Vice President at Diversified Investment Advisors, says changing the DOL's introductory text to note that "the performance indicates a specific point-in-time time frame, and may change significantly when alternative time frames are reviewed, would be beneficial." Unfortunately, the "snapshot-in-time" anomaly is a structural fault in most government performance reporting regulations, but remains unaddressed. By encouraging what behavioral economists call "recency," the recommended disclosure format may inadvertently cause 401(k) plan sponsors to promote inappropriate decision making on the part of employee investors. As a result, the new rule may actually increase fiduciary liability of 401(k) plan sponsors.

Table 1—Variable Return Investments						
Name/ Type of Option Web Address	Average Annual Total Return as of 12/17/10			Benchmark Index/Lipper Category		
	1yr.	5yr.	10yr.	1yr.	5yr.	10yr.
Equity Funds						
(1) Growth Fund of America/Large Cap Growth www.americanfunds.com	13.46%	2.16%	2.67%	S&P 500		
				15.80%	1.80%	1.40%
				Large Cap Growth		
				17.11%	2.01%	-0.38%
(3) EuroPacific Growth/ International Large Cap Growth www.americanfunds.com	8.67%	5.80%	6.42%	MSCI EAFE NR USD		
				7.54%	2.00%	3.46%
				International Large Cap Growth		
				12.90%	3.70%	3.86%
(4) SSgA S&P 500 Index/ S&P 500 Index www.ssgafunds.com	15.62%	1.63%	1.21%	S&P 500		
				15.80%	1.80%	1.40%
				S&P 500 Index		
				15.14%	1.25%	0.85%
(5) Vanguard Index 500/ S&P 500 Index www.vanguard.com	15.79%	1.78%	1.34%	S&P 500		
	15.66%	1.68%	1.26%	15.80%	1.80%	1.40%
	15.79%	N/A	N/A	S&P 500 Index		
				15.14%	1.25%	0.85%
(6) Fidelity Contrafund/ Large Cap Growth www.fidelity.com	19.86%	4.65%	5.77%	S&P 500		
				15.80%	1.80%	1.40%
				Large Cap Growth		
				17.11%	2.01%	-0.38%
(7) Fidelity Diversified International/ International Large Cap Growth www.Fidelity.com	9.89%	2.19%	5.98%	MSCI EAFE NR USD		
	10.55%	0.38%	5.10%	7.54%	2.00%	3.46%
	10.18%	0.09%	4.78%	International Large Cap Growth		
	9.39%	-0.71%	3.90%	12.90%	3.70%	3.86%
	9.41%	-0.66%	3.98%			
	9.87%	-0.14%	4.50%			
(8) Vanguard Institutional Index/ S&P 500 Index www.vanguard.com	15.79%	1.79%	1.38%	S&P 500		
	15.81%	1.82%	1.40%	15.80%	1.80%	1.40%
				S&P 500 Index		
				15.14%	1.25%	0.85%
(9) Fidelity Spartan 500 Index/ S&P 500 Index www.fidelity.com	15.75%	1.75%	N/A	S&P 500		
	15.75%	1.75%	1.27%	15.80%	1.80%	1.40%
				S&P 500 Index		
				15.14%	1.25%	0.85%
(10) Dodge & Cox Stock/Large Cap Value www.dodgeandcox.com	13.76%	-0.15%	6.19%	S&P 500		
				15.80%	1.80%	1.40%
				Large Cap Value		
				12.80%	0.35%	2.93%
Bond Funds						
(2) Pimco Total Return/ Intermediate Bond Fund www.pimco.com	6.32%	7.65%	6.88%	Barclays Cap. Aggr. Bd.		
	7.40%	7.79%	7.31%	4.91%	5.80%	5.84%
	7.05%	7.97%	7.30%	Intermediate Investment Grade		
				6.34%	5.16%	5.35%

Besides the problem of recency, the sample chart does not employ what the SEC already requires — a graphical depiction of performance in addition to a tabular version of the data. Different people read better in different environments. Some like numbers while some prefer graphs. This sample chart shows a bias against those who like images.

By using BrightScope's Top Ten list, where all classes of funds were massed together, we quickly discovered a very important omission in this table — the ticker of the mutual fund.

It's also apparent the use of benchmarks, while perhaps helpful for sophisticated investors, may be too much out-of-context information for the casual investor. We can easily imagine these investors asking, "What does it mean for different funds to have different benchmarks?" The chart does not offer an explanation. If we use just the standard index benchmarks, like the S&P 500 or EAFE, we omit how well the fund does versus its peers. On the other hand, using an index benchmark does give us a quick way to compare an actively managed fund with an index fund alternative — but only if that fund does as well as the index (which almost by definition cannot occur although Vanguard comes real close). Jeffrey M. Siegel, Vice President, United Wealth Management Group, worries that frequent changes in standard indices may skew long-term comparisons. He points out the "membership in the S&P has changed over the past few years, with car companies out and financial companies in, so the very nature of the S&P as a measuring device of risk has changed somewhat."

He's also concerned about the ambiguity of some index labels. "For example, to say 'Russell Midcap' does not indicate whether it is the Russell 3000, 2500, 2000, 1000 or even the Russell Midcap Index, which only holds the bottom 800 stocks of the Russell 1000," says Siegel.

Using fund categories provided by rating agencies like Lipper might offer more information, especially when comparing funds within the same category. The risk here, of course, comes about when the rating agency mis-categorizes a fund. Morningstar, which doesn't have a multi-cap category, is more likely to do this than Lipper, but Lipper does shift funds between categories based on its — not the fund's — investment criteria. A couple of changes do suggest themselves. The first is to group all similar funds together. The second is to include something like the Lipper ranking (i.e., "A," "B," "C," "D" or "E") which immediately tells the reader where the fund ranks (in the case of Lipper, by quintile) among its peers.

Perhaps the best (and possibly most radical) solution to benchmarking would be to reject it altogether. After all, thirty years ago, before the ascendency of modern portfolio theory from academia to the industry, investors — both professional and individuals — focused more on the forest of total return rather than the trees of asset classes and style boxes. The traditional measurement of specific target returns would replace the panoply of benchmarks that have arisen over the last three decades. After all, it's likely investors more intuitively understand their personal need to achieve a certain Goal-Oriented Targeted return than try to translate the relative relevance of an arbitrary index or style box. Because this idea is possibly too radical, we'll not include it in our revised comparison chart.

By adding the Lipper letter rankings, we discover another issue with the chart. Many of the index funds got straight A's, yet some of the active funds with lower letter grades actually produced higher returns. In the end, it is this absolute performance which investors desire, not relative performance. This represents the best reason to compare returns in terms of Goal-Oriented Return targets.

Name/ Type of Option Web Address	Fund Ticker	Average Annual Total Return as of 12/17/10			Benchmark Index/Lipper Category		
		1yr. (Rank)	5yr. (Rank)	10yr. (Rank)	1yr.	5yr.	10yr.
Equity Funds							
(1) Growth Fund of America/Large Cap Growth www.americanfunds.com	AGTHX	13.46% D	2.16% C	2.67% A	S&P 500 15.80%　1.80%　　1.40% Large Cap Growth 17.11%　2.01%　　-0.38%		
(3) EuroPacific Growth/ International Large Cap Growth www.americanfunds.com	AEPGX	8.67% D	5.80% A	6.42% A	MSCI EAFE NR USD 7.54%　2.00%　3.46% International Large Cap Growth 12.90%　　3.70%　　3.86%		
(4) SSgA S&P 500 Index/ S&P 500 Index www.ssgafunds.com	SVSPX	15.62% A	1.63% A	1.21% A	S&P 500 15.80%　1.80%　　1.40% S&P 500 Index 15.14%　1.25%　　0.85%		
(5) Vanguard Index 500/ S&P 500 Index www.vanguard.com	VFIAX	15.79% A	1.78% A	1.34% A	S&P 500 15.80%　1.80%　　1.40% S&P 500 Index 15.14%　1.25%　　0.85%		
	VFINX	15.66% A	1.68% A	1.26% A			
	VIFSX	15.79% A	N/A N/A	N/A N/A			
(6) Fidelity Contrafund/ Large Cap Growth www.fidelity.com	FCNTX	19.86% B	4.65% A	5.77% A	S&P 500 15.80%　1.80%　　1.40% Large Cap Growth 17.11%　2.01%　　-0.38%		
(7) Fidelity Diversified International/ International Large Cap Growth www.Fidelity.com	FDIVX	9.89% D	2.19% D	5.98% B	MSCI EAFE NR USD 7.54%　2.00%　3.46% International Large Cap Growth 12.90%　　3.70%　　3.86%		
	FDVIX	10.55% D	0.38% E	5.10% B			
	FDVAX	10.18% D	0.09% E	4.78% B			
	FDIBX	9.39% E	-0.71% E	3.90% C			
	FADCX	9.41% E	-0.66% E	3.98% C			
	FADIX	9.87% D	-0.14% E	4.50% B			
(8) Vanguard Institutional Index/ S&P 500 Index www.vanguard.com	VINIX	15.79% A	1.79% A	1.38% A	S&P 500 15.80%　1.80%　　1.40% S&P 500 Index 15.14%　1.25%　　0.85%		
	VIIIX	15.81% A	1.82% A	1.40% A			
(9) Fidelity Spartan 500 Index/ S&P 500 Index www.fidelity.com	FUSVX	15.75% A	1.75% A	N/A .	S&P 500 15.80%　1.80%　　1.40% S&P 500 Index 15.14%　1.25%　　0.85%		
	FUSEX	15.71% A	1.72% A	1.27% A			
(10) Dodge & Cox Stock/Large Cap Value www.dodgeandcox.com	DODGX	13.76% B	-0.15% D	6.19% A	S&P 500 15.80%　1.80%　　1.40% Large Cap Value 12.80%　0.35%　　2.93%		
Bond Funds							
(2) Pimco Total Return/ Intermediate Bond Fund www.pimco.com	PMBIX	6.32% C	7.65% A	6.88% A	Barclays Cap. Aggr. Bd. 4.91%　5.80%　5.84% Intermediate Investment Grade 6.34%　5.16%　　5.35%		
	PTSAX	7.40% B	7.79 B	7.31% A			
	PTTRX	7.05% B	7.97% A	7.30% A			

WILL DOL'S NEW MUTUAL FUND FEE DISCLOSURES MISLEAD 401(K) INVESTORS?

In the originally proposed Model Comparative Chart for its new 401(k) disclosure rule, the DOL's sample Model Comparative Chart included a second part devoted solely to fee and expense information. This chapter will focus on this second part — Fee and Expense Information — specifically, its suggested layout for Table 3. We used data from the top ten most widely held mutual funds in 401(k) plans as identified by BrightScope to populate Table 3. Much of this data was obtained through Fidelity's mutual fund data center. Although all the information is useful, its presentation may expose the investor to some dangerous decision making shortcuts. We'll explain why this might increase fiduciary liability, offer some easy-to-implement alterations, and point out which data points 401(k) plan sponsors cannot alter.

Here's the DOL's suggested language for this part: "Table 3 shows fee and expense information for the investment options listed in Table1 [and Table 2]. Table 3 shows the Total Annual Operating Expenses of the options in Table 1. Total Annual Operating Expenses are expenses that reduce the rate of return of the investment option. Table 3 also shows Shareholder-type Fees. These fees are in addition to Total Annual Operating Expenses."

The DOL suggests this language following Table 3: "The cumulative effect of fees and expenses can substantially reduce the growth of your retirement savings. Visit the Department of Labor's Web site for an example showing the long-term effect of fees and expenses at http://www.dol.gov/ebsa/publications/401(k) employee.html. Fees and expenses are only one of many factors to consider when you decide to invest in an option. You may also want to think about whether an investment in a particular option, along with your other investments, will help you achieve your financial goals."

Table 3—Fees and Expenses			
Name / Type of Option	**Total Annual Operating Expenses**		**Shareholder-Type Fees**
	As a %	Per $1000	
Equity Funds			
(1) Growth Fund of America/Large Cap Growth www.americanfunds.com	0.69%	$6.90	This fund has a 12(b)-1 fee of 0.25% and a front end load of 5.75%.
(3) EuroPacific Growth/ International Large Cap Growth www.americanfunds.com	0.85%	$8.50	This fund has a 12(b)-1 fee of 0.25% and a front end load of 5.75%.
(4) SSgA S&P 500 Index/ S&P 500 Index www.ssgafunds.com	0.18%	$1.80	This fund has a 12(b)-1 fee of 0.25% and there are no loads in this fund.
(5) Vanguard Index 500/ S&P 500 Index www.vanguard.com	0.07% 0.18% 0.07%	$0.70 $1.80 $0.70	All the classes in this fund have no 12(b)-1 fee and no loads.
(6) Fidelity Contrafund/ Large Cap Growth www.fidelity.com	1.01%	$10.10	This fund has no 12(b)-1 fee and no loads.
(7) Fidelity Diversified International/ International Large Cap Growth www.Fidelity.com	0.99% 1.04% 1.31% 2.07% 2.06% 1.55%	$9.90 $10.40 $13.10 $20.70 $20.60 $15.50	Two classes of this fund have no 12(b)-1 fee and no loads; One class has a 12(b)-1 fee of 0.75% and a front end load of 5.75%; One class has a 12(b)-1 fee of 1.00% and a back end load of 5.00%; One class has a 12(b)-1 fee of 1.00% and a back end load of 1.00%; and, one class has a 12(b)-1 fee of 0.75% and a front end load of 3.5%.
(8) Vanguard Institutional Index/ S&P 500 Index www.vanguard.com	0.05% 0.02%	$0.50 $0.20	All the classes in this fund have no 12(b)-1 fee and no loads.
(9) Fidelity Spartan 500 Index/ S&P 500 Index www.fidelity.com	0.07% 0.10%	$0.70 $1.00	All the classes in this fund have no 12(b)-1 fee and no loads.
(10) Dodge & Cox Stock/Large Cap Value www.dodgeandcox.com	0.52%	$5.20	This fund have no 12(b)-1 fee and no loads.
Bond Funds			
(2) Pimco Total Return/ Intermediate Bond Fund www.pimco.com	0.50% 0.50% 0.46%	$5.00 $5.00 $4.60	All the classes in this fund have no 12(b)-1 fee and no loads.

Once again, the lack of tickers stands out. It's also immediately clear the DOL should have included columns for 12(b)-1 fees, front-end loads and back-end loads rather than relying on text. In addition, it's unclear why the DOL decided to separate the fee information from the performance information. "The lack of a comparison of applicable fund averages, or a notation explaining the relationship between investment type and fees (for example, international equity options tend to be more expensive than short-term bond options), may result in a participant making an inappropriate decision," says William A. Noyes, Vice President at Diversified Investment Advisors. Noyes adds, "The concern is how much will a participant understand? The Fees and Expenses table includes operating expenses in a percentile format as well as per a $1,000 investment. This may be difficult for some investors to understand. The additional shareholder-type information — while important — will likely further confuse some participants. A primary concern is that participants may elect to utilize the investment option with the highest historical performance or, alternatively, the lowest fees only because they don't fully understand the relationships or impact of either. As a result, what is intended to help participants, may hurt them as their decisions are driven by confusion and data overload."

Jeffrey M. Siegel, Vice President, United Wealth Management Group, likes the table because "wrap fees are now going to be much more clearly indicated, which may give independents a better chance at attacking cases that were solely the province of big wire houses or large plan administrators." However, Siegel feels "it should be clearly disclosed if there are no fees to move within funds in a family. Sometimes the simplest answer is to buy into a family of funds that let you move around within them at no additional fee rather than have a different family for each class of fund."

Ary Rosenbaum, Managing Partner at The Rosenbaum Law Firm P.C., wonders if the table contains too much information to be digested. He also offers this insight: "In light of the Edison case, it would be nice if the fund expenses chart would note the other share classes and whether there is an institutional share class available for the plan at a lower cost. It's great for plan sponsors to know about the share class fees, but it is almost useless if they don't know if there is a cheaper share class of the same fund that the Plan may be qualified for."

We've tried to put these ideas together to create a modified table. The only piece of data we couldn't easily find was an important one — Siegel's transaction fee data. That information depends on the platform and service vendor; therefore, we cannot display it in a generalized example like the one we're using. The next page shows what the new table looks like.

As Noyes suggest, ideally this information would appear side-by-side with the performance information in Table I. Rosenbaum sums up the thinking of many experienced professionals when he says, "The DOL fee disclosures are good for the industry. However, how long and how much will it cost plan providers to provide this information and will plan sponsors actually take the time to read these disclosures? It's been my view that fee disclosure will actually create more fiduciary liability because plan sponsors who ignore fees in breaching their fiduciary role now have no excuse not to know about fees since the information will be provided."

Name / Type of Option	Fund Ticker	Total Annual Operating Expenses As a % / Per $1000 [Lipper Peer Group Average]		Shareholder-Type Fees 12(b)-1 Fees / Front End Load / Back End Load [Lipper Peer Group Average] (where relevant)		
Modified Table 3—Fees and Expenses						
Equity Funds						
(1) Growth Fund of America/Large Cap Growth www.americanfunds.com	AGTHX	0.69% [0.89%]	$6.90 [$8.90]	0.25% [0.19%]	5.75% [1.42%]	-
(3) EuroPacific Growth/ International Large Cap Growth www.americanfunds.com	AEPGX	0.85% [0.92%]	$8.50 [$9.20]	0.25% [0.17%]	5.75% [1.12%]	-
(4) SSgA S&P 500 Index/ S&P 500 Index www.ssgafunds.com	SVSPX	0.18% [0.14%]	$1.80 [$1.40]	0.25% [0.01%]	-	-
(5) Vanguard Index 500/ S&P 500 Index www.vanguard.com	VFIAX VFINX VIFSX	0.07% 0.18% 0.07% [0.14%]	$0.70 $1.80 $0.70 [$1.40]	- - -	- - -	- - -
(6) Fidelity Contrafund/ Large Cap Growth www.fidelity.com	FCNTX	1.01% [0.89%]	$10.10 [$8.90]	-	-	-
(7) Fidelity Diversified International/ International Large Cap Growth www.Fidelity.com	FDIVX FDVIX FDVAX FDIBX FADCX FADIX	0.99% 1.04% 1.31% 2.07% 2.06% 1.55% [0.89%]	$9.90 $10.40 $13.10 $20.70 $20.60 $15.50 [$8.90]	- - 0.75% 1.00% 1.00% 0.75% [0.19%]	- - 5.75% - - 3.75% [1.42%]	- - - 5.00% 1.00% - [0.05%]
(8) Vanguard Institutional Index/ S&P 500 Index www.vanguard.com	VINIX VIIIX	0.05% 0.02% [0.14%]	$0.50 $0.20 [$1.40]	- -	- -	- -
(9) Fidelity Spartan 500 Index/ S&P 500 Index www.fidelity.com	FUSVX FUSEX	0.07% 0.10% [0.14%]	$0.70 $1.00 [$1.40]	- -	- -	- -
(10) Dodge & Cox Stock/Large Cap Value www.dodgeandcox.com	DODGX	0.52% [0.72%]	$5.20 [$7.20]	-	-	-
Bond Funds						
(2) Pimco Total Return/ Intermediate Bond Fund www.pimco.com	PMBIX PTSAX PTTRX	0.50% 0.50% 0.46% [0.52%]	$5.00 $5.00 $4.60 [$5.20]	- - -	- - -	- - -

SHOULD WHAT DOL'S NEW REGS REVEAL ABOUT MOST WIDELY HELD 401(K) MUTUAL FUNDS WORRY PLAN SPONSORS?

Sometimes you're just not lucky in the hand you're dealt. In our previous chapters, we've shown what the new DOL mutual fund disclosure requirements look like using the ten most widely held 401(k) mutual funds for our test drive. Unfortunately, when asked, Brightscope could not provide us tickers since they aggregated all share classes. As a result, we reported on all share classes of these funds. In addition, since Brightscope reported only generic data, we couldn't determine if plan sponsors negotiated more favorable rates (such as removal of any loads). Still, we found the DOL's model comparison tables (modified slightly as identified in earlier chapters) revealed several interesting and significant issues that could cause worry in the typical 401(k) plan fiduciary.

One of the most glaring questions rising from the analysis using the DOL's model comparison chart starts at the very top. How could such a high cost/poor performing fund like the Growth Fund of America sit as the most widely held 401(k) mutual fund. Lipper gave them a "D" 1-year rating and a "C" 5-year rating. In addition, the fund has a 12(b)-1 fee and a 5.75% load. From everything a 401(k) fiduciary must consider, this fund best represents a poster child of what should NOT be done, not glorified as the most widely used mutual fund. How could this contradiction exist?

Charles Massimo, President of CJM Fiscal Management, says the "American funds are on just about everyone's platform (they pay to be there) and brokers get paid very well to sell these funds." Roger Wohlner adds, "The Growth Fund has not done well over the past several years, but has a solid longer-term track record." Indeed, with a 10-year Lipper rating of "A," it appears the best days of the Growth Fund are well behind it. Wohlner wonders if we can accurately assess which class 401(k) plans actually use. He says, "Using the American funds as an example, I am skeptical that plans are using the share classes with front-end loads. Now expenses can be another issue. As I understand it, retirement plans invest in the R share class. The fees are fairly reasonable starting with R4 and above." Again, Brightscope could not provide that level of detail in their listings. (If you want to learn more about the good, the bad and the ugly of R shares, read Wohlner's June 28, 2010 post, "American Funds—The Secret Sauce for 401(k) Plans?")

But the poor equity performance is not limited to the Growth Fund. Ironically, the comparison of the most widely held funds may explain the widely held perception that actively managed mutual funds perform worse than passively managed funds. Newly released Lipper numbers (for periods ending 12/31/2010) show that in at least 10 or 11 (of 12) Lipper categories, the average actively managed fund has beaten the average S&P 500 index fund in each of the 1-year, 3-year, 5-year and 10-year time periods. (Similar results appeared last year and were profiled in "Does the 'Lost Decade' Signal the End of Passive Investing?" *FiduciaryNews.com*, January 5, 2010.) Massimo sees the preponderance of these lower-performing funds (only the Fidelity Contrafund consistently beat the S&P 500 Index funds) as the result of "better marketing and brand familiarity [making them] available on more platforms."

From the DOL's model comparison chart, the data clearly shows, in terms of focusing on a fund's expense ratio, that it really counts when comparing similar index funds. The SSgA S&P 500 Index carries the highest expense ratio and 12(b)-1 fees among all the index funds. It's not surprising then that it also features the worst performance among all the index funds. It is surprising, however, that the SSgA S&P 500 Index stands as the most widely held 401(k) index fund. Wohlner sees this as a problem and warns, "Sponsors and consultants need to be diligent about insisting they are in the most advantageous index share class. For example, Vanguard has made the Signal share class more widely available to plans, but you have to ask for it."

We can see from the DOL's model comparison chart how blindly focusing on a fund's expense ratio can easily mislead when looking at actively managed funds (or between funds of different classes). The fund with the highest expense ratio (Fidelity Contrafund) also has the best and most consistent performance. "Fees should never be the deciding factor," says Massimo, "but they should definitely be part of the decision." Massimo attributes the overemphasis on fees to "a world of investors being uneducated about the issues that matter most."

So, what are we left to conclude from our little test drive of the DOL's new mutual fund disclosure requirements? Although laden with shortcomings, some minor tweaks to the DOL's model comparison chart prove most revealing when applied to the most widely held 401(k) mutual funds. It clearly shows many 401(k) plans hold sub-par and expensive funds. With the most widely held 401(k) funds possessing both 12(b)-1 fees and loads, it's apparent there's a real need for a level playing field in terms of the fiduciary standard and possibly also the outright elimination of the DOL's Frost National Advisory Opinion (which exempts fiduciaries from the prohibited transaction violation caused by the use of 12(b)-1 fees).

Massimo says, "Unfortunately most plan trustees are in the dark about the 'true' cost of owning mutual funds." Still, he doesn't think plan sponsors should throw in the towel or hide their collective heads in some collective sand. "A trustee needs to understand they are personally liable for legal issues arising from their 401(k) plan. They should request an independent, unbiased fee analysis every two to three years." Massimo concludes bluntly, "While many want to solely blame Wall Street for many of the issues facing the 401(k) industry, plan trustees and HR directors need to take some of the blame themselves for not being better informed and/or educated when it comes to matters that can impact their 401(k) plans."

Wohlner sums up the thinking of numerous commentators when he says, "We absolutely need a tough, uniform fiduciary standard, especially as it applies to 401(k) plans."

The question remains: Do the new DOL mutual fund reporting requirements even come close to satisfying the need for a "tough, uniform fiduciary standard" or do they merely add to the worries of 401(k) plan sponsors?

SECTION SEVEN:

– EDUCATION –

JUST BECAUSE YOU CAN'T MAKE A HORSE DRINK DOESN'T RELIEVE YOU OF YOUR FIDUCIARY DUTY TO LEAD HIM TO WATER

THE 4 ESSENTIAL ELEMENTS OF A SUCCESSFUL 401(K) PLAN EDUCATION PROGRAM

The key to success for any 401(k) plan is disciplined execution, and the key to disciplined education is instruction for both the employees and the plan sponsors. Unfortunately, education, despite its importance, often falls to a lower priority status in the busy-ness of business and life. Worse, it can easily be misapplied by having the wrong people leading the effort. Indeed, in many cases, education is frequently left to the devices of vendors rather than the plan sponsor. Why? Simply because they haven't taken the time to pinpoint the key components of a successful 401(k) plan education program. For that reason, we present the four critical elements right here.

In plans that permit employee-directed investing, ensure education is:

1. **Consistent and Regular** — This means the terminology used in all plan literature is consistent with the terminology used in the education program. If the plan's education program talks about goals in terms of the modern investment objectives, then the plan's website cannot continue to refer to the traditional investment objectives. (If you're unfamiliar with the difference between the two, read the chapter "401(k) Plan Sponsors: Is Your Investment Policy Statement Still Using Outdated Language?" on page 170.) Similarly, an education program should be a regular event and scheduled at a convenient time for employees.

2. **Tied to Investment Policy Statement** — An IPS that can't be understandably articulated to the plan sponsor through education is not worth its salt. Likewise, a well-drafted IPS that isn't

understandably articulated to employees through education isn't worth anything, either. The IPS drives the investment philosophy of the plan and should also provide a handy blueprint for a successful education program. (For those interested in learning more, read the chapter "How Should a 401(k) Plan Sponsor Construct an Appropriate Investment Policy Statement?" on page 175.)

3. **Covers both Administration and Investments** — Sure, the quarterback gets to do all the commercials, but he wouldn't be where he is if it weren't for his linemen. Similarly, everyone always wants to talk about investments, but the problems 401(k) plan participants face aren't due to a lack of good long-term investments, they're mainly due to inadequate savings. The mechanics of savings begins with understanding the administrative functions of the plan and carries through how participants determine their broad investment strategy.

4. **Customized to the Plan's Employees** — Many investment professionals once thought the need to understand plan demographics disappeared as we migrated from pension and traditional profit sharing plans to participant directed 401(k) plans. That can't be further from the truth. Not only do we need an array of investment options geared to people of different ages and different economic backgrounds, but the plan's education program needs to address the different learning styles of the different generations.

Let's focus on this last item for a moment. Organizational development scholar Dr. Morris Massey says, "People develop values and outlook based on their world and their experiences from birth to about age 10." What does this mean for a 401(k) plan education program?

It means, very roughly, each generation comes with a different value system and a different way of understanding things.

Take a look at just one example to understand the ramifications when it comes to delivering a 401(k) education program that employees of different generations will embrace. We'll use the example of communications. The oldest workers prefer to communicate using the phone. Those not quite as old may be more comfortable with email. A younger still group forsakes email and relies mostly on texting. The youngest generation has moved beyond texting and instead uses Skype, Twitter or Facebook to communicate with one another.

Now imagine how the different generations feel about saving, spending and investing. Think about the events that might have shaped their views. Those coming of age in the go-go 60's or the Reagan Revolution of the 1980's might treat stock investing differently than those whose first experience was the stagnant 70's or the credit crisis of the last few years. Their willingness to invest for the long-term might be skewed by events of their youth.

Similarly, and this crosses the generations, different people respond differently to different investment styles. Some people like words and pictures. Others like numbers and formulae. Some people want to see a graph while (less often, at least according to behavioral research) others prefer tables.

Being able to speak to different styles and values in one program represents the greatest blueprint to success for any 401(k) plan education program. While education might best be left to professional teachers, 401(k) plan sponsors might not find that a viable option. The four key elements presented here offer a few simple steps every plan sponsor can easily afford to take. The next chapter will offer more specific examples from real world situations.

THE PRIMARY OBJECTIVE OF A SUCCESSFUL 401(K) EDUCATION PROGRAM

Julius Caesar once said "Experience is the teacher of all things." The irony for 401(k) investors, however, lies in the truth that experience only comes with age, and successful retirement investment requires time. Learning the power of compounding at age 60 does little to help. Investors must learn this secret of success in their 20's or 30's. One simple sensational strategy sums it up: Savings.

"A 401(k) is first and foremost a SAVINGS tool... you save before you spend," says Chuck Miller, a consultant in financial services communications from the greater Chicago area. "The more time you spend on finding ways to create an education program that emphasizes how participants can save more," he says, "will help them more than all the investment education you may impart."

We've seen the fruits of disciplined savings in our very first chapter "Hooray for the 401(k)!" The book's opener detailed how ordinary workers became millionaires merely by consistently saving in their companies' 401(k) plans. They started saving early and contributed often. They have proved to an often cynical world the 401(k) plan can go beyond its original intent to merely supplement other retirement income sources. For these people, their 401(k) assets have grown large enough to become the primary vehicle to sustain them during retirement.

These investors had the same advantage as all employees with 401(k) plans. The difference is they seized this opportunity with a vengeance while their co-working brethren did not. The primary objective of all 401(k) education programs should be to produce workers who reach retirement with the assets they need.

A successful education program, therefore, presents through a clear process the instructions employees must follow to successfully retire. Any good program will address both administrative and investment issues. It's important this program is tailored to the plan's Investment Policy Statement as well as the demographics specific to the company. Remember, the style of teaching is potentially different for different generations.

But all these factors must act as individual lenses, each focused on one thing: Savings. Let's see how this works in the three typical types of education programs developed by every 401(k) plan.

Trustee Education — This program is designed specifically for the plan sponsor and the plan's designated trustees. It should be taught by an expert or experts in both regulatory issues and behavioral finance. The administrative side of this education program should focus on how the regulatory framework can be used to do two things: increase plan participation among employees and maximize their contributions. The investment side of this education program should focus primarily on how to incorporate behavioral finance techniques in the plan design (including the Investment Policy Statement) to encourage more employees to participate and to encourage employees to maximize their contribution rate.

New Entrant Orientation Education — This program is designed specifically for new or newly eligible employees. It should be taught by an experienced teacher — not just an entertaining presentation artist. The teacher needs to know how to respond to different learners in different situations, but also be very patient as these students will probably know little to nothing about personal finance. The administration side of this education program concentrates on explaining to the new entrant which people (both internal employees and outside vendors) offer which plan services. For example, the employee will need to know who to contact in Human Resources for certain specific questions and who to contact at the recordkeeper for other specific questions. The investment side of this education program, although speaking to long-term investing in a general way, should emphasize how to determine retirement needs and the best savings strategies.

Ongoing Education — This program, more likely a series of seminars, is designed specifically for veteran employees who have been participating in the plan for some time. It should, like the New Entrant Education Program, be taught by a teacher. Because these students should have more experience with personal finance matters, this teacher should be capable of extending the lesson to a more advanced stage. The administrative side of this education program should go beyond the identification of the personnel involved in the 401(k) plan service. Instead, it should highlight how employees can independently use available systems (including web-based systems) to increase their deferral rates. The investment side of this education program should concentrate on updating the employee's retirement needs and improving their savings strategy. Advanced sessions can also begin to reveal how behavioral finance studies can be used to help them avoid making common investment mistakes.

While it's easy to isolate an objective, the real world can present challenges. We will address these in the next chapter.

THE MOST COMPELLING CHALLENGES IN 401(K) EDUCATION

According to the Profit Sharing Corporation of America's most recent Annual Survey of Profit Sharing and 401(k) Plans, nearly one in four eligible employees do not contribute to their 401(k) plan. It's hard to believe 25% of American workers are independently wealthy, but that's pretty much the only reason they shouldn't be actively contributing to their company's 401(k) plan. In addition, the survey also reveals only 63% of the assets are invested in equities. In terms of old school financial planning, this implies the average age of all participants is 63 years old, another doubtful if not sarcastic conclusion.

How can something — the 401(k) — so right be so terribly ignored?

The problem can start right at the top. "If the plan sponsor says it's not important, it's awfully hard to convince them otherwise," says Courtenay Shipley, President of Shipley Capital Advisory in Nashville, Tennessee. "You might be able to explain that it's the "right" thing to do, it helps with limiting their liability, or it's in their best interest for employee morale-building and attracting and retaining employees theoretically. But, it's not required by ERISA," she continues.

How do you convince a reluctant plan sponsor of the importance of education? "Show them a sample from the many studies illustrating the abysmal state of financial literacy among adults," says Duane Thompson, Senior Policy Analyst at fi360 in Pittsburgh, Pennsylvania. Thompson agrees with Shipley when he says, "If they have a strong interest in reducing employee turnover, this is one of the ways to differentiate themselves from other employers. Of course," he adds, "in the current economic climate, employee turnover is probably not a big problem."

Thompson's insistence on going the financial literacy route has its merits given its appeal to the fiduciary duty of the 401(k) plan sponsor. "If a plan sponsor knows most of her employees do not have enough basic knowledge to begin being successful — and decides to skip education — is that decision in the best interest of participants?" asks Dennis Ackley, President of Ackley Associates in Lees Summit, Missouri.

Once the plan sponsor overcomes the threshold of reluctance regarding education, things don't get any easier. The first challenge is to determine the right syllabus. "In the early 1980's," says Ackley, "many supplemental savings plans were renamed '401(k) retirement plans.' To support these plans, mutual fund sales materials were modified and also renamed — 'retirement education.' No adult-education experts were involved, no pilot testing was done and no successful education programs were used as models. That's how it started. That's how it stayed."

The second challenge is finding the proper teacher to discuss savings and investing. James Watkins, III, CEO/Managing Member at InvestSense, LLC in Atlanta, Georgia says, "Unfortunately, most 401(k) education programs I've reviewed are presented by employees of service providers whose conflicts of interest prevent both proper disclosure of and education on such topics." Watkins feels investment discussions fall prey to a generic cookie-cutter approach. "Most education plans I have reviewed just parade a bunch of meaningless, multi-color pie charts before plan participants and say 'pick one,' with little, if any, explanation of the importance of using correlation of returns to reduce overall portfolio volatility," he says. He also worries the issue of fees isn't framed properly. "Again," says Watkins, "based on my experience, this information is not discussed. At best, the education program simply advises participants to try to reduce costs. Again, the participants lose in the battle of best interests."

Even if the plan sponsor finds the perfect teacher, a 401(k) education program can fall victim to common misconceptions employees have about their 401(k) plan. Worse, as Steven Kaye, President of American Economic Planning Group, Inc. in Warren, New Jersey, points out, these misconceptions can infect even the highest levels of the company. Kaye says the most common misconceptions of plan sponsors include "their responsibilities as a sponsor, as fiduciaries, embedded costs, their potential liabilities, committee expectations, focus of DOL audits and how much more education participants need."

Thompson adds a further worry. "Some small plan sponsors have the impression they are getting administrative services for free," he says. Fortunately, the DOL's new Fee Disclosure Rule might address that. Thompson says, "When 408(b)2 disclosure kicks in mid-summer of 2012, that impression will change."

At the employee level, the greatest misconception is ignoring the need to save for retirement. Even those who do participate in their 401(k) plan often do not contribute enough to secure an adequate retirement, although they're quick to ask advice on how much to defer. "Most financial pros say it's 17% — if employees wait to age 45 to save," says Ackley. He adds, "The Center for Retirement Research says it's 31%. Obviously, contributing for a future income could be one of the most difficult financial efforts employees will ever make. The inconvenient truth about 401(k)s is that employees must be personally motivated to learn how to use the plan and to take the difficult steps to fund their account."

What can be done to help employees and plan trustees "unlearn" common investment mistakes and illusions?

"We insist on trustee education and bring in an ERISA attorney every two to five years depending on the client," says Kaye. "For the participants we offer one-on-ones (free half-hour consultations) with CFP® professionals who are RIA's (fiduciaries)."

Watkins believes it's important to address the problem of *di-worse-ification.* "I think the biggest 'unlearn' 401(k) educators face is getting plan participants and trustees to think of diversification in terms of 'effective' diversification," he says. Watkins would prefer investors look at "reducing portfolio volatility through the use of correlation of returns, instead of the commonly held perception of diversification in terms of just the number and the classification of investments in the portfolio."

On the opposite end, we have investors, frightened by recent news, fleeing the market at just the wrong time. Thompson would "point to the huge market downturn in 2008, and rebound six months later." He says "It probably wasn't pretty, looking at year-end statements for either year, but if you panicked and left the market before March 2009, you missed a huge opportunity to recover a significant part of your losses." More generally, Thompson thinks an overactive investor does not serve himself well. As an example, he would point out "the huge gap between overall mutual fund performances and that of investors making market-timing mistakes by chasing returns."

If employees should chase returns, what should employees chase? A practical goal-oriented target focused on the investor's precise retirement needs might be a better alternative. Why don't we see education programs emphasizing goal-oriented targets? "One reason," says Ackley, "is the old mutual fund presentations and supplemental thrift plans — the framework of 401(k)s — never focused on account targets." He asks, "Don't employees need to discover that a $100,000 account is likely to generate less than $400 a month in future income. Isn't it best to know this at age 25 — not 65?"

Ackley cannot contain his passion on this issue. He continues, "Show them if they had $100,000 at age 65 and they wanted it to last 25 years, say to age 90, they can get a realistic idea of the annual income by dividing 25 into $100,000. How much is that a month? Is this advice or just grade-school math? Is it something employees need to know to help them get a good start? I realize I've ignored inflation, investments and a host of other things. But we're just getting started. And shouldn't the key question be, 'Is this realistic and understandable?' not 'Is this precise?' We need more 35-year-olds — and fewer 65-year olds — with $50,000 401(k) accounts."

"For beginners," he says, "I believe we need to focus more on contributing and much less on investing. Certainly, investing is important...but it should come in the second phase of the education."

Finally, what happens when an employee mentions he has a personal adviser that offers conflicting advice? Thompson has yet to see specific examples of this. "My sense is this happens rarely, since the vast majority of plan participants do not have a personal advisor, and most plans have not yet begun to offer advice under the new fiduciary adviser safe harbor," he says.

But such a conflict will eventually occur if it hasn't already. "One best practice is to encourage participants to use outside advisors (and teach the difference between a sales relationship and a fiduciary relationship and to check credentials — registered rep vs. registered advisor) and stress that the plan education is general concepts and not customized to the individual ... and everyone is different," says Kaye.

Ackley doesn't fear this potential conflict. In fact, it appears he invites it. "Actually, I think it's fine," he says. "It reinforces what I believe they should be discovering — there is no single-right answer and no risk-free future. Hiding risks is a leftover idea from a paternalist past. It's unfair to allow employees to believe they can find a precise, correct number and a risk-free approach. The Society of Actuaries has a list of a couple dozen serious risks — any one of them could derail a person's retirement."

Now that we've identified some obstacles, the obvious question is: How do we overcome them to create a successful 401(k) education program? The answer lies in the final chapter in this section.

SUCCESSFUL 401(K) EDUCATION PROGRAMS — DOES YOURS MEASURE UP?

There's only one thing worse than all the infamous misconceptions on the part of the investing public and 401(k) plan sponsors putting 401(k) education success behind the eight ball. And that's poorly executed 401(k) education programs. It's true 401(k) plan sponsors have a fiduciary duty to give the beneficiaries of the plan the best chance for success. And it's true a good 401(k) education program goes a long way towards encouraging investors to attain that success. But is it fair to expect 401(k) plan sponsors — who are often neither investment experts nor education experts — to know the difference between a good 401(k) education program and a bad one?

With this in mind, I asked industry experts to share their experiences in the ugly, bad and good of 401(k) education programs. What they reveal may hit too close to home for some, surprise others and downright embarrass many. They found some popular techniques habitually fail to lead employees down the primrose path. Do any of these stories sound familiar to you?

What's an example of an improper method of education? "Doing nothing," says Duane Thompson. "The state of financial literacy today is so low that almost anything helps. Of course, plan sponsors should aspire to more than that," he adds.

Courtenay Shipley, President of Shipley Capital Advisory, in Nashville, Tennessee, describes an improper method of education as "passing out enrollment booklets and expecting folks to read the material and fill out the forms." She says, "We live in a world that pulls us in every direction and demands we carve out time for everything we do. Let's be realistic — that enrollment booklet will end up in a pile on the kitchen table never to be revisited again!"

Some symptoms of less than satisfactory means of education include "those delivered on the Internet only, those taught at too high or too low of a level, those presented less than once a year, and those only focusing on investments and not tying it into personal goal achievement," says Steven Kaye.

General education can only achieve so much. Chuck Miller, a consultant in financial services communications from Chicago, echoes Kaye's comments when he says, "The lack of information severely limits any onsite investment advice program. A personal advisor will have substantially more information about a family's circumstances and finances."

Dennis Ackley believes many 401(k) education programs fail because "they don't incorporate adult learning theory and techniques into their education program for adults." He believes retirement education is adult education. "Google 'adult education techniques and principles' and see how many of the key things mentioned are evident in your retirement education." He says, "You probably won't find many. That's just one reason retirement education isn't working well."

Sometimes, though, plan sponsors need to have an education plan fail in order to find out what can lead to success. Shipley tells us this story: "An advertising firm client was failing testing and was concerned about employees not taking advantage of the plan and the match. After some investigating and surveys, the underlying issue was their creative people were being given materials that appealed more to left-brained, data/numbers-oriented, linear thinkers. As a result, there was a general feeling it was boring and too hard to understand." Shipley explains, to improve the process, the firm "shortened the length of group meetings, used different materials that incorporated less industry-jargon while featuring more pictures and covered big-picture concepts. One-on-one meetings followed these group meetings in order to help employees apply concepts to their individual situation. The result: an increase from 64% to 90% in participation and the following year no refunds had to be given."

Kaye concurs with the idea of one-on-one meetings and views this solution as the best example of a successful method of education. He lauds companies who commit themselves to "providing participants who are too bashful to ask questions in public — or want to bring in a spouse — to free counseling by professionals who act as fiduciaries."

Ackley says, "The single most important element of learning is a motivated learner." He says the key to a successful education program "is to make beginning 401(k) education simple enough for the students to explain what they learned. If they cannot explain it, they didn't learn it." He contends 401(k) education programs should be created "for the beginners, not for financial pros — they don't come to the 401(k) meetings anyway."

Alas, no two 401(k) plans are alike so it's impossible to say there's one best formula for success in designing a 401(k) education program. A better fix is to define how one should measure success, but even this can be tricky. "A 401(k) plan sponsor can't really measure retirement readiness since the plan doesn't have access to much of the information required to make a reasonable evaluation," says Miller. "There's a whole lot more to gauging income in retirement than a future 401(k) balance," he adds. Still, Miller believes a form of success measurement does exist. He says, "Since savings is the primary goal of your education program, an increasing level of contributions would be the key metric."

Shipley is willing to consider other criteria. "Success is measured by the results of the program or campaign, with the desired outcome planned in advance," she says. Shipley indicates this can include something soft like HR receives fewer visits regarding 401(k) questions, or something more solid like an increase in participation or more appropriate investments. Kaye includes participation, level of contribution and investment mix to his list. He also measures success simply "by how many show up for the meetings."

Because he doesn't feel a universal definition of good retirement education exists, Ackley puts the onus of measurement on the teacher. He says, "Plan sponsors must ask the provider, 'When you're delivering great education, what will our employees know...and how will you measure that for us?'"

Which leads us to our last question: What is the best way to deliver education programs?

In terms of the teacher, "for a 401(k) education program to be truly beneficial to plan participants, I believe that the program must be presented by a truly independent and objective adviser," says James Watkins, III, CEO and Managing Member at InvestSense, LLC in Atlanta, Georgia.

In terms of media, Lana Burkhardt, President at Lana Burkhardt & Associates in Harrisburg, Pennsylvania, says, "My experience with building 401(k) plan participant programs is that the delivery of in-person, webcast or video are much more impactful than sending printed educational materials. Individuals tend to access and learn from these forms of educational materials and respond with higher participation levels in their programs." Kaye adds that any in-person presentation should be supplemented with web/cell access as well and include workbooks.

In the end, the delivery mechanism of a 401(k) education program is really a communications strategy. Shipley says this communications strategy "needs to target how employees learn: visual, aural, kinesthetic, pictorial, interactive, in a group, on their own, etc..." She adds that developing an associated set of analytics to determine what motivated whom to action should be included in this strategy.

Whatever strategy is ultimately selected, "the method of delivery should not be determined by cost," says Ackley. "Rather, the delivery method should be selected by its effectiveness in creating knowledgeable 401(k) operators. If it takes employee meetings, that's what you must do. If you find an effective website, that's great." For Ackley, plan sponsors should do whatever works for them and their employees.

Perhaps it is most instructive to end where we began by circling back to educating the folks most responsible for providing a successful 401(k) education program — the 401(k) plan sponsor. We'll leave Bert Carmody, Investment Consultant at MillenniuM Investment and Retirement Advisors, LLC in Atlanta, with the final word. He says "Fiduciary education for plan sponsor/ fiduciaries remains a work in progress. Having conducted numerous plan sponsor fiduciary educational sessions, it is a balance between informing on fiduciary obligations, new/existing regulations and not scaring them into terminating the plan. The real challenge is trying to change fiduciary behavior and sometimes little steps have to be made to convince plan fiduciaries the mission is credible, they can accomplish it, and the benefits outweigh the costs."

ACT III:

– THE DÉNOUEMENT –

SECTION EIGHT:

– THE BEST SOLUTION –

HOW TO PUT IT ALL TOGETHER

4 LIABILITY-REDUCING STRATEGIES FOR TODAY'S 401(K) PLAN SPONSOR

Among the many important items outlined in *401(k) Fiduciary Solutions* are the following regulatory issues 401(k) plan sponsors need to know right now:

1) The 401(k) Investment Advice Rule issued by the DOL in December 2011;
2) The Universal Fiduciary Standard (expected to be defined by both the DOL and the SEC later in 2012); and,
3) The Modification of 12(b)-1 Fees (still pending from the SEC).

These three issues linger like a ticking time bomb. They're out there. They're going to go off at some point. We just don't know when. Plan fiduciaries need to get ready for them. Many 401(k) plan sponsors appear to have taken an "ostrich" approach. Unfortunately, ignorance is no excuse for the law. Plan sponsors need to know what's going on, lest they risk a troubling surprise. These are serious issues and the astute fiduciary can prevent unanticipated future liabilities by taking action right now.

What can the typical 401(k) fiduciary do to better prepare for the possible consequences of these impending regulatory changes? Here's the straightforward advice: Be aware, or be at risk.

Here are four liability-reducing strategies for today's 401(k) Plan Sponsor:

1. **Understand the duties and responsibilities of being a fiduciary.** The first plan is to understand what it means to function as a fiduciary. Too often,

people who act as fiduciaries don't recognize they are fiduciaries. Essentially, anyone in any position that has an impact on somebody else's assets serves as a fiduciary. It's not just the named trustee, the company's owners or its top executive officers. Fiduciaries can include HR personnel, a member of the investment committee, someone who works with or hires the recordkeeper, and, in fact, just about anybody who holds the authority to hire and fire any of these employees.

2. **Familiarize oneself with the appropriate DOL literature.** The second strategy you'll want to undertake is to familiarize yourself with the DOL literature. The DOL does not replace the normal professional advice fiduciaries often seek. It does, however, begin to frame the important issues and suggest the types of questions the 401(k) plan sponsor ought to ask these professionals. At the very least, the DOL literature represents an excellent source of training. For a list of some of these links, take a peek at the "Government Resources" tab in the lower part of the right-hand column on the Home Page of *FiduciaryNews.com.*

3. **Keep up with the news and any regulatory changes.** There's a lot of news, ideas and issues coming from any variety of sources, not just the DOL. Such information can be obtained from journals, news agencies, professional societies and even local chambers of commerce. Much of this is available for free on the Internet.

4. **Conduct a preliminary plan diagnostic and review to check for any fundamental compliance exposures.** This item represents the most

comprehensive strategy. These are identified and outlined in the next two chapters.

Once adopted, the three pressing regulatory changes outlined earlier can and will require 401(k) plan sponsors to re-evaluate their retirement plan's service providers. The burden will likely be placed on plan trustees and fiduciaries to uncover, disclose and probably even eliminate all forms of conflicts of interest. If there's one thing you should take away from this book, it's this: Change happens and it happens continually in this industry. As a fiduciary, you don't want to be surprised by this change. So, the best thing to do is to be prepared.

5 CRITICAL COMPONENTS OF A
PLAN DIAGNOSTIC TEST

Conducting a period plan diagnostic test is often seen as an easy way for the typical 401(k) fiduciary to reduce fiduciary liability. An ERISA plan trustee or fiduciary will usually hire an independent fiduciary consultant to conduct a comprehensive plan fiduciary diagnostic test. A plan fiduciary diagnostic test, to effectively reduce fiduciary liability, must thoroughly examine each of these five critical components of fiduciary liability:

1. **State & Federal Regulatory Compliance** — 401(k) plans fall under the Employee Retirement Income Security Act (ERISA) as maintained by United States Department of Labor (DOL). In addition, certain states may add further regulatory burdens (or opportunities) to the plan for the fiduciary to meet. It's good to obtain a comprehensive regulatory compliance checklist from your plan's employee benefits attorney prior to conducting your plan fiduciary diagnostic test.

2. **Service Vendor Fees & Conflicts of Interest** — State and federal fiduciary laws generally state the fiduciary must act solely for the benefit of beneficiaries. The fiduciary, therefore, has an obligation to seek the most favorable fee arrangements. In addition, the fiduciary has the duty to ensure personal and vendor conflicts of interest do not interfere with what's best for beneficiaries. Unfortunately, many vendor conflicts of interest lay hidden in complex packages. In general, the DOL expects the 401(k) fiduciary to: Review the service

providers' performance; Read any reports they provide; Check actual fees charged; Ask about policies and practices, such as trading, investment turnover, and proxy voting; and, Follow up on participant complaints.

3. **Integrated Investment Policy Statement** — While the DOL does not require a plan to have a written investment policy statement, the DOL does state "The maintenance by an employee benefit plan of a statement of investment policy designed to further the purposes of the plan and its funding policy is consistent with the fiduciary obligations set forth in ERISA section 404(a)(1)(A) and (B)." Once plan trustees adopt an investment policy statement, it becomes a legal guideline for the plan. Therefore, it is critical the investment policy statement be drafted in a manner that integrates it fully into the existing documentation of the plan. Too often, the plan adopts an off-the-shelf investment policy statement provided by a vendor. Ironically, adopting such investment policy statements may actually increase fiduciary liability.

4. **Investment Due Diligence** — Even if a 401(k) plan satisfies the diversification requirements of 404(c), the DOL still hold the plan fiduciary responsible for monitoring and selecting those investments. If one exists, the investment policy statement provides a clear roadmap for the 401(k) fiduciary to follow regarding the selection and monitoring of investments. In addition, regular due diligence reports must be consistent with this roadmap. With a clearly written roadmap, the 401(k) fiduciary can reduce fiduciary liability. Without a clearly written roadmap, it may be difficult for the ERISA

fiduciary to successfully defend investment due diligence actions during a DOL audit.

5. **Trustee & Employee Education** — Section 404(c) does not require employers to offer employee education. According to the DOL, if an employer or vendor merely provides general financial and investment education, then it is not acting as a fiduciary. On the other hand, if the employer hires a professional investment adviser to provide individual advice to employees, both the selection of that vendor and the vendor itself takes on fiduciary liability. This vendor selection falls under the same issues as #2 above, especially the conflict of interest concerns.

Does the 401(k) plan fiduciary need to conduct this diagnostic test alone? Definitely not! There are plenty of independent fiduciary consultants — lawyers, accountants and registered investment advisers — capable of undertaking a thorough and comprehensive test on your behalf. The key attribute here, however, (and aside from relevant experience), is "independent." An existing service provider likely isn't the ideal candidate when it comes to an independent fiduciary review.

This short chapter can come nowhere near the comprehensiveness required for an effective plan fiduciary diagnostic test. This kind of test goes far beyond the independent audit requirements of larger plans. Many ERISA plan sponsors often delegate this testing to a competent independent fiduciary consultant.

The diagnostic test represents a mere momentary snapshot of the plan. Ideally, plan sponsors will want to adopt a system to ensure the plan operates most efficiently and effectively on an ongoing basis. This ultimate fiduciary solution is presented in our final chapter.

THE 7 MOST VITAL ACTION STEPS 401(K) FIDUCIARIES MUST ADDRESS RIGHT NOW

Are you a 401(k) fiduciary looking for ways to reduce your personal fiduciary liability? The United States Department of Labor (DOL) doesn't expect the Employee Retirement Income Security Act (ERISA) fiduciary to always produce favorable outcomes for retirement plan beneficiaries. Rather, the DOL expects the 401(k) fiduciary to carefully document and prudently execute all aspects of the retirement plan.

In this spirit of prudent due diligence, ERISA plan sponsors must address the following seven vital action steps and incorporate them into an ongoing system to help best ensure the plan continues to operate smoothly, effectively and successfully:

1. **Identify, document and understand the true cost of all plan services.** These costs can be borne by the employer, plan, and participant. The DOL considers costs a big issue, so benchmark plan costs against fellow employers in comparable peer groups. There are several reliable independent rating services available for this purpose.

2. **Secure improved financial disclosure from plan service providers, including the identification of any potential conflicts of interest.** If you're paying 12(b)-1 fees or participating in revenue sharing programs, you need to know that. If one of your current service providers is affiliated with another of your service providers, you need to know that. It's not necessarily going to get you into trouble if this situation exists — at least right now — but you ought to know of these facts. Again, an independent fiduciary consultant can help plan sponsors navigate

through the often murky waters of hidden fee arrangements, and believe me, the murkiness doesn't necessarily disappear with the implementation of the DOL's Fee Disclosure Rule.

3. **Create, implement and maintain an Investment Policy Statement (IPS) that is consistent with compliance standards.** If you don't have an IPS, make one. If you've got one and you haven't looked at it recently, take a look at it and see if it needs to be updated. Make a point to review the IPS every few years. As before, this is an area where the required expertise normally falls outside the realm of the plan sponsor's knowledge, so hiring an investment adviser or fiduciary consultant will help.

4. **Create, implement and maintain an Investment Due Diligence process that is consistent with the compliance standards set forth in your IPS.** Again, this isn't something that you just do once. Unlike the IPS, which you might look at every few years, the Due Diligence process is ongoing and generally documented on (probably no more than) a semi-annual basis. These plan-level reports check to make sure the investment choices are still consistent with the plan demographics the plan sponsor placed into the IPS. But the Due Diligence process goes beyond picking investment options. It should include the proper transfer and handling of funds by the payroll processor, recordkeeper and custodian. When these service providers are independent parties, the plan sponsor benefits by having each one keep an eye on the others.

5. **Create, implement and maintain a participant and trustee education framework that is consistent with compliance standards.** Part of this process includes what you, as a plan fiduciary, are doing right now (i.e., reading this book). Another

part of this process involves participant education. This can come from your enrollment meetings, regular employee meetings and even be a part of your plan's implementation of the Investment Advice Rule. There are lots of different options available when it comes to participant education, but they are almost all more effective when experts are hired to handle the process. A word of warning here, though. These experts should be intimately familiar with the implications of the research in behavioral finance discussed throughout this book. Effective education primarily addresses the psychology of saving, not, as many falsely guess, investing intricacies.

6. **Upgrade, implement and maintain an employee Investment Advice policy consistent with the new DOL compliance standards.** The key take-away from the DOL's guidelines is to assure any advice is "level-fee," meaning the fee remains the same regardless of the investment recommendation.

7. **Create, implement and maintain a system to keep track of recent news on compliance issues and continually monitor plan investment options.** By this we mean to formalize the process. It's also a barefaced plug for *FiduciaryNews.com*, a wonderful source for keeping abreast of the latest goings-on in the world of the ERISA fiduciary.

I hope, after reading lo so many pages, I've successfully conveyed the sense of the ERISA fiduciary business, both from the point of view of the service provider and the plan sponsor. It's normal for plan sponsors to feel overwhelmed by the regulations, procedures and knowledge required to operate a retirement plan. That's why so many hire professionals to handle specific chores. In the end, it might be the best investment the plan makes.

ACT IV:

– THE WRAP-UP –

SECTION NINE:

– APPENDICES –

THE SECTION OF THE BOOK YOU'LL MOST LIKELY BOOKMARK

9 FREE ONLINE DOL RESOURCES FOR 401(K) PLAN SPONSORS

Where's the best place for 401(k) plan sponsors to go for free help on their fiduciary duties and responsibilities? The United States Department of Labor (DOL) regulates institutional retirement plans. Many guidelines come from the Employee Retirement Income Security Act (ERISA), but subsequent legislation (including possibly new Congressional action) also sets down regulations.

The DOL has put together several free online "booklets" and "fact sheets" to assist and inform 401(k) plan sponsors and fiduciaries. Here's the sticking point every fiduciary must know. Since the DOL specifically warns their booklets are not intended to provide legal, tax or investment advice, these generic summaries do not replace the need to hire appropriate consultants.

1. **Fiduciary Education Campaign: Getting It Right — Know Your Fiduciary Responsibilities** (http://www.dol.gov/ebsa/fiduciaryeducation.html) — The Employee Benefits Security Administration (EBSA) created the Fiduciary Education Campaign as a compliance assistance initiative for employers and service providers. Many of the booklets cited here are part of this campaign.
2. **Meeting Your Fiduciary Responsibilities** (http://www.dol.gov/ebsa/publications/fiduciaryresponsibility.html) — To meet their responsibilities as plan sponsors, employers need to understand some basic ERISA rules. ERISA sets standards of conduct for all plan fiduciaries (which includes any employee or vendor that has some function related to the management of plan assets). This publication

provides an overview of the basic fiduciary responsibilities applicable to retirement plans under the law.

3. **What You Should Know About Your Retirement Plan**
   (http://www.dol.gov/ebsa/publications/wyskapr.html) — This comprehensive booklet provides ten chapters and an extensive glossary. It's an excellent (though exhaustive) starting point.

4. **Tips For Selecting And Monitoring Service Providers For Your Employee Benefit Plan**
   (http://www.dol.gov/ebsa/newsroom/fs052505.html) — This fact sheet contains a dozen helpful hints for the 401(k) plan sponsor seeking to hire another professional in any field to assist with the creation, operations and monitoring of the plan and its investments.

5. **Selecting And Monitoring Pension Consultants**
   (http://www.dol.gov/ebsa/newsroom/fs053105.html) — This fact sheet offers ten questions every 401(k) plan sponsor should ask any candidate seeking to provide investment management services to the plan.

6. **Selecting An Auditor For Your Employee Benefit Plan**
   (http://www.dol.gov/ebsa/publications/selectinganaudito r.html) — For plans with 100 or more participants, Federal law requires the plan sponsor to hire an independent auditor to review the plan as part of their annual Form 5500 filing. This booklet features ten questions to ask potential candidates.

7. **Staying Up-To-Date with Changes In Filing Your Plan's Annual Return/Report Form 5500**
   (http://www.dol.gov/ebsa/publications/gettingreadyforch anges.html) — This fact sheet offers a quick snapshot of the changes in Form 5500 for the all

filings made after January 1, 2010 (i.e., the 2009 plan year).

8. **Reporting and Disclosure Guide for Employee Benefit Plans**
   (http://www.dol.gov/ebsa/pdf/rdguide.pdf) — This 21-page booklet (actually a .pdf file) offers a comprehensive overview of all reporting requirements in an easy-to-read format.

9. **Understanding Retirement Plan Fees And Expenses**
   (http://www.dol.gov/ebsa/publications/undrstndgrtrmnt. html) — The DOL believes 401(k) plan sponsors need to better understand and evaluate their plan's fees and expenses. This booklet focuses on those fees and expenses specific to 401(k) plans.

10 USEFUL DOL TIPS FOR EMPLOYERS WITH RETIREMENT PLANS

The following is excerpted from the United States Department of Labor (DOL) booklet *Meeting Your Fiduciary Responsibilities.*

Understanding fiduciary responsibilities is important for the security of a retirement plan and compliance with the law. The following tips may be a helpful starting point:

1. Have you identified your plan fiduciaries, and are they clear about the extent of their fiduciary responsibilities?
2. If participants make their own investment decisions, have you provided sufficient information for them to exercise control in making those decisions?
3. Are you aware of the schedule to deposit participants' contributions in the plan, and have you made sure it complies with the law?
4. If you are hiring third-party service providers, have you looked at a number of providers, given each potential provider the same information, and considered whether the fees are reasonable for the services provided?
5. Have you documented the hiring process?
6. Are you prepared to monitor your plan's service providers?
7. Have you identified parties in interest to the plan and taken steps to monitor transactions with them?
8. Are you aware of the major exemptions under ERISA that permit transactions with parties-in-interest, especially those key for plan operations (such as hiring service providers and making plan loans to participants)?

9. Have you reviewed your plan document in light of current plan operations and made necessary updates? After amending the plan, have you provided participants with an updated SPD or SMM?
10. Do those individuals handling plan funds or other plan property have a fidelity bond?

10 QUESTIONS THE DOL WANTS THE ERISA FIDUCIARY TO ASK ABOUT 401(K) FEES

The Department of Labor (DOL) has placed on its website a helpful guide for the typical 401(k) plan fiduciary seeking to reduce personal liability when it comes to 401(k) plan fees. Titled "A Look at 401(k) Plan Fees," the site attempts to address the common questions regarding 401(k) plan fees a fiduciary might have.

Perhaps the most important piece of advice offered by the DOL warns the 401(k) plan fiduciary that "there is no easy way to calculate the fees and expenses paid by your 401(k) plan due to the number of variables involved." You might be surprised who the DOL suggests trying to find the answers to the following ten questions from. (Hint: Try asking your plan's service providers.)

401(k) Fees Checklist
(from the DOL's *A Look at 401(k) Plan Fees*)

1. What investment options are offered under your company's 401(k) plan?
2. Do you have all available documentation about the investment choices under your plan and the fees charged to your plan?
3. What types of investment education are available under your plan?
4. What arrangement is used to provide services under your plan (i.e., are any or all of the services or investment alternatives provided by a single provider)?
5. Do you and other participants use most or all of the optional services offered under your 401(k) plan, such as participant loan programs and insurance coverages?

6. If administrative services are paid separately from investment management fees, are they paid for by the plan, your employer or are they shared?

7. Are the investment options tracking an established market index or is there a higher level of investment management services being provided?

8. Do any of the investment options under your plan include sales charges (such as loads or commissions)?

9. Do any of the investment options under your plan include any fees related to specific investments, such as 12(b)-1 fees, insurance charges or surrender fees, and what do they cover?

10. Does your plan offer any special funds or special classes of stock (generally sold to larger group investors)?

Bear in mind, the DOL provides this information primarily as a helpful tool for employees, not fiduciaries. Indeed, the DOL directs the employee to ask the 401(k) plan's administrator to provide the answers to the above questions. That means fiduciaries better prepare themselves to know the answers.

There is one more instructive piece of advice the DOL offers: "Keep in mind that the law requires the fees charged to a 401(k) plan be 'reasonable' rather than setting a specific level of fees that are permissible. Therefore, the reasonableness of fees must be determined in each case." A fiduciary cannot hide behind lower fees if the investment option does not appear reasonable.

YOUR 401(K) COMFORT CHECKLIST

Federal and State Compliance

- ☐ 404(c) Review
- ☐ Prudent Investor Act Review
- ☐ Thorough Documentation
- ☐ Suitable Transfer Frequency
- ☐ Appropriate Investment Options
- ☐ Provides Required Communications
- ☐ Periodic Plan Review and Update
- ☐ Successful Implementation

Independence of Service Providers

- ☐ Plan Counsel
- ☐ Plan Accountant
- ☐ Plan Custodian/Directed Trustee
- ☐ Plan Recordkeeper
- ☐ Plan Investment Adviser
- ☐ Plan Co-Fiduciary (Consultant)
- ☐ Corporate Attorney
- ☐ Corporate Accountant
- ☐ Payroll Processer
- ☐ Paying Agent

Appropriateness of Investment Policy Statement

- ☐ Consistent with Corporate Goals
- ☐ Avoids MPT Mistakes
- ☐ Thoroughly Documented
- ☐ Clearly Written & Understood
- ☐ Trustees' Education
- ☐ Provides Plan's Mission
- ☐ Accommodates All Employees
- ☐ Provides Meaningful Objectives

☐ Properly Addresses Risk
☐ Properly Addresses Demographics
☐ Identifies Method of Evaluation
☐ Review/Update Periodically

Investment Option Due Diligence and Monitoring

☐ Documented Selection Process
☐ Documented Monitoring Process
☐ Uses Post-MPT Techniques
☐ Analyzes at least 20 Critical Parameters
☐ Options in Line with Objectives
☐ Options are Materially Unique
☐ Review Options vs. Benchmarks
☐ Uses Consistent Risk/Return Wording
☐ Use Industry-Accepted Sources
☐ Documented Independent Evaluation

Education

☐ Consistent Program Design
☐ Program Implementation
☐ Clear Process for Instructions
☐ Investment Education
☐ New Entrant Orientation
☐ Ongoing Educational Seminars

Index:

12480403R00170

Made in the USA
Charleston, SC
08 May 2012